VEGETARIAN COOKING FOR HEALTHY LIVING:

An Ultra Low-Fat Nutrition Guide For Living Well

D1457075

BY MARY TER MEER, BS AND
JAMIE GATES GALEANA, MS, RD, LD

First Edition

APPLETREE PRESS, INC.
Mankato, Minnesota

Appletree Press, Inc.
151 Good Counsel Drive, Suite 125
Mankato, MN 56001
Phone: (507) 345-4848 Fax: (507) 345-3002

The reader is cautioned to consult with his or her physician and/or registered dietitian prior to consuming or serving any of the foods produced in this cookbook. The recipes given in this text were developed to help readers/cooks adopt an ultra low-fat vegetarian eating pattern and are not intended as a substitute for any treatment prescribed by a physician. This book is intended as a reference and cooking book only, not as a medical guide for self-treatment.

CATALOGING-IN-PUBLICATION DATA
Ter Meer, Mary, 1931-
    Vegetarian cooking for healthy living : an ultra low-fat nutrition guide for living well / by Mary Ter Meer and Jamie Gates Galeana, Mankato, MN : Appletree Press, Inc. c1997.

    262 p. : col. Ill.; 23 cm.

    Includes glossary and indexes.

    Summary: An ultra low-fat vegetarian nutrition guide with more than 130 original and creative recipes that require no exotic ingredients and follows the heart reversal guidelines advocated by Dean Ornish, M.D. Full nutrient analysis.

    ISBN 0-9620471-9-8

    1. Vegetarian cookery. 2. Cookery (Vegetables). 3. Low-fat diet-Recipes. I. Title.
II. Galeana, Jamie Gates, 1963-

TX837   97-074491
641.5636   CIP

Editor:	Linda Hachfeld
Copy Editors:	Samantha Massaglia and Gretchen Nelson
Assistants:	Jennifer Breutzman
Graphic Design:	Douglas Allan
Photo Stylist:	Lisa Fechter
Food Stylist:	Linda Hachfeld
Cover Design:	Douglas Allan
Photography Studio:	Taylor Corporation

Cover Photo: *Tortilla Black Bean Casserole,* page 73 and *Szechuan Asparagus with Vermicelli,* page 96.

Printed in the United States of America

Acknowledgements

I am grateful to my daughter, Anne, who introduced me to the Ornish Program. She was my biggest cheerleader, never wavering in her support for this project.

My husband, Dave, has my unending gratitude. He spared me by not mentioning his food preferences, endured refrigerator overload and endless grocery lists, and he was my chief bottle washer. He was always there for me.

Special thanks to Jamie Gates Galeana, MS, RD, LD, without whom there would be no cookbook. Her skills as a nutritionist, writer, and editor were a tremendous asset to the book.

Special thanks for the loving efforts of my sisters and their husbands: Ellen and Don Frisinger, and Elaine and Pete Longjohn. They kept the postman busy and the telephone ringing with ideas, recipes to adapt, and much needed encouragement and enthusiasm.

I thank Duncan Beaman for his counsel on the legal aspects of book publishing.

My sincere appreciation to these dear friends who shared and tested recipes, offered feedback, and sought to contribute to the good health of the reader: Kay Bosworth, Lee Corp, Carol Derks, Rose Dichter, Allan and Alice Gulker, Rainey Haskins, Jeanne Hammond, Nel Kastner, John and Kitty Lindbert, Dot Murtaugh, Shirley Tindall, Christine Welsh, Ellie Wright and Dorothy Voss.

Any large project needs a bit of humor along the way. I thank Bill Voss for a good laugh and seven-year old Alice Peterson whose grandmother sent me her recipe for Watermelon Popsicles:

take water melon remove seeeds put water melon in blender mix till lickwdde put in popcacale frams freese for a wile take out and Eat!

Mary Ter Meer

Acknowledgements

Special thanks to my husband and family for supporting me in bringing this book to fruition.

Thank you to Dave and Mary Ter Meer, who prove that healthy eating and lifestyle change can be a truly positive experience, and particularly to Mary for trusting me as her co-author and source of accurate nutrition information.

Jamie Gates Galeana, MS, RD, LD

Table of Contents

FOREWORD 7

INTRODUCTION 9

CHAPTER 1
What this Book Can Do for You................................11

CHAPTER 2
Nutrition and Lifestyle 17

CHAPTER 3
Stocking the Ultra Low-Fat Vegetarian Kitchen 35

CHAPTER 4
Fabulously Fit Main Dishes: Beans and Legumes......53

CHAPTER 5
Fabulously Fit Main Dishes: Grains and Pasta 75

CHAPTER 6
Fabulously Fit Main Dishes: Vegetables: Main Dish 101

CHAPTER 7
Hearty Sandwiches and Substantial Soups, Stews,
Chilies and Chowder..125

CHAPTER 8
Salads: Away with the Iceberg Lettuce! 149

CHAPTER 9
Energizing Breakfasts 171

CHAPTER 10
Bread and Muffins 183

CHAPTER 11
Desserts To Live For...199

REFERENCES & SUGGESTED READING 225

APPENDIX A
Metropolitan Height/Weight Chart 227

APPENDIX B
Sample Menus 228

APPENDIX C
Food Label and Nutrient Claims 234

APPENDIX D
Commercial Food Buying Guide 239

APPENDIX E
Enjoying Food Away From Home 251

SUBJECT INDEX 257

FOOD AND RECIPE INDEX 259

Foreword

Five years ago, my family experienced a tragedy that changed our lives forever. My husband, Dave, suffered a heart attack. Fortunately, he survived, but in order to preserve his health, it was necessary to develop a new lifestyle for our family and ourselves.

According to our doctor, Dave was an unlikely candidate for a heart attack, even though his blood cholesterol level was 240. He did not smoke, did not have high blood pressure, and wasn't overweight. In addition, there was no history of heart disease in Dave's family, and we had both carefully followed the American Heart Association's dietary recommendations for the past ten years.

A month before his heart attack, Dave experienced a sharp pain between his shoulder blades. The pain was brief, so we dismissed the problem. A few days later, Dave felt another, more severe pain. Again, we assumed it was nothing serious. Shortly after that, Dave was overcome by a third pain and checked into the hospital. Later that night, he experienced his first heart attack. If he had remained at home, Dave wouldn't be with us today.

Our doctor explained the severity of Dave's problems. The left descending coronary artery contained many blockages, and none of the well-known procedures for treating heart problems of this kind were possible.

A month later, Dave had another heart attack, which further elevated the risk that my husband would never lead a normal life again. Fortunately, Dave responded well to medication and his recovery went smoothly. He enrolled in Cardiac Rehabilitation, a successful program aimed at helping cardiac patients recover from heart disease. However, in spite of all these efforts to stabilize Dave's condition, so much seemed to be out of our control. We felt helpless about preventing heart disease from taking its toll on our family.

Our lives changed for the better when our daughter introduced us to *Dr. Dean Ornish's Program for Reversing Heart Disease*. We had everything to gain, and nothing to lose, so we gratefully embraced Dr. Ornish's book and lifestyle changing program. We particularly focused on our eating habits.

Realizing the need for immediate action, we began looking for new ways to prepare healthy foods. Over time, my family and I adapted old recipes, shopped at health food stores, and scoured supermarket shelves looking for new and acceptable products. We also purchased a fat-counting guide to calculate the amount of fat present in foods.

Our results were worth the time and effort it took to change our lifestyle. Dave's cholesterol dropped from 240 to 176, and he has been able to participate in activities he enjoyed before his heart attack. In addition, we experienced the unexpected benefit of significant weight loss. I had been a yo-yo dieter most of my adult life, but as a result of our change to the Ornish program, I lost 35 pounds and have kept them off for five years.

Inspired by our success, other family members have begun preparing the recipes we developed and have reduced their fat intake.

The following chapters include tips for drastically changing your lifestyle, tips for eating out and travelling, and many other suggestions for daily food preparation. We hope that these recipes and tips aid your journey toward a healthier lifestyle. Enjoy!

Mary Ter Meer
Co-author

Introduction

I met Dave and Mary Ter Meer in 1992, while working as a clinical dietitian on the cardiac floor of a local hospital. A cardiologist recommended that I see Dave, who had recently suffered a heart attack. The Ter Meers expressed their willingness to do anything to confront heart disease and accepted the diet that I suggested. The diet allowed no more than 30% of its calories to be from fat, was low in saturated fat, and followed American Heart Association guidelines.

For most people, switching to a diet this restrictive seemed like a death sentence in itself. Forget the heart attack or coronary bypass surgery — giving up the high-fat foods they loved was sure to kill them well before heart failure took its toll!

The Ter Meers wanted to go even further. They investigated Dr. Dean Ornish's dietary guidelines, which advocate extremely low-fat foods and require phenomenal lifestyle changes in order to reduce heart disease. I was skeptical. Many of my patients had to be coerced into making the smallest strides toward the more liberal American Heart Association guidelines; reducing their fat intake to 10% was even more difficult.

Three years later, I discovered that the Ter Meers had successfully implemented Dr. Ornish's diet and had achieved fabulous results! Dave had lowered his cholesterol level, and both were feeling better and dropped extra pounds. Mary Ter Meer wanted to share her positive experience and the recipes that she had developed.

Based on Dr. Ornish's recommended dietary guidelines, *Vegetarian Cooking for Healthy Living* contains delicious recipes that are low in fat and cholesterol, yet high in flavor and nutrition. This book, while not a replacement for Dr. Ornish's research, seeks to complement his guidelines and provide invaluable nutrition information.

We don't offer never-ending restrictions. Instead, we present lots of realistic suggestions for what you CAN do. Here's to your good health!

Jamie Gates Galeana, MS, RD, LD
Co-author

Chapter 1
What This Book Can Do For You

What is ultra low-fat eating and how can it enhance your life? *Vegetarian Cooking for Healthy Living* answers these questions and explains how to choose and prepare low-fat foods that taste great. If you are interested in dramatically changing your eating habits to improve your health and to enhance many other aspects of your life, this book can help you.

The eating style promoted in *Vegetarian Cooking for Healthy Living* should not be viewed as a diet that you go on to reach some goal and then drop once your goal is achieved, but should be a lifestyle change that becomes as much a part of life as waking each day. When healthy changes become a true lifestyle change, they are not laborious, count-the-days till it's over restrictions. They are positive enhancements that leave you feeling better and enjoying your newfound way of eating. But let's start at the beginning: what is an ultra low-fat lifestyle and why should you adopt it?

An ultra low-fat diet is, essentially, a low-fat vegetarian diet. The concept of vegetarianism has changed a lot over the years. In the 1960's, it was often viewed as a kind of social movement. However, vegetarianism has come a long way from bean sprouts, carrot juice and social protest. It has become a distinct cuisine in its own right. Simply stated, vegetarians choose not to eat any meat, fish, or poultry or their by-products, and may also avoid eggs and dairy products. Instead, they supplement their diet with many other foods, including fruits, vegetables, nuts, seeds, legumes and whole grain products.

While numerous approaches to vegetarianism exist, *Vegetarian Cooking for Healthy Living* focuses on low-fat, lacto-ovo vegetarianism. This diet consists of broad-based plant foods, egg whites, and nonfat dairy products like milk, cheese and yogurt. We offer a variety of recipes, as some contain no eggs or dairy products while others may include nonfat chicken broth.

Vegetarianism has become increasingly widespread in the United States and the reasons for choosing this lifestyle vary. Many choose it for a number of ethical and political reasons. A significant number of people eat vegetarian food for two simple reasons: it tastes great and it improves their health.

The health benefits of a low-fat vegetarian diet are significant. Research indicates that abstaining from animal products is in the best interest of the human body. A 1993 Position Paper of the American Dietetic Association states:

> A considerable body of scientific data suggests positive relationships between vegetarian diets and risk reduction for several chronic degenerative diseases and conditions, including obesity, coronary artery disease, hypertension, diabetes mellitus, and some types of cancer . . . It is the position of the American Dietetic Association that vegetarian diets are healthful and nutritionally adequate when appropriately planned.

In addition to decreasing risk of cancer, particularly of the breast, colon, and prostate, another benefit of low-fat vegetarianism is protection against heart disease. The American Heart Association (AHA) and other health organizations recommend that only 30 percent of our daily calories come from fat. (A typical American diet contains between 37 and 40 percent fat.) We designed the recipes and recommendations for a low-fat vegetarian lifestyle in this book to go beyond the AHA guidelines and adhere to those outlined in a revolutionary book called *Dr. Dean Ornish's Program for Reversing Heart Disease,* by Dean Ornish, M.D.

The Ornish program requires patients with heart disease to drastically alter their lifestyle and diet. For example, Dr. Ornish believes that only 10 percent of a patient's daily calories should come from fat. As a result, his patients have experienced less chest pain, lowered blood cholesterol levels, reversed coronary artery blockages, reduced blood pressure, and experienced weight loss as well as an improved sense of well-being. In accordance with Dr. Ornish's dietary plan, all but one of the recipes in *Vegetarian Cooking for Healthy Living* contain a maximum of four grams of fat.

You don't have to have heart disease to benefit from this type of lifestyle, however. It's equally important to think preventively. By reducing your fat intake, you will preserve the good health you experience today. An ultra low-fat diet is also beneficial in losing and maintaining weight, is an excellent diet for fueling active bodies, and just plain leaves you feeling good.

A diet that is high in fat, particularly saturated fat, and cholesterol results in a number of physiological processes that promote heart and other diseases. Here are simplified explanations.

High levels of fat in the diet result in high levels of lipids (fats) in the blood and blood cholesterol is comprised of these lipids. As they circulate through the bloodstream they encounter damaged areas of the artery wall and can stick to these areas. This leads to the buildup of fatty plaques in the arteries, called atherosclerosis or hardening of the arteries. These plaques grow larger over time and can close off the artery completely. Pieces of these plaques may break off and become lodged in a narrowed blood vessel. These processes lead to heart attack or stroke.

By reducing the amount of fat and cholesterol in your diet you can reduce the lipids that circulate in your bloodstream, thus reducing the buildup of arterial plaques and decreasing your risk of heart attack or stroke.

An ultra low-fat vegetarian diet is also beneficial in preventing heart disease by promoting weight loss and maintenance. Losing weight (when overweight) results in fewer circulating fats and cholesterol in the blood, and decreases stress on the heart by reducing the work it must do to allow the body to perform even the simplest of tasks.

The physiology of weight loss and maintenance can be stated fairly simply. Foods consist of carbohydrates (also called starches and sugars), protein and fat. A gram of fat contains nine calories, while carbohydrate and protein each contain only four calories per gram. That's less than half the amount of fat! If you decrease the amount of fat in your diet, replacing it with foods high in carbohydrates, for example, you can eat twice as much food without gaining weight! If you are overweight and replace the high fat foods in your diet with low-fat carbohydrates and protein, you will lose weight.

Part of this also has to do with metabolism of these nutrients. Fat is fat. It is very easily stored as fat when eaten. Eating more calories than you need from carbohydrate and protein will also be stored as fat, but the process is different. Eating excess carbohydrate or protein requires more caloric energy to break them down into a form to be stored as fat. It is not as direct a process as when you eat excess fat.

A simple principle of weight loss: if the body is using more calories than it's taking in weight loss will occur. Increasing activity and embarking on a regular exercise program will help achieve this. Gaining muscle is an added benefit of exercise and, while it may first appear as weight gain on the scale, it's a desirable gain. The increase in muscle will increase metabolism so that the body is burning more calories even when at rest.

When considering the successfulness of adopting ultra low-fat eating, don't focus on the goal of weight loss alone. Consider the nutritious foods that you eat and how they make you healthier, how much better you feel overall and the more fit body that you're getting through healthy nutrition and exercise habits.

As if preventing heart disease and promoting weight loss weren't enough, there are theories as to why an ultra low-fat vegetarian diet decreases cancer risk.

High levels of certain fats circulating throughout the body appears to cause oxidative damage to cells by free radicals. This damage leaves cells susceptible to any carcinogens to which they are exposed, opening the door for cancer development. In addition, toxic substances are stored in body fat. So if your high fat diet includes a lot of animal products, as most do, your cells would be exposed to carcinogens that an animal has stored in its fatty tissues. Avoiding most animal products limits this exposure. Besides the decreased fat intake, an ultra low-fat diet relies heavily on a variety of fruits and vegetables, all great sources of the antioxidants and phytochemicals that will reduce damage by free radicals.

If you are a very active person, even a professional athlete, an ultra low-fat diet is an excellent way to fuel an active body. Carbohydrate is the body's main source of fuel, with a constant supply being necessary for fueling active muscles and for brain function. Though fat is burned as fuel during aerobic exercise (like cycling, swimming, walking), carbohydrate is the factor that limits how long you are able to exercise. Because your body only stores limited amounts of carbohydrate, it's important to regularly consume a high carbohydrate diet. An ultra low-fat vegetarian diet is ideal.

These are very simple explanations for complex processes. Keep in mind, this book is written as a guide for getting started on an ultra low-fat diet and as a tool for motivation and support. Living a low-fat diet lifestyle can be very rewarding in terms of your health and your general feeling of well-being. We're not suggesting that an ultra low-fat vegetarian diet is a magic panacea but it is certainly a ticket to an improved lifestyle and optimal health.

We've organized *Vegetarian Cooking for Healthy Living* in a manner that provides a complete picture of a low-fat vegetarian lifestyle. **Chapter 2: Nutrition and Lifestyle** expands on the practicalities of low-fat vegetarianism and explains how they relate to overall good health. This chapter discusses methods of getting enough protein and other essential nutrients. **Chapter 3: Stocking the Ultra Low-fat Vegetarian Kitchen**, explains how to set up your kitchen for efficient low-fat vegetarian cooking. Information on purchasing foods, cooking methods, seasoning and substitutions can be found in **Chapter 3**. The **Appendices** contain information such as a height and weight table, 14 sample menus built around the recipes in this book, methods of effectively reading product labels, tips for maintaining a low-fat vegetarian lifestyle while away from home, and a list of low-fat commercial food products.

It's true, low-fat vegetarian food is delicious, and there are many ways to prepare unique, flavor-filled meals. In fact, with a few variations, recipes that contain high-fat products can be converted into recipes that aren't harmful to your body. That's the approach we take in this book; we've designed a number of vegetarian low-fat recipes that are easy to prepare and that are enjoyable to eat. All the recipes that appear in *Vegetarian Cooking for Healthy Living* were developed using broad-based plant foods that focus on beans, legumes, grains, pasta, vegetables, fruits, nonfat dairy products and egg whites. We then go a step further and explain how to incorporate our suggestions into your lifestyle.

We encourage you to view this book as a springboard to new eating habits rather than as a mere list of recipes. Whether your goal is to become a low-fat vegetarian or whether you'd simply like to add some healthful low-fat vegetarian recipes to your culinary repertoire, *Vegetarian Cooking for Healthy Living* can help you. Regardless of the reason for choosing to live a low-fat lifestyle, as with any lifestyle change, it should be because you have made the choice to do so. If it is something you truly want to do for yourself you will be much more successful and satisfied with your choices. You're not just making a lifestyle *change;* you're making a lifestyle *enhancement.*

Chapter 2

Nutrition and Lifestyle

Now that you've decided to alter your lifestyle, perhaps you're wondering about the practicalities of such a change. How does one begin to implement new habits? Can an ultra low-fat vegetarian lifestyle meet your nutritional needs? Perhaps you wonder whether you'll constantly feel hungry, and worry that your favorite high-fat foods will be replaced with tasteless alternatives. We address each of these concerns in this chapter.

Transitioning to New Eating Habits

Change is rarely easy, even when a desirable goal awaits us. Removing favorite foods from a diet is especially difficult. Not only do we enjoy the taste of certain foods; we may also have an emotional attachment to many of them. Fortunately, the human body readily adapts to change. You weren't born with a taste preference for fat, and your taste buds can be trained to prefer the taste of low-fat foods. Before long, the high-fat foods that you used to enjoy will be much less appealing.

There are two schools of thought on changing dietary habits: the "cold turkey method" and the "Rome wasn't built in a day" method. You need to decide what works best for you. Many people prefer the cold turkey method. Although it may be difficult at first, you will notice more immediate results in improving your health and lipid profiles, and in the long run it's more effective.

Mary Ter Meer offers her thoughts on going cold turkey:

> Cold turkey is just that – cold turkey! It's that simple. One of the first things I did was begin a systematic search for the fat in our kitchen and then got rid of it. I immediately threw away bottles of oil and stick margarine. Then, I replaced various items in my cupboards with homemade products or nonfat items available in the stores. I was surprised at the large number of acceptable nonfat products.

We continued transitioning to a low-fat meatless diet by removing meat, poultry and fish from some of our favorite dishes, such as spaghetti, chili, and lasagna. We replaced the meat with beans, pasta, and vegetables. Our family and friends also began sending us recipes to adapt and ideas they thought would be useful.

During that time, I kept a daily log of the food we ate, paying particular attention to the amount of fat in the foods. I also purchased a fat counter, which proved invaluable. I used it to determine where fat occurred in our diet. To my surprise, I found that fat occurs naturally in food. It doesn't need to be added.

The cold turkey approach got tempting high-fat foods out of the house, and gave them visible results from the start. There is no better reinforcement than quick, visible results - feeling better, looking better and lower cholesterol levels.

The "Rome wasn't built in a day" approach advocates a gradual transition to low-fat foods, perhaps by achieving a couple of new low-fat goals each week. Proponents believe that since preferences aren't formed overnight, they can't be changed overnight. Although this method is somewhat easier to implement, it's much more difficult to maintain. Opponents believe that continuing to keep some high-fat foods in your home makes it difficult to permanently eliminate them from your diet.

Whichever method you choose, try not to be too hard on yourself. Changing your lifestyle is often a matter of trial and error. If you make mistakes along the way, simply pick up where you left off, note your accomplishments and envision your future goals.

Vegetarian Diets: Fact and Fiction

A vegetarian diet offers an endless variety of fresh, flavorful foods. By removing fat from meals, you begin to taste the food itself. Unfortunately, the typical American diet has degenerated to the point that the real flavor of foods is masked by fat, salt and sugar added in preparation.

Some vegetarian diets are not necessarily healthy, either. Generally, fat, salt and sugar are not restricted from vegetarian cuisine; therefore, many vegetarian snacks, such as ice cream and candy bars, wouldn't be recommended for someone following the Ornish program. It's also important for vegetarians to eat a wide variety of foods to meet their nutritional needs. We hope that *Vegetarian Cooking for Healthy Living* helps you experiment with new foods and old favorites.

Dr. Ornish's dietary plan offers two diet programs. For persons who already have heart disease, he recommends the Reversal Diet. For others, the Prevention Diet may be sufficient. You should consider your own health and lifestyle when determining which is best for you. If not sure, consult with your physician or registered dietitian. Regardless of which you choose, any of the recipes in *Vegetarian Cooking for Healthy Living* can be enjoyed as part of the diet lifestyle.

The Reversal Diet (which is primarily what the Ter Meers' have followed) excludes all animal products except for egg whites and nonfat dairy products such as skim milk, nonfat yogurt, and nonfat cheese. It also follows these principles:

- limit fat intake to ten percent of daily calories
- limit fat intake to monounsaturated and polyunsaturated fats, and little saturated fat
- limit use of oils
- limit cholesterol to five milligrams a day
- calories are not restricted
- diet is very high in fiber
- limit alcohol consumption
- eliminate caffeine
- salt and sugar may be used in moderation

Dr. Ornish's Prevention Diet is more liberal. If you don't have heart disease and your other risk factors are low, then some additional fat and cholesterol in your diet is acceptable. Dr. Ornish recommends first eliminating high-fat foods from your diet and then gradually decreasing your fat intake.

Vegetarian Cooking for Healthy Living uses these guidelines as a reference point. We are a bit more liberal in that we use cocoa (which contains caffeine), do not restrict sodium in all of the recipes, and suggest a number of low-fat convenience products like canned beans and tomatoes, sauces, boxed soy-based protein mixes and grain mixes. With hectic lifestyles, they can make the difference between eating healthier or grabbing what you can.

The Vegetarian Food Guide Pyramid (please see next page) is a great guide for building your ultra low-fat vegetarian diet. Keep in mind, however, that you probably want to avoid the low-fat dairy products shown in the pyramid and choose nonfat varieties. In addition, peanut butter, shown in the meat alternative group, is high in fat and not usually part of an ultra low-fat diet.

THE VEGETARIAN FOOD PYRAMID

A Daily Guide to Food Choices

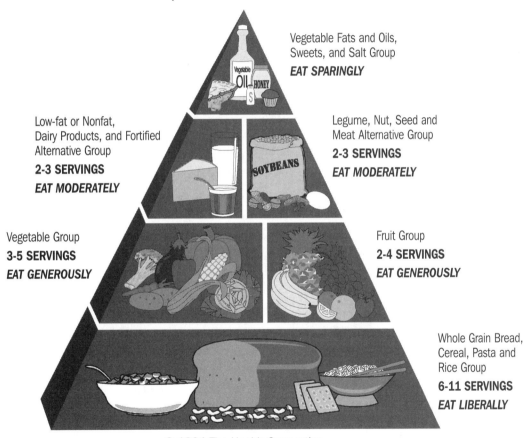

Vegetable Fats and Oils,
Sweets, and Salt Group
EAT SPARINGLY

Low-fat or Nonfat,
Dairy Products, and Fortified
Alternative Group
2-3 SERVINGS
EAT MODERATELY

Legume, Nut, Seed and
Meat Alternative Group
2-3 SERVINGS
EAT MODERATELY

Vegetable Group
3-5 SERVINGS
EAT GENEROUSLY

Fruit Group
2-4 SERVINGS
EAT GENEROUSLY

Whole Grain Bread,
Cereal, Pasta and
Rice Group
6-11 SERVINGS
EAT LIBERALLY

© 1994 The Health Connection.

The Vegetarian Food Guide Pyramid is available as a poster and as
handouts from the Health Connection. 1-800-548-8700.

The following sections contain in-depth nutrition information and explain how to further streamline your low-fat vegetarian diet.

Fats

As previously stated, the elimination of unnecessary fat from your diet is an integral part of the Ornish program and of our recipes and lifestyle suggestions. Your body does, however, need one tablespoon of polyunsaturated linoleic acid each day (approximately 14 grams of fat). But you don't need to actively seek this kind of fat. Even though fruits, vegetables, whole grain foods, and dried beans and legumes are essentially considered "fat-free", eating a variety of these foods each day provides enough linoleic acid. Other fats that your body needs can be synthesized from carbohydrates and proteins.

It's important to have a basic understanding of different types of dietary fat. Studies show it's not only the amount of fat in your diet that you should be concerned with, but the type of fat can impact your health. Keep in mind that most foods contain a combination of polyunsaturated, monounsaturated and saturated fats.

It is particularly important to avoid saturated fat as it significantly increases blood cholesterol levels. Some studies indicate that saturated fat plays a much greater role in raising blood cholesterol than does the actual cholesterol in foods. Because saturated fats are found primarily in animal products (meat, chicken, dairy foods and egg yolks) they are fairly easy to avoid on a vegetarian diet.

Significant amounts of saturated fats occur in only a few plant foods: coconuts, palm and palm kernel oils, for example. Avocados, nuts, and seeds also contain saturated fat, although a much larger percentage of their fat is monounsaturated. In his Reversal Diet, Dr. Ornish suggests not using nuts and seeds but you may find it acceptable to use them in moderation.

Fats can be checked visually to determine whether they are saturated. Any fat that is solid at room temperature is saturated and should be avoided, including vegetable shortening and some margarines. Although both products begin as polyunsaturated oils, they go through a process called hydrogenation, which adds additional hydrogen atoms to their chemical structure that makes them more solid. It also produces substances called trans-fatty acids, which raise blood cholesterol levels.

Most of the fat found in plant based foods is either poly or monounsaturated. In the past, doctors believed that polyunsaturated oils helped decrease cholesterol levels. An individual who replaced the saturated fat in their diet with polyunsaturated fat might show improvement in blood cholesterol. Many thought this meant they could use these fats (like corn, safflower, sunflower, sesame and peanut oils) liberally. While polyunsaturated fats are preferable to saturated fats, any fat used in excess is harmful. Polyunsaturated fats have also been linked to certain types of cancer as they produce metabolic by-products that cause oxidative damage to cells.

It is most desirable to use products with monounsaturated fats in food preparation. Olive and canola oils contain acceptable levels of monounsaturated fats. Canola oil may be the best choice as it also contains only about half the amount of saturated fat as does olive oil.

In order to determine your daily fat intake, we suggest keeping a food log. Carry a small notepad and write in it consistently. Be sure to write down everything you eat in a 24-hour period, and be complete. Everything you consume should be entered in the log, including sauces and condiments, portion sizes and how the food was prepared. Ideally, you should keep the record for three days, preferably two weekdays and one day of the weekend. We all tend to eat differently on our days off and when we socialize.

Next, using one of the references on page 225, list the amount of fat and saturated fat in each item. At the end of the day, total each column. This will give you an idea of your total fat and saturated fat intake for the day. To get a more accurate idea of your intake, average these totals for the three days. A registered dietitian can assist you with the analysis.

Once you know how much fat you're eating, determine how much you *should* be eating. If you already know approximately how many calories you eat in a day, and you don't need to gain or lose weight, the rest is easy. When you keep your food log, also write down the calories in your food, total them for each day, and average the three days. This will determine your average caloric intake.

Multiply this number by .10 if you want to follow Ornish's reversal diet, or by .20 if you want to follow a more preventative diet. Then divide by 9. For example, if you eat approximately 2000 calories per day and want your fat intake to be no more than 10 percent, you would be limited to 22 grams of fat per day.

You can also determine your caloric intake by using the reasonable body weight method. This method is especially useful if you need to lose or gain weight because the amount of fat that you eat is based on your goal weight instead of your actual weight. The Metropolitan Height and Weight Tables are provided in **Appendix A**, along with instructions for determining your reasonable body weight (RBW). For a diet of no more than 10% fat, divide your RBW by 6. For no more than 20% fat, divide your RBW by 3. If your RBW is 140 pounds, for example, you would limit your fat intake to 23 grams per day to achieve your goal of 10%.

Remember that you also have a fat minimum. If you are not meeting your minimum needs, you may need to add a little canola oil to make up the difference, perhaps as a teaspoon of oil on your salad. If you need assistance, contact a registered dietitian for further information on determining your reasonable body weight or fat intake, or *Dr. Dean Ornish's Program for Reversing Heart Disease.*

Participants starting a low-fat vegetarian diet frequently experience significant weight loss. Many have found that such a diet provides more food than they can eat, yet their weight loss continues. For many people, this type of weight loss is a positive side-benefit of a low-fat vegetarian diet. However, if weight loss becomes a problem, seek the advice of a registered dietitian or physician.

Proteins

Your body needs some protein each day. Specifically, it needs amino acids, the building blocks that make up protein. Dietary protein supplies amino acids so that the body can make its own proteins. These needs can be very easily met by a vegetarian diet.

Following is a sampling of protein needs for healthy people based on weight (needs would vary for pregnant and nursing women, children, certain athletes, and some medical problems):

- 125 pounds - needs approximately 45 grams
          of protein a day
- 150 pounds - needs approximately 55 grams
          of protein a day
- 200 pounds - needs approximately 73 grams
          of protein a day

Most Americans get 100 or more grams of protein a day, well above their needs for building and repairing body tissue.

Excess dietary protein is undesirable. First of all, much of this excess comes from animal products, high in cholesterol and saturated fat. Secondly, calories from excess protein will be stored as excess fat. Finally, when protein is metabolized, one of the byproducts is excess nitrogen. This must be excreted by the body, puts a heavy load on kidneys and can eventually lead to kidney damage.

Dietary proteins are complete or incomplete. Amino acids are essential or non-essential. Complete proteins are found in animal and soy products, and contain all the essential amino acids which cannot be synthesized by the body. Most plant proteins are incomplete, lacking one or more essential amino acids. By combining incomplete protein foods in your diet you get complete proteins.

In the past, the medical community believed that only animal products could supply the eight essential amino acids to make a complete protein. Now we know that eating a wide variety of plant-based foods throughout the day, not necessarily at the same meal, helps meet both your energy and protein needs.

Many of the recipes in this book offer complete protein, either through the use of soy-based meat substitutes or dairy products, or by a combination of complementary vegetable proteins. Some examples include:

Beans/Legumes + Cereals/Grains

Bean and Pasta Stew
Bean Lasagna
Beans and Vegetables with Rice
Blackeyed Peas and Corn
Corn, Bean and Rice Goulash
Crêpes with Hearty Bean Filling
Italian Pasta Salad
Lentil Patties with Tomato Chutney
Minestrone Salad

Minestrone Soup
Pasta and Bean Salad
Picanté Black Bean Casserole
Potato, Bean and Rice Soup
Spanish Rice and Beans
Summer Macaroni Salad
Tortilla Black Bean Casserole
Vegetable Stew with Cornmeal
   Dumplings

Vegetables/Green Leafy Vegetables + Whole Grains/Cereals

Cabbage Rolls
Penne with Artichokes and Leeks
Roasted Vegetable Strata
Szechuan Asparagus with Vermicelli
Vegetable Kabobs over Rice
Vegetable Lasagna
Vegetable Pita Sandwich
Vegetable Stir-Fry
Veggie Submarine Sandwich

Soy Protein + Whole Grains

Cornbread Hot Tamale Pie
"Ground Beef" Casserole
Sloppy Joes
Tofu Stuffed Shells
Tostadas

Whole Grains/Cereals + Nonfat Dairy Products

Banana Yogurt with Granola
Broccoli and Mostaccioli
Broccoli Ricotta Crêpes
Calzones
Creamy Fettuccine
Mosquito Coast French Toast

Pita Pizza
Polka Dot Chili
Raspberry Parfait
Rice Pudding
Strawberry Crêpes
Tomato Lasagna Rollups

Fiber

Besides being low in fat and cholesterol, the recommended diet includes foods high in dietary fiber. Eating a high fiber diet helps lower your blood cholesterol level, decrease constipation, aid weight control, and prevent cancers of the colon and breast. Fiber, often referred to as "roughage", is the indigestible portion of foods, found particularly in fruits, vegetables, dried beans and peas, and whole grains. Most Americans ingest approximately ten grams of fiber a day. The recommended amount is 25–35 grams a day.

A high fiber diet can be very useful in losing weight. High fiber foods take longer to digest than refined foods, so it takes longer to get hungry after eating them. Fiber also causes a slower release of glucose into the bloodstream, providing a more constant flow of fuel into your brain and body. When choosing grain products, it's important to note that whole grains are best and should be the foundation of your diet. These grains are unrefined and closest to their natural state. Foods that experience less processing are more nutrient-dense. Processing grains like wheat, barley, corn, rice, and oats usually removes most of their fiber. For that reason, it's important to choose products like bread made from 100% whole-wheat flour, whole-wheat pasta, brown rice instead of white, whole-oat cereal instead of refined, and whole cornmeal instead of degermed.

Several cautions accompany a high fiber diet. Fiber can interfere with the absorption of zinc, calcium, copper, iron, magnesium and other trace minerals. (A multi-vitamin and mineral supplement can help replenish them.) A change to a high-fiber diet should be done gradually. As you increase the amount of beans, whole grains, fruits and vegetables in your diet, also increase your fluids. If not, you'll become constipated. Try to drink at least eight glasses of non-caffeinated beverages each day.

Fruits and Vegetables

Once you've built the base of your diet with whole grains, add at least two to four servings of fruit and three to five servings of vegetables each day. In addition to providing fiber, they are loaded with a variety of vitamins and minerals. Citrus fruits, kiwi, strawberries, tomatoes and broccoli, for example, are great sources of vitamin C. Fruits and vegetables that are yellow-orange and deep-green in color are good sources of beta-carotene.

Vitamin C and beta-carotene appear to act as anti-oxidants in the body, inhibiting cancer formation and decreasing the arterial damage that can lead to the build-up of artery clogging plaques. Instead of focusing on one specific nutrient, however, be assured that fruits and vegetables contain a variety of compounds that act as anti-oxidants in the body, and by eating a wide variety, you won't miss any of them.

Fruits and vegetables add a lot of color and flavor to foods. Try experimenting with new varieties. If you are eating fruits and vegetables with a wide range of colors, you know you are getting a wide variety of vitamins, minerals and other beneficial non-nutritive substances.

Additional Vegetable Sources

Although whole grains and vegetables offer plenty of protein, alternative vegetable sources are available. The following sources deserve special attention:

• **Dried beans and Peas**: Black (turtle) beans, navy, pinto, kidney, cannellini, pink, adzuki, garbanzo (chickpeas), white, mung, and soy beans, split, green, and black-eye peas, and lentils (see Glossary of Beans, page 55).

Each of these products also provides iron, calcium, potassium, and phosphorous and fiber. And, they are an excellent source of complete protein when combined with grain products like corn, rice, and pasta.

• **Tofu and Soybean Derivatives**: Protein, calcium, magnesium, and zinc can all be found in tofu and other soybean derivatives.

Research indicates that the use of these products helps lower cholesterol and decrease cancer risk. Tofu, also known as soybean curd, is the most commonly known soybean product. Tofu and other soybean products blend well with other products because they have little flavor of their own and take on the flavor of the foods and seasonings with which they are cooked.

Texturized vegetable protein (TVP) is a protein that is extracted from soybeans. It works well as a meat substitute in dishes like chili, meatless pasta, or any dish that calls for ground beef or turkey. The texture of TVP is remarkably similar to that of ground meat, which allows you to eat some of your favorite dishes without the fat and cholesterol. If vegetarians eat some type of dried bean or soybean product combined with a whole grain each day, they can be assured of getting adequate protein. (See **Appendix D** for further information on brand specific meat alternatives).

Egg Whites and Nonfat Dairy Products

As mentioned previously, Dr. Ornish's Reversal Diet allows egg whites and nonfat dairy products. The nonfat dairy products, like skim milk or plain nonfat yogurt, are limited to one cup (eight ounces) a day, which provides the daily recommendation of 5 milligrams of cholesterol. Egg whites are also an excellent source of protein and are cholesterol-free so their use is unlimited.

If you choose to follow a more liberal low-fat diet, then additional nonfat dairy products can be used. With moderate use they slightly increase your cholesterol intake. Products such as nonfat sour cream or ricotta cheese contain little or no cholesterol and are fat-free. Choosing to use nonfat dairy products a bit more liberally can boost protein intake for people with increased needs and will provide additional calcium. Sometimes, using even a tablespoon of additional nonfat cheese, sour cream, or cream cheese can be satisfying while adding diversity to meals.

Salt and Sodium

Most Americans get too much sodium (a component of salt) in their diets, around 5000–6000 milligrams a day. The National Academy of Science recommends sodium intake be limited to 2400 milligrams a day. Consider that a teaspoon of salt contains about 2000 milligrams of sodium.

This high sodium intake doesn't come solely from the salt shaker, but from processed foods (packaged, canned and fast foods, for example), many of which have salt or sodium added as a preservative or flavor enhancer. Because a low-fat vegetarian diet relies on a lot of fresh foods, your sodium intake will probably decrease without many other changes.

If you have high blood pressure you should limit salt intake.

You should also limit salt and sodium intake if you have a problem with fluid retention and swelling (edema). If unsure of how much salt or sodium you should be using, contact your physician or registered dietitian.

Sugar

We have a preference for sweets even as infants. Sugar is the body's most basic energy source and a basic compound of food. The primary fuel used by the brain and preferred by muscle, our bodies need a constant supply to function optimally.

You may have heard that sugar robs your body of nutrients, causes hyperactivity in children, causes diabetes and more. None of these is true. Sugar usually only becomes a problem when overeaten, leaving little room for other foods. This is because sugar is a significant source of no other nutrient than calories. A lot of sugary foods are not the best choice when trying to eat an optimal, nutrient dense diet.

This reference to sugar includes honey, white and brown sugar, unbleached sugar, and other sweeteners, all essentially the same. There is nothing wrong with using sugar in moderation, but you'll want to cut back if you find you're using it on everything. Unless you have diabetes, or your physician or dietitian has recommended you avoid added sugars for another reason, it is preferable to use regular sweeteners instead of artificial sweeteners.

Nutrient Concerns

Vitamin B12

Since vegetarian diets limit animal products, it can be difficult for vegetarians to receive enough vitamin B12. However, by eating eight ounces of plain, nonfat yogurt or drinking skim milk each day, you can meet your needs.

Calcium

Nonfat dairy products also provide calcium, riboflavin and vitamin D. Milk and dairy products are often touted as the best source of calcium, but green leafy vegetables also contain significant amounts of calcium. Among other things, calcium intake decreases the risk of developing osteoporosis, a disease that causes bones to lose calcium, become brittle and subsequently break.

Osteoporosis is prevalent in American society, where intake of animal protein is too high. A diet high in animal protein causes bone to release calcium, which is then excreted. Even though the calcium intake of this low-fat vegetarian diet is not very high, needs are decreased with the decreased consumption of animal protein. Your body will use calcium more efficiently.

Iron

Vegetarian diets sometimes limit iron intake as the iron found in plant-based foods is not as easily absorbed as that from animal products. By eating iron-fortified breads and cereals and dark-green leafy vegetables, you can increase your iron intake. Dried beans and dried fruits such as raisins, apricots, or prunes also provide iron. Since vitamin C helps the body absorb iron more efficiently, try eating iron-rich foods along with a glass of juice or food high in vitamin C.

Nutrient Supplements

If you do not eat a wide variety of foods, or regularly take medication, we recommend taking a vitamin-mineral supplement. Women, especially, also need to take a daily calcium supplement. The body easily absorbs both calcium carbonate and calcium gluconate. You should not, however, view a supplement as a solution to a diet that is chronically inadequate. In general, a daily multi-vitamin that contains iron and trace minerals and meets one hundred percent of the U.S. Recommended Daily Allowances is adequate.

We hope that the discussion in this chapter has given you a clearer idea of what it means to switch to a low-fat vegetarian diet. The initial difficulty of giving up high-fat foods is quickly out-weighed by the benefits of low-fat foods: improved health, an increased culinary repertoire and weight loss. The change should be enjoyable and long-lasting.

Flavor with Fresh and Dried Herbs

The Bountiful Cupboard

Chapter 3

Stocking the Ultra Low-Fat Vegetarian Kitchen

Chapter 3 guides you in creating a culinary environment where you can cook low-fat vegetarian foods that look appealing and don't require more effort than high-fat foods. We'll explain which ingredients should be in your kitchen, how to organize your kitchen for efficient cooking, the equipment you'll need and how to prepare low-fat vegetarian meals. We'll also offer some tips for purchasing the freshest produce, reducing your time in the kitchen, methods of attractively presenting foods and seasoning the foods that you prepare.

Preparing Your Culinary Environment

Tips for Purchasing Ingredients

Knowing where to shop and what to purchase play an important role in stocking a nutritious low-fat vegetarian kitchen. Fruits, vegetables, grains, rice, pastas and organic products are important items to have on your kitchen shelves and in your refrigerator.

When shopping for fruits and vegetables, try to purchase fresh produce. If fresh produce isn't available, frozen varieties can also be used. Canned fruits and vegetables provide some nutrients, but not as many as fresh and frozen products, and usually have less flavor as a result of processing. Canned vegetables are also high in added sodium unless you purchase 'no salt added' varieties.

When selecting fresh fruits and vegetables, always look for unbruised, firm produce that is free of mold. If the fruits and vegetables have lost turgor (are limp or mushy), they are old or suffering from improper storage and are losing nutrients. In such an instance, try to choose a frozen variety. Also, look for bright colors. For example, a dark red strawberry has more nutrients than a pale strawberry.

Buying produce locally helps ensure freshness. Most produce in supermarkets is shipped from all over the United States and the world. While this offers a fabulous variety of produce, it means that produce has traveled a distance and has likely lost some of its nutrients. (Fruits and vegetables lose nutrients from the moment they are picked.) A local farmer's market or organic farm can provide excellent produce. The selection may be somewhat limited by season, but the freshness of the just-picked produce makes up for a lack of variety.

When purchasing grains, look for those in an unprocessed state, particularly whole grains as they contain more fiber. (If you buy grains in bulk from bins, be sure to wash them thoroughly.) Packaged grain mixes should be avoided because they are often high in sodium and added fat. Instead of buying a flavored rice mix, for example, buy quick-cooking brown rice which can be cooked in fat-free chicken broth with wild rice and parsley. If you have the time, add some baby peas or minced red pepper and carrots.

Most stores also sell boxed pastas and rice mixes that contain little sodium. We recommend the Bean Cuisine® brand. Fantastic Foods® rice, Marrakesh Express® couscous and Indian Harvest® rice blends also work well. (Please see **Appendix D** for suggested commercial mixes along with addresses and/or phone numbers.) If you choose a brand that requires added oil, decrease the fat content by decreasing or omitting the oil and adding fat-free broth instead.

Organic products offer another nutritious option. While the organic label is no guarantee, these products usually contain lower levels of chemical residues because they are grown without the use of chemical fertilizers and pesticides. Look for organic produce, organically grown cereals and grains, canned beans and products made with organically grown foods. Organic produce often has greater flavor than non-organic fruits and vegetables.

Most large supermarkets carry the ingredients you need to prepare your kitchen for low-fat vegetarian cooking. If you have trouble finding a particular item, talk to the store manager. While some large corporations offer healthier lines of food, many smaller companies specialize in producing foods that are, for example, low-fat, high-fiber and made with whole grains and organic ingredients. Some supermarkets shelve these foods in a special section. Instead of offering fat-free broth or rice mixes in their respective aisles, they may all be shelved in a "health food" aisle.

Also try shopping health food stores. While sometimes more expensive, they offer a wide variety of healthy products. Be sure to read labels since not all products in a health food store are low-fat.

Some Essential Ingredients

A functional ultra low-fat vegetarian kitchen contains a number of basic items. Keeping them on hand streamlines your food preparation and also eliminates the excuse of not having what you need to create a healthy meal. The following is a list of basics to keep on your kitchen shelves. Be sure to add your favorites and eliminate those you don't like. Also, in addition to these dry goods and dairy products, a refrigerator full of fruits and vegetables greatly expands your low-fat vegetarian meal options. (For a list of recommended brand-name products and addresses of the companies that produce them, see **Appendix D**):

- **beans (canned)** - black, pinto, kidney, great northern, butter, lima, navy
- **beans (dried)** - navy, pinto, lima, black-eyed peas
- **broth** - nonfat chicken and vegetable
- **crackers** - fat-free or matzoh
- **evaporated skim milk**
- **fat-free, cholesterol-free fat replacement** - Butter Buds®, Molly McButter®, Lighter Bake®, and nonfat cooking sprays.
- **flour** - whole-wheat, all-purpose, bread, rye
- **fruit (canned in juice)** - pineapple, mandarin oranges
- **fruit (dried)** - apricots, cranberries, prunes, raisins
- **grains** - barley, couscous, cornmeal, oatmeal
- **lentils and split peas**
- **juices** - orange, apple, pineapple, low-sodium tomato and V-8®
- **Midland Harvest®** - Burger 'n Loaf® mix (note: these products are 100% vegetable protein and very low in fat). Some of the varieties in this series include mixes for making casseroles, chili, tacos and sloppy Joes. The Ground Beef

Casserole recipe in this cookbook uses the Burger 'n Loaf Herb 'n Spice® mix. The Taco Filling and Dip® is used in the Tostados.

- **noodles** - egg-free
- **pastas** - include some whole-wheat and vegetable varieties, mostaccioli, macaroni, fettuccine, linguine, spaghetti, angel hair, rotini
- **Pioneer Biscuit Mix®**
- **potatoes** - try assorted varieties like Yukon Gold® and Redskin®
- **rice** - brown, wild, white
- **salad dressings** - assorted nonfat varieties, many make good marinades
- **sun-dried tomatoes** (without oil)
- **Texturized Vegetable Protein®** (TVP) - This product enables you to easily adapt all your recipes that require meat. For example, unflavored TVP granules are used in the Hot Tamale Pie, Sloppy Joes and the Mashed Potato Pie.
- **tomatoes** (canned) (whole and crushed) - either 16 ounces or 28 ounces
- **spices** (We suggest purchasing them gradually as they can be expensive.) - allspice, basil, bay leaves, caraway seed, chives, celery seed, chili powder, cinnamon, cloves, dill weed, cumin, fennel, garlic powder, ginger, Italian seasoning, dry mustard, nutmeg, mint, minced onion, onion powder, oregano, parsley, paprika, red pepper (cayenne), ground black pepper and peppercorns, poppy seeds, rosemary, summer savory, thyme, tarragon, Mrs. Dash®, lemon pepper, salt-free Spike®
- **vinegar** - rice, apple cider, raspberry, balsamic
- **dairy** - cheese (nonfat, less than five milligrams of cholesterol per serving), Eggbeaters® (or other nonfat cholesterol-free egg substitute), ricotta cheese (nonfat, less than five milligrams of cholesterol per serving)
- **sour cream** - nonfat, cholesterol-free
- **yogurt** - nonfat, five milligrams of cholesterol per serving

Reorganizing Your Workspace

Increasing the number of products that you keep on your kitchen shelves and in your refrigerator may require some reorganizing of your kitchen space. Positioning plastic baskets on top of the hydrator drawers in the refrigerator doubles the storage space for fruits and vegetables. The meat drawer can then be used for storing nonfat cheese and packaged foods that require refrigeration. Placing the foods that you use often and in quantity, such as rice, dried beans, pastas and flour in stackable canisters saves space. You may also need additional space for a variety of canned goods including staples like canned tomatoes, beans, pasta sauce and nonfat chicken and vegetable broth. A well-stocked kitchen enables you to prepare the recipes in this book as well as some of your other favorites.

Equipment

You don't need to purchase a lot of new or special kitchen equipment to begin a low-fat vegetarian lifestyle, but there are some items that make low-fat cooking easier. To get started, we suggest purchasing the following equipment:

- **blender or food processor** - great for chopping, puréeing and blending foods. It can also be useful when you blend yogurt cheese or other fat-free dairy products for dips and sauces. A large food processor is also useful if you cook in large amounts. Otherwise, a regular blender works well.

- **stainless steel steamer basket** - essential for cooking vegetables without fat. Simply fill the bottom of a pan with water, place the steamer in the pan, fill the steamer with vegetables, cover and steam on high until vegetables achieve desired texture. Steamed vegetables are particularly healthy because they retain most of their nutrients and their original bright colors, unlike vegetables that are boiled in liquid or fried at high temperatures. If you want to go a step further, purchase a microwave steamer. Vegetables steamed in the microwave retain even more nutrients than those steamed conventionally.

- **salad spinner** - makes salad preparation easier. Simply wash your salad greens, place them in the salad spinner, and drain off the liquid. Use only what you want and leave the rest in the salad spinner in the refrigerator. Doing so keeps the salad greens crisp and ready to use for several days.

- **nonstick cookware** - essential because it eliminates the need to add fat during food preparation.

- **sharp knives and suitable cutting boards** - imperative because a low-fat vegetarian diet requires cutting and chopping of many fresh fruits and vegetables. Keep several cutting boards of different sizes on hand and keep your knives sharp. If you don't feel comfortable using a sharpening stone, buy a sharpening tool for your knives. Some chefs believe in sharpening knives every time they are used.

You may also find these items helpful when cooking:

- **colander and/or strainer**
- **cheesecloth and/or large coffee filters** - for making yogurt cheese
- **fat separator** - for skimming any fat off of soups and broths
- **cheese grater** - for shredding or grating vegetables and citrus zest
- **plastic or nonstick utensils** - for use with nonstick cookware
- **plastic freezer containers** - for freezing foods prepared in quantity or advance
- **five quart pot** - for preparing soups, rice and pasta in large quantities (you might even want an eight or twelve quart pot if you like to prepare soups in large quantities for freezing)
- **nonstick baking pans**

Cooking Methods

Now that you have purchased some basic ingredients and have arranged your kitchen for efficient vegetarian cooking, you're ready to begin preparing some low-fat vegetarian foods. As you begin cooking, the methods that you use play an important role in producing truly low-fat meals. First, forget deep or pan-frying foods! Instead, you'll want to steam, poach, broil, bake, grill, sauté, stir-fry and microwave your low-fat vegetarian foods.

Second, remember that nonfat cooking spray is essential for low-fat cooking. You can eliminate the need for oil when sautéing or stir-frying by spraying the pan with nonfat cooking spray before heating. You will find this particularly useful, for example, when quickly sautéing onions or garlic, when cooking egg whites or liquid egg substitutes or grilling a sandwich. Also, use it to coat baking pans to keep baked goods from sticking instead of greasing a pan with oil or shortening. Spraying foods with nonfat cooking spray before baking also facilitates browning.

Baking

Baked goods and desserts can be included in a low-fat diet if substitutions are made for some high-fat ingredients. Several new products make low-fat substitutions easy. For example, Lighter Bake®, a fruit purée, works well as a substitute for oil in cookies and breads. You can eliminate all of the shortening in a recipe and substitute with half the amount of Lighter Bake®.

Fruit purées make good fat substitutes. You may need to experiment a little, but in general, fruit purée can be substituted for an equal measure of oil. It's important to use a fruit that doesn't impart too much of its own flavor to the finished product. Prune and pear purées as well as applesauce are particularly unobtrusive. Occasionally, nonfat plain yogurt can be substituted for oil. Usually, yogurt should be substituted in equal amounts but some recipes require further adjustments.

Egg whites or a fat-free, cholesterol-free egg product should always be substituted for eggs in a recipe. Two egg whites or ¼ cup egg substitute are equivalent to one whole egg. If you need to use more than ¾ cup egg substitute in a recipe, you should reduce the amount of other liquids in the recipe by two tablespoons.

Sugar in a recipe can be decreased by half without affecting the end product. First, try reducing it by ¼, check the results and decrease the amount gradually the next time you make the recipe.

Salt can also be reduced and sometimes eliminated entirely. Cut back gradually as it may affect the degree to which a baked item rises. Begin by reducing the salt content by half.

Substituting whole-wheat flour for all or part of the regular flour in a recipe increases the fiber and nutrient content of baked goods. Begin by substituting one half of the white flour. If you are satisfied with the results, try substituting a little more next time. Items made with whole-wheat flour often seem heavier, but your taste buds will gradually adjust to the new texture. Unbleached all-purpose flour can also be used in place of regular white flour.

Flavor Boosters

The use of fresh fruits and vegetables in your cooking automatically adds a lot of flavor to your food. However, you can further increase the flavor of your foods through skillful use of herbs, spices, extracts, imitation flavorings and juices and broths.

Fresh herbs have a flavor all their own and greatly enhance the taste of food. When using fresh herbs, you can use up to three times more than dried herbs. Try growing your own herbs or purchase a few fresh bunches at the supermarket. Home gardeners particularly like basil, parsley, chives and dill. These herbs flourish in indoor gardens, on lanais, balconies or window sills. Freshly cut herbs also impart greater flavor than the dried varieties, although either will achieve the desire effect of adding flavor to foods. To release the flavor of dried herbs, pinch them between your fingers.

The world of extracts and imitation flavorings contains many exciting options. Maple extract added to Grape Nuts® cereal, for example, creates a product much like walnuts and can be used in baking. Try using butter flavoring in recipes that call for a stronger essence of butter. Almond and vanilla extracts also taste delicious in baked items.

Liquefying Butter Buds® or Molly McButter® according to package directions creates a useful imitation for butter. A drop or two of imitation butter flavoring intensifies flavor and can be drizzled over vegetables, pancakes, or any other food you seek to enhance with fat-free butter flavor.

Ordinary nonfat, cholesterol-free mayonnaise increases in flavor when combined with minced garlic or freshly ground pepper, capers, chives, chopped onions, chili sauce, salsa, horseradish, snipped parsley or basil. A handful of chopped fresh basil blended with ⅓ cup nonfat mayonnaise and a teaspoon of vinegar or lemon juice makes a wonderful spread for sandwiches or dressing for potato salads.

For rice or pasta being served as a side dish, add fat-free chicken or vegetable broth for more flavor. Some nonfat, low sodium varieties are available (see **Appendix D**).

If you desire a hint of meat flavor in your recipes, use imitation bacon pieces. Always choose a low-fat, cholesterol-free product like Bac'n Pieces® or Baco's®. Imitation bacon pieces have a distinct meat flavor, so smaller portions can be used.

To achieve heightened flavor when not using oil or fat in cooking, use garlic, mustard, onion, vinegars, hot pepper sauce, fresh herbs and spices, fruit juices, zest of lemon, lime or oranges, and commercial salt-free herb 'n spice seasoning mixes. They can be used as a substitute for omitted salt.

Roasted red peppers also improve many foods such as casseroles, vegetables, salads and sandwiches. They add fabulous flavor and color to meals. (see Food Preparation Guidelines later in this chapter for more information.)

The cooking liquids from vegetables can later be used to sauté vegetables or cook rice and as a base for soups. Low-sodium tomato and V-8® juice, fruit juices and nonfat chicken broth also increase moisture and flavor.

Time Savers

Planning ahead takes only a few minutes and makes food preparation much easier. Using the following time-saving tips will leave you more time to enjoy the foods that you prepare.

When making a casserole, double the recipe and freeze one. You might as well make two while you have the time and ingredients at hand.

Make good use of the automatic timer on your oven, or use a crock-pot. Dinner will be ready when you get home. Care must be taken with recipes that include egg or dairy products. If they are left unrefrigerated for a long time before cooking, they can spoil.

When you're chopping vegetables for a stir-fry, chop some extra to keep in the refrigerator for snacking. Cook large batches of white and brown rice. Package for freezing in two-cup portions of either white or brown rice. Or, if you prefer, freeze one cup of brown and one cup of white rice together for persons who haven't become accustomed to the nuttier flavor and heavier texture of high-fiber brown rice. Then, when you need rice, thaw and serve.

When cooking rice, it helps to dextrinize brown rice, which shortens cooking time and makes the rice lighter and fluffier. To dextrinize, heat uncooked brown rice in a dry frying pan over medium heat, stirring often to keep it from burning. Heat it until the rice becomes slightly darker and begins to smell nutty. At this point, the rice is ready to cook as directed. Omit butter and salt and reduce the cooking time to 25 minutes (instead of 45–50 minutes). Some newer varieties of brown rice cook in less time.

Potatoes are a staple and should be kept on hand. Bake potatoes along with casseroles or whenever you're using the oven. They can then be reheated quickly in the microwave. The microwave should be used for cooking whenever possible. It greatly reduces cooking time and helps preserve the nutrients in foods.

When making crêpes for a recipe, make them in quantity and freeze them between pieces of wax paper. When thawed, they can be used to make a delicious dinner or dessert.

Take advantage of the many varieties of salad greens and precut vegetables in the produce section of the supermarket. Many are even pre-washed which saves a great deal of time during food preparation. Likewise, try precut varieties of fresh melon and pineapple, also found in the produce section.

Food Presentation

The experience of eating involves all the senses, and the appearance of food has a great impact on whether we think it tastes good. Luckily, a vegetarian diet never has to lack color due to the wide variety of fruits and vegetables available. For example, imagine bright red peppers or the appealing colors of oranges, carrots and sweet potatoes. Also, consider the variety of deep green vegetables and salad greens and even the pink, black and speckled colors of beans. The colors are endless and create a feast for the eyes.

The presentation of food on a plate is also very important. Food, including garnishes, should be arranged attractively. Instead of the overused sprig of parsley, considering using:

- fresh sprigs of mint or dill
- a slice of citrus beside an entrée or dessert
- chopped red pepper sprinkled lightly on top of a salad or over an entire plate of food
- fat-free croutons floating in soups
- shredded carrots sprinkled around the edge of a plate
- fresh sprouts spread around a sandwich or over a baked potato (sprouts can be substituted by a thinly curled or chopped green onion)
- powdered sugar sprinkled over a plate under and around a dessert
- raspberries or a strawberry fan placed beside a scoop of fruit sorbet
- finely chopped fresh parsley or basil sprinkled like confetti over a plate before pasta is served

The plates on which you serve your food also make a difference. Try serving a plain dessert on your finest china. Eating nonfat plain yogurt with fresh berries out of a fine glass sherbet dish or crystal champagne glass suggests more indulgent tastes than a cereal bowl. Colored service-ware also makes a difference. For example, pasta with a bright-red marinara sauce served on a cobalt-blue plate is striking.

Seasonings

Bread Crumbs

Bread crumbs can be used in a variety of capacities. To prepare them, bake stale bread crusts at 225°. When the bread crumbs are thoroughly dry, process them in your blender or food processor. Next, season them with a mixture of your favorite dried herbs or garlic powder. The seasonings stick together better if the crumbs are first sprayed lightly with a nonfat cooking spray. The dried bread crumbs stay fresh for several weeks in a tightly-sealed container in the refrigerator. Seasoned bread crumbs, crushed cereal, matzoh or nonfat crackers are good choices for topping off a casserole. Spray lightly with a nonfat cooking spray to aid in browning.

Roasted Red Peppers

Roasted red peppers add both color and flavor to casseroles, sandwiches, dips and salads. To roast peppers, broil them for approximately 20 minutes or until the skins are black and blistered. Turn them every five minutes. Then, place them in a paper bag to steam for 15 minutes. When the peppers are cool enough to handle, peel off the skin, trim the seeds and use them as you wish. Roasted peppers stay fresh for up to two weeks if placed in water in the refrigerator.

Vegetables

Advances in agriculture and shipping make a wide variety of fresh vegetables available. Don't be afraid to experiment with different combinations or vegetables, or to substitute one vegetable for another. Always thoroughly wash vegetables before use to rid them of any pesticides or fertilizer residues.

Suggestions for Seasoning Vegetables

We recommend using chopped onion, green and red peppers, garlic, fresh parsley and cilantro to season vegetables. A splash of lemon or lime juice and vinegar also add pizzazz. Used alone, lemon juice enhances the natural flavor of a vegetable.

Following is a list of seasonings that taste particularly good with specific vegetables:

asparagus	garlic, lemon juice, onion, tarragon, vinegar
beans	caraway, cloves, cumin, mint, onion, green or red peppers, savory, tarragon, thyme
beets	basil, caraway, dill, savory, thyme
brussels sprouts	basil, caraway, dill, savory, thyme
cabbage	celery seed, caraway, dill, tarragon
carrots	cinnamon, cloves, mint, sage, tarragon, basil, parsley, dill
cauliflower	dill, rosemary, tarragon
corn	allspice, green peppers, black pepper
cucumbers	basil, dill, garlic, vinegar
greens	lemon juice, onion, vinegar
peas	mint, mushrooms, onion, parsley, dill, basil
potatoes	chives, basil, dill, garlic, onion
squash	allspice, dill, cinnamon, cloves, ginger, nutmeg
tomatoes	basil, bay leaf, onion, tarragon, thyme, vinegar (red wine or balsamic)
zucchini	basil, dill, garlic, onion, oregano

Vinegars

Vinegars have been a staple ingredient for innumerable years. It only takes a small amount of vinegar to impart a lot of flavor. Vinegars also come in many varieties with significant differences in taste.

Rice wine vinegar is less acetic and subtler in flavor, so it has more uses than other varieties. Balsamic vinegar, with its rich color and aromatic scent, occupies the other end of the spectrum and should be used in smaller amounts. White and red wine vinegars are also available and enhance many foods.

Supermarkets carry many excellent herbal vinegars which can

also be prepared at home. To do so, pour hot red or white wine vinegar, or even plain white vinegar, in sterile jars and add sprigs of fresh herbs and spices. In a month your vinegar will be ready. Add your favorite herbs and spices to tailor the vinegar to your liking. We recommend using fresh sprigs of your favorite herbs and spices with combinations of garlic cloves, freshly ground pepper, bay leaves, lime or lemon juice, mustard or mustard seed, or fresh dill. There's really no limit to the combinations that you can try.

Keep some vinegars on your kitchen shelves for future use. They need to steep for at least a month. Once they've done so, they can be used in a number of ways. For example, vinegars used in marinades taste wonderful. Marinated beans and vegetables served chilled with orzo and rice are also delicious.

When raspberries are in season, raspberry vinegar is always a favorite. To prepare raspberry vinegar, bring white vinegar to a simmer and add raspberries that have been rinsed and cooled. Maintain a proportion of two cups of vinegar to one pint of berries. Cool, cover and allow them to steep in your refrigerator or a cool place for two or three days. After the vinegar has steeped, strain the raspberries out and the raspberry vinegar is ready for use in your favorite recipes.

You can add a touch of sugar, honey or other seasonings, or make vinaigrette by adding a small amount of nonfat plain yogurt or nonfat sour cream to your vinegar. The lightly sweetened result is a wonderful fat-free, low-sodium complement to vegetables. A splash of raspberry vinegar tastes particularly refreshing over cooked green beans.

Yogurt Cheese

Yogurt cheese provides an excellent nonfat substitute for cream cheese, sour cream and mayonnaise. It adds a rich taste to foods without adding fat. As you begin to incorporate it into your food preparation, you'll be amazed at its versatility.

To make your own yogurt cheese, use any nonfat plain yogurt that has not had a stabilizer or gelatin added. Most common supermarket brands work well for this purpose. A 32-ounce carton of yogurt yields

1 to 1½ cups of yogurt cheese, depending on how long it is drained.

To drain yogurt cheese, line a strainer or colander with cheese-cloth or a large coffee filter and spoon yogurt into the strainer. Cover and place it over a bowl in the refrigerator overnight, allowing the whey (the liquid) to drain out. Then, discard the liquid. Store the resulting yogurt cheese in the refrigerator if not used immediately.

Yogurt cheese can be used without alteration as a spread on canapés or bagels. When chives are added, it becomes a topping for baked potatoes. When mixed with salsa, it becomes a dip for raw vegetables. Also, follow the recipe for any cheesecake-like desserts, substituting the yogurt cheese for regular cream cheese. Yogurt cheese can also be sweetened lightly with honey or sugar and served with fruit in rolled-up crêpes.

Oils, Margarines and Imitations

Chapter 2 provides an explanation of the types of fats. From that discussion, you know that highly monounsaturated fats are best for your health and are found, for example, in olive and canola oils. These oils can be used in food preparation. You should also look for them when reading the label of a prepared product. Regardless of what type of oil you use, keep in mind that a tablespoon of oil contains 14 grams of fat, so all oils should be used sparingly.

Olive oil has a distinct flavor and should be used only when you wish to highlight that flavor in your foods. For example, it would be a great addition to a pasta or rice dish, but would be less appealing (if not distasteful) in many baked breads and muffins. Darker olive oils have a stronger taste. For a lighter taste, try canola oil. It is usually the preferred oil for baked items. If you have a recipe that calls for margarine, try substituting one of these liquid oils instead. They can often be added without affecting the outcome of the recipe. When cooking at a high temperature, use oil instead of margarine because margarine releases carcinogens when cooked at high heat.

When preparing a recipe that calls for oil, try cutting it in half. If this is successful, you may find that you can eliminate it entirely. Margarines can usually be successfully substituted for butter in recipes. Some "light" or fat-free margarines may not work well as butter substitutes for cooking at high temperatures because they have a high water content, which can affect the outcome of baked goods. Always look for margarine with liquid canola oil as the first ingredient. See **Appendix C** for more information on label reading.

Nonfat cooking sprays make it easier to prepare foods without added fat. Although nonfat cooking sprays contain oils, spraying them allows you to use a small and insignificant amount of oil. Use nonfat cooking spray whenever a cooking pan or utensil needs to be oiled, and for sautéing and stir-frying. For example, spraying it on vegetables and potatoes that you plan to bake helps them brown and crisp without adding fat.

When sautéing a dense vegetable, you may need more moisture than the cooking sprays provide. Try adding a tablespoon or two of fat-free chicken or vegetable broth, water or wine to help steam the vegetables. This process also improves the vegetables' flavor.

Liquefied artificial butter sprinkles (Molly McButter® or Butter Buds®) serve a variety of purposes. They can be drizzled over vegetables, or can replace butter that is included primarily for taste. The **Pumpkin Pie** recipe (see page 221) called for two tablespoons of melted extra-light margarine. We adapted the recipe by using two tablespoons of liquefied butter sprinkles and ¼ teaspoon of butter flavoring. This eliminated 12 grams of fat without sacrificing flavor.

Substitutions

Many of your favorite recipes can be adapted to fit within the ultra low-fat or nonfat guidelines by making some simple substitutions. Use the following guidelines as a starting point:

INSTEAD OF:	TRY:
Milk	Skim Milk*
Cream or half and half	Evaporated skim milk
Shortening or oil in baking	Fruit purées
White flour	All, or half, whole-wheat flour
Oil for sautéing	Fat-free broth
Cream cheese	Yogurt cheese or fat-free cream cheese
Sour cream	Plain nonfat yogurt or fat-free sour cream

1 cup buttermilk or sour milk	Measure 1½ tbsp. vinegar into 1-cup measuring cup and add skim milk to equal 1 cup
1 whole egg	2 egg whites or ¼ cup nonfat, cholesterol-free egg substitute
Egg yolk for white sauce	Add a little egg substitute to a white sauce to achieve cream color
½ cup margarine	⅓ cup canola oil
1 tablespoon margarine	2¼ teaspoons canola oil
1 ounce baking chocolate	3 tbsp. nonfat cocoa powder plus 1 tbsp. canola oil, or cocoa powder and a fruit purée

*Use a nonfat, cholesterol-free coffee creamer (like nonfat Coffeemate®) to enrich skim milk in some of your recipes.

There are a number of ingredients that you can use as thickeners for sauces and soups: Puréed cooked vegetables such as broccoli, onions, peppers, potatoes and beans; leftover pasta puréed in a nonfat broth; tofu blended with a small amount of water. Other more common thickeners include flour, cornstarch, or arrowroot.

Sodium Reduction

As discussed in the first section of this book, sodium may or may not be something that you are trying to cut back on. Sodium occurs naturally in foods, and you get plenty of it without ever adding any. Following are some ways that you can cut back on sodium in your food preparation.

- Buy 'no salt added' or low sodium varieties of canned vegetables or processed foods when available.
- Rinse and drain all regular canned vegetables and beans before cooking or serving them.
- Avoid pre-packaged mixes. They usually contain a lot of added sodium.
- Rely on herbs and spices for adding flavor to your food. Put away the salt shaker!
- Try salt-free seasonings like Mrs. Dash®, lemon pepper, and salt-free Spike®.

- Use garlic or hot sauce to eliminate the need for salt without compromising taste.
- Make your own vegetable or chicken broth without added salt. Avoid using bouillon or dried soup mixes.
- Try to eliminate salt from recipes. Begin by omitting half, then, if the results are acceptable, eliminate it entirely the next time.

A Word About the Recipes

Nutrient Analysis of Recipes

Each recipe has been analyzed with the Nutritionist III® software program. Values are provided for calories, grams of fat, protein, carbohydrate and fiber and milligrams of cholesterol and sodium. Dietary exchanges for those managing their weight or diabetes are provided along with the nutrient analysis.

Preparation tips or notes are given along the side of many recipes to help the reader acquire ingredients or understand the recipe method.

As used in the recipes herein, the designation ® refers to registered trademarks for products that are not manufactured or sold by the publisher or the authors. The owners of such trademarks have no affiliation with the publishers or authors.

Chapter 4

Fabulously Fit Main Dishes: Beans and Legumes

Once a person accepts the philosophy that a well balanced diet need not include meat, the possibilities for entrées are endless.

The entrées in this chapter are built on a foundation of beans, other legumes and grains. The increasing availability of meat substitutes, such as texturized vegetable protein (TVP) and soybean curd (tofu), provide a great source of non-animal protein and allow for greater variety and creativity in vegetarian entrées.

When decreasing fat in favorite dishes, remember to add more liquid when cooking without meat juices, added oils or other fat. Good liquid replacements include fat-free broth, juice, wine, water or flavored vinegars.

Beans

Beans are a very versatile food and will soon become a staple in your kitchen. They're a powerhouse of good nutrition, come in many varieties and are inexpensive.

Beans are actually a member of the legume family, the best source of plant protein, of which there are many thousands of varieties. High in fiber, low in fat, and a good source of iron and calcium, legumes are edible seeds that grow in pods, and include split peas and lentils as well as beans. They are treated as vegetables when fresh, but collectively as legumes when dried. Lima beans and black-eyed peas are good examples of this.

In preparation, first remember to pick over all dried beans or peas, removing any small stones or other foreign particles, then rinse. To shorten cooking time (by hours, actually), all beans should be soaked. The only exceptions are split peas, lentils and black-eyed peas. You can use either the overnight or quick method.

To soak beans overnight, simply place the beans in a large pot, cover with water, cover with a lid and soak. You can leave them sitting on the stove if you wish, but placing them in the refrigerator will help prevent them from souring. After soaking, drain and they're ready to use.

For the quick soaking method, place beans in water in a large pot and bring to a boil over high heat. Boil gently for five minutes, turn off the heat, and let them soak, covered, for one to two hours, then drain.

Draining the water that the beans are soaked in will help get rid of a lot of the substances that tend to cause gas, as they leach into the water during soaking. Also, changing the water several times during the soaking period will have the same effect. If you find that eating beans causes your gastrointestinal system to suffer too much from gas, you may want to try a product called Beano®. Sold in supermarkets and drugstores, it helps digest the naturally occurring sugars in the beans that are the culprit in causing gas and bloating.

If you can't find the time to soak beans, you will find many varieties available canned. These tend to have a lot of salt added during processing, so be sure to drain and rinse thoroughly in order to decrease the sodium if that is a concern for you.

When beans are ready to be cooked, place them in a heavy pot with three cups of water for each cup of soaked beans, or four cups of water for each cup of unsoaked beans. Bring them to a boil over high heat, then reduce the heat, cover, and simmer until tender.

When cooking in hard water, it may be necessary to add ⅛–¼ teaspoon baking soda to the cooking water per cup of legumes. Also note that acidic ingredients, like vinegars or tomato sauce, should not be added until the legumes are tender. If added too early, the beans or peas will not soften properly.

The following glossary of beans will guide you in your selection, while the cooking chart will enable you to cook beans to just the right texture.

Glossary of Legumes: Beans, Peas, and Lentils

Adzuki - Also called azuki. A small red or brownish bean frequently used in Japanese or Chinese food, somewhat sweet and with a soft texture, it is often mixed with brown rice or other grains.

Anasazi Bean - Native to southwestern United States, they are a maroon and white speckled bean that can be used in place of pinto beans.

Black Bean - Native to Carribean and Latin America cuisine. A small, oval, dark black bean, with soft texture and earthy taste, they are popularly used in black bean soup and black beans and rice.

Black-eyed Pea - Also known as cowpea, it is not really a pea but a bean popular in cooking of the southeastern United States. Creamy in color with a single black spot on the skin, this medium-sized bean has a firm texture and mild flavor. Fresh black-eye peas are especially tasty.

Broad Bean - Also called fava beans, they are a staple of Mediterranean and Middle Eastern cooking used in casseroles, soups and stews. Large, flat, brown, oval beans somewhat resembling the lima in shape, they have a firm, mealy texture with thick skins that must be removed before eating.

Cannellini Bean - These large white kidney beans, a favorite in Italian casseroles, soups and sauces, are most popularly purchased as a canned variety.

Chickpea - Also called garbanzo beans in Latin American cooking and cecis in Italian cooking, they are also popular in Indian and Middle Eastern cuisine, known widely as the legume used to make hummus spread. They are round, about the size of a small hazelnut, creamy yellow to tan colored, with a firm texture and nutty taste.

Cranberry Bean - A medium-sized oval bean, beige or light brown with splashes of pink or red spots on their skin, and a mild nutty flavor. Traditionally used in New England baked beans.

Flageolets - Widely used in France, these are actually immature kidney beans, pale green in color.

Garden Pea - This legume is most commonly eaten fresh, as a vegetable, and does not require long cooking times as do other legumes. They are green, round, and sweet, varying in size from tiny "baby peas" to the larger, more mature pea. Snow peas and sugar snap peas are varieties of green pea whose pods may be eaten.

Great Northern Bean - A large, kidney shaped white bean, firm and very mild-flavored. Good in soups and casseroles.

Green Bean - Usually eaten as a vegetable, this common bean is the young, green form of the kidney bean.

Kidney Bean - Available as white or various shades of red, this bean is named for its oval, kidney shape, has a soft and somewhat meaty texture, and tastes rather bland. It is a good choice for chili, soups and casseroles.

Lentil - Frequently used in Indian, Mediterranean and Middle Eastern cuisines, they are grown in many varieties. Brown and green lentils are the most common in the United States. They are small, round, and flat, with a taste of pepper that can sometimes lend a "bite" to their flavor. They do not require presoaking, cook quickly and are commonly used in soup or as a side dish.

Lima Bean - These are often eaten as a fresh green bean as well as prepared from dried beans, probably most familiar as the bean used in succotash. They are either small, oval, green baby limas with a mild taste and soft texture, or larger beans sometimes called Fordhook or butter beans with a thicker skin and more white in color.

Mung Bean - Also called golden gram or green gram. Popular in Asian cuisine, this is a tiny bean, about half the size of a pea, usually green, yellow, or brown in color. With a somewhat sweet taste, they are most often eaten sprouted and raw, especially in salads or on sandwiches, but can be cooked quickly.

Navy Bean - Also called pea beans or small white beans, these are a small, roundish, more dense and mildly flavored version of the Great Northern bean, ranging in color from white to tan. Most commonly used in soups or baked beans.

Pigeon Pea - A small red or brownish pea common to African and Carribean cuisine. It has a rather strong taste, but is good mixed with a mild rice.

Pinto Bean - Common to cuisine of Mexico and the southwestern United States, they have the highest fiber content of any legume. Small or medium-sized, pale beige or pinkish oval beans, covered with brown speckles, they have a mild, earthy flavor.

Red beans - Popular in the Cajun dish of red beans and rice, these are a medium-sized oval bean, light red in color, with a rich flavor.

Soybean - A staple of Asian cuisine and the world's leading legume crop, it is high in protein and fat, being the only legume to provide complete protein. It is a round, firm bean with very little flavor and, although it can be eaten fresh in soups or side dishes, it is most often processed into other forms for more popular use. Soybeans are commonly used as a protein or meat supplement. Products include tofu, tempeh, texturized vegetable protein, soy sauce (tamari), miso, soymilk, soy cheese and soybean oil. Because the flavor is so bland, it is recommended to be prepared with other foods that will impart a stronger flavor.

Split Peas - They split apart once they have been dried and their skins removed, thus their name. Though these are available as either yellow or green peas, they are not eaten fresh like green peas. Popular in Indian cooking and well known in the United States for split pea soup, they don't require presoaking and cook quickly.

Legumes:
Cooking Times and Yields (for uncooked, soaked beans)

LEGUME	COOKING TIME	YIELD (cups)
Anasazi beans-1 cup	2 hours	2
Adzuki beans-1 cup	1–1½ hours	2
Black(turtle) beans-1 cup	1½-2 hours	2
Black-eye peas(cowpea)-1 cup	1 hour	2
Cannellini beans-1 cup	1½ hours	2
Chickpea(garbanzo bean)-1 cup	1½–2 hours	2½
Cranberry beans-1 cup	1½–2 hours	2½
Fava(broad) beans-½ cup	30–40 minutes	1
Flageolet beans-½ cup	1–1¼ hours	1½
Great northern beans-1 cup	1–1½ hours	2¼
Kidney beans-1 cup	1½ hours	2
Lentils*-1 cup	30-45 minutes	2
Lima beans-1 cup	¾-1 hour	2
Mung beans-½ cup	35-45 minutes	2
Navy beans-1 cup	1½ hours	2
Pinto beans-1 cup	1½–2 hours	2
Red beans-½ cup	1 hour	1½
Soybeans-1 cup	2–3 hours	2½
Split peas*-1 cup	30–45 minutes	2

(these do not require presoaking)

Bean Lasagna

9 X 13" BAKING DISH; 12 PORTIONS

2 medium onions, diced
4 cloves garlic, minced
½ 1b. mushrooms, diced
2 teaspoons oregano
1 teaspoon basil
¼ cup fresh parsley, snipped
½ teaspoon salt
1 16-oz. can (2 cups) pinto beans, drained, reserving ½-cup liquid
4 cups Italian style stewed tomatoes
9 lasagna noodles
3 cups nonfat cottage cheese
1 cup nonfat Mozzarella cheese, grated
Nonfat olive oil cooking spray

Sauté onions, garlic and mushrooms over medium heat in a skillet sprayed with nonfat olive oil cooking spray. Add spices and reserved liquid from the beans. Simmer for 5 to 10 minutes. Add beans and tomatoes. Cover and simmer for 10 minutes or until slightly thickened.

In a large deep saucepan, cook lasagna noodles until tender. Drain, rinse and separate to prevent sticking. Heat oven to 350°.

In separate bowl, combine cottage cheese with Mozzarella cheese.

Spray a 9 x 13-inch pan with cooking spray and assemble lasagna by layering ⅓ noodles, ⅓ cheese, ⅓ of tomato/bean mixture. Repeat twice. Bake at 350° for 40 minutes or until hot and bubbly.

NUTRITION INFORMATION PER SERVING

Serving Size: 1 portion

Calories: 194
Protein: ....15.5 g
Carbohydrate: ....31.5 g
Fat:......................................1 g
Cholesterol: ....7 mg
Sodium: ....711 mg
Fiber: ....1 g

Dietary Exchanges:
1½ starch, 2 vegetable and
1 very lean meat

N o t e :

Friendship® cottage cheese is a nonfat as well as cholesterol-free product, that works well in this recipe.

Beans and Vegetables with Rice

To shorten preparation time, cook large separate batches of brown and white rice. Package them for freezing in 2-cup packages; 1 cup brown and 1 cup white. When you're ready to prepare a recipe just defrost and it's ready to use.

4 PORTIONS

2   cups rice (half brown and half white rice, thawed)
1   cup chopped onion
3   cloves garlic, minced
2   medium tomatoes, diced
2   small zucchini or summer squash, chopped
½   teaspoon oregano
½   teaspoon cumin
¼   teaspoon salt
1   16-oz. can (2 cups) chili hot beans
     Pepper and Tabasco sauce to taste
     Nonfat cooking spray

Thaw rice and heat in microwave or oven until ready to use.

Sauté onions and garlic in pan sprayed with nonfat cooking spray. Add tomatoes, zucchini and seasonings. Cover and simmer until vegetables are tender. Add the beans and heat thoroughly. Season to taste and spoon onto the hot rice.

NUTRITION INFORMATION PER SERVING

Serving Size: 1 portion

Calories: 245
Protein: ....10 g
Carbohydrate: ....53 g
Fat:.................................2 g
Cholesterol: ....0 mg
Sodium: ....518 mg
Fiber: ....8 g

Dietary Exchanges:
  2 starch and 3 vegetable

N o t e :

If you don't have the prepared rice packets in your freezer, cook rice to equal 2 cups when cooked.

Black Beans and Rice

A very satisfying meal when served with a green salad and a whole grain bread.

6 PORTIONS

3 cups dried black beans, picked over and rinsed
6 cups nonfat chicken broth, divided
1 cup diced celery
1 large onion, chopped
4 cloves garlic, minced
½ cup uncooked white rice
⅛ teaspoon cayenne pepper
2 cups stewed tomatoes, cut up
3 bay leaves
1 teaspoon salt
2 to 4 peppercorns
   Salt-free Spike® or similar product to taste
½ cup nonfat powdered milk
6 tablespoons nonfat, cholesterol-free sour cream.
   garnish: green onions, frozen peas or sliced radishes

NUTRITION INFORMATION PER SERVING
Serving Size: 1 portion
Calories: 345
Protein: ....24.5 g
Carbohydrate: ....61.5 g
Fat: ....2 g
Cholesterol: ....1 mg
Sodium: ....942 mg
Fiber: ....8 g
Dietary Exchanges:
3 starch, 2 vegetable, 1 very lean meat and ½ skim milk

Preparation Tip:

Thin with a bit of water if the beans are too thick.

Soak beans overnight. Drain, rinse and cook with 4 cups broth until tender, about 2 hours. Sauté celery, onions and garlic until soft; add to the beans. Add rice, cayenne pepper, tomatoes, bay leaves, salt, peppercorns and 1½ cups broth, reserving ½ cup broth for later. Cook 1 hour.

Stir the powdered milk into the remaining broth and add to the beans. Bring to serving temperature and serve in large soup bowls garnished with a tablespoon of sour cream, green onions, frozen peas or sliced radishes.

Broccoli and Tofu Bake

Silken tofu has a smooth texture and a sweetness resembling fresh cream.

8 X 8" BAKING DISH; 4 PORTIONS

1 cup chopped onion
2 cloves garlic, minced
2 cups broccoli flowerets
1 cup chopped mushrooms
1 tablespoon water
¼ cup nonfat, cholesterol-free egg substitute
2 egg whites
1 10-oz. pkg. soft silken tofu (such as Mori Nu®)
1 tablespoon yellow mustard
1 teaspoon dried basil
⅛ teaspoon nutmeg
¼ teaspoon salt
⅛ teaspoon black pepper
2 tablespoons nonfat Parmesan cheese
   garnish: red pepper rings
   Nonfat cooking spray

NUTRITION INFORMATION PER SERVING

Serving Size: 1 portion

Calories: 113
Protein: ....13 mg
Carbohydrate: ....11 mg
Fat:.............................2.5 mg
Cholesterol: ....2.5 mg
Sodium: ....321 mg
Fiber: ....less than 0.5 g

Dietary Exchanges:
2 vegetable and 1 lean meat

Sauté onion and garlic in a skillet sprayed with a nonfat cooking spray. Add broccoli, mushrooms, and 1 tablespoon water or nonfat broth. Cover, reduce heat and steam until broccoli and mushrooms are just tender. Place in an 8 x 8-inch baking dish sprayed with nonfat cooking spray.

In a blender, combine egg substitute, whites, tofu, seasonings and cheese. Blend for 2 minutes, scraping down the sides, until mixture is smooth. Pour over broccoli mixture. Garnish each corner with a red pepper ring and bake at 350° for 35 minutes or until center is firm.

Crêpes with Hearty Bean Filling

8 PORTIONS

2 16-oz. cans (4 cups) great northern beans, drained and mashed, reserving liquid
1 cup chopped onion
1 cup grated carrots
3 cloves garlic, minced
¼ cup fresh parsley, snipped
1 teaspoon Mrs. Dash® or similar product
   Black pepper to taste
   Tabasco Sauce (optional)
8 **Whole Wheat Crêpes** (page 193)
   Sweet and Spicy Tomato Sauce (page 123)
   Nonfat cooking spray

NUTRITION INFORMATION PER SERVING

Serving Size: 1 crêpe with sauce

Calories: 260
Protein: ....14.5 g
Carbohydrate: ....51 g
Fat:.....................................1 g
Cholesterol: ....0.5 mg
Sodium: ....204 mg
Fiber: ....3 g

Dietary Exchanges:
2 starch, 1 vegetable, 1 fruit and 1 very lean meat

Drain and partially mash beans. In a skillet sprayed with vegetable cooking spray, sauté the onions, carrots and garlic until tender. Add the onion mixture and all remaining ingredients to the beans adding liquid as necessary to keep the mixture from being too stiff.

Place approximately ⅓ cup of filling on each crêpe. Roll, place seam side down in a baking dish and bake at 350° for 20 minutes or until hot. Top with **Sweet and Spicy Tomato Sauce** (see page 123). Makes filling for 8 crêpes.

Fulla Beans Casserole

8 PORTIONS

¾ cup firmly packed brown sugar
½ cup white vinegar
1 teaspoon dry mustard
1½ teaspoons salt-free Spike® or similar product
2 medium onions, sliced and separated
1 16-oz. can lima beans, drained and rinsed
1 16-oz. can kidney beans, drained and rinsed
1 16-oz. can vegetarian, nonfat baked beans
1 16-oz. can butter beans, drained and rinsed

In saucepan, blend together sugar, vinegar, mustard and Spike®; bring to a boil. Add onions, reduce heat and simmer until onions are just tender.

Pour beans into a 2-qt. baking dish, add vinegar mixture and stir gently. Cover and bake 1 hour at 350°. Uncover to finish baking if beans are too juicy.

NUTRITION INFORMATION PER SERVING

Serving Size: 1 portion

Calories:	302
Protein:	13 g
Carbohydrate:	61.5 g
Fat:	less than 1 g
Cholesterol:	0 mg
Sodium:	254 mg
Fiber:	8 g

Dietary Exchanges:
3 starch and 2 vegetable

Lentil Casserole

Prepare a tossed salad while this casserole bakes and you're ready for dinner.

2-QT. BAKING DISH; 8 PORTIONS

1¾ cups dry lentils, rinsed and picked over
3 quarts water
2 bay leaves
3 cloves garlic, minced
2 large onions, chopped
2 cups sliced or shredded carrots
1 cup sliced mushrooms
½ cup sliced celery
½ cup chopped red pepper
½ cup tomato sauce
2 cups Italian tomatoes, drained and cut up
½ teaspoon dried salt
¼ teaspoon dried pepper
½ teaspoon dried basil
¼ teaspoon sage
1 teaspoon thyme
1 cup nonfat Cheddar cheese, shredded
    Nonfat cooking spray

NUTRITION INFORMATION PER SERVING

Serving Size: 1 portion

Calories: 96
Protein: ....8 g
Carbohydrate: ....17.5 g
Fat: ....0.5 g
Cholesterol: ....2 mg
Sodium: ....466 mg
Fiber: ....1 g

Dietary Exchanges:
1 starch and 1 vegetable

In large kettle, combine lentils, water and bay leaves. Bring to a boil, reduce heat and simmer 30 minutes. Drain and set aside. Sauté garlic and onions in a large skillet sprayed with a nonfat cooking spray.

Add remaining ingredients to onion-garlic mixture except the cheese; add lentils and mix well. Place in a 2-qt. baking dish, cover and bake for 1 hour at 375° Remove cover, sprinkle with cheese and continue baking for 5 to 10 minutes or until cheese is melted.

NUTRITION INFORMATION
PER SERVING

Serving Size: 1 pattie

Calories: 223
Protein: ....11 g
Carbohydrate: ....32 g
Fat: ....6 g
Cholesterol: ....0 mg
Sodium: ....468 mg
Fiber: ....2 g

Dietary Exchanges:
2 starch, 1 vegetable and 1 fat

Serving Note:

These patties freeze well. Place 4 of the patties in an 8 x 8-inch baking dish, cover with chutney, and they're ready to go right from the freezer, to the oven, to the table.

Lentil Patties with Tomato Chutney

These patties may be served on buns with lettuce, tomato, sprouts and nonfat, cholesterol-free mayonnaise.

8 PATTIES

1   cup dry lentils, rinsed and picked over
2   cups water
½   cup chopped celery
1   cup chopped onions
½   cup chopped walnuts
2   cups dry bread cubes or crumbs
¼   cup nonfat, cholesterol-free egg substitute
2   egg whites
1   cup low-sodium tomato sauce
½   teaspoon garlic powder
½   teaspoon thyme
2   teaspoons Worcestershire sauce
½   teaspoon salt
¼   teaspoon pepper
    Nonfat cooking spray
    Tomato Chutney (page 122)

Cook lentils in boiling water for 45 minutes to 1 hour. Drain.

In a skillet sprayed with nonfat cooking spray, sauté celery and onions. Remove from heat. Add all ingredients, mixing well to form 8 patties. Consistency should be easy to handle so add the tomato sauce a bit at a time. With oven set at 350°, place patties on a cookie sheet and bake 15 minutes on one side and 15 minutes on the other. Serve with **Tomato Chutney** (see page 122).

Picanté Black Bean Casserole

The combination of seasonings, particularly the cloves, make this casserole very tasty. If your taste buds require more "heat" use medium or hot picanté sauce.

8 PORTIONS

1 large onion, coarsely chopped
3 cloves garlic, minced
1 16-oz. can (2 cups) black beans, rinsed and drained
2 cups stewed tomatoes, undrained
½ cup mild picanté sauce
1 teaspoon chili powder
1 teaspoon cumin
½ teaspoon basil
⅛ teaspoon cloves
¼ teaspoon oregano
4 cups cooked rotini, orzo or your favorite pasta
½ cup fresh parsley, snipped
1 cup shredded nonfat Cheddar cheese
  Nonfat cooking spray
  garnish: nonfat, cholesterol-free sour cream

NUTRITION INFORMATION PER SERVING

Serving Size: 1 portion

Calories:	178
Protein:	11 g
Carbohydrate:	32 g
Fat:	1 g
Cholesterol:	2 mg
Sodium:	544 mg
Fiber:	2 g

Dietary Exchanges:
2 starch and 1 vegetable

Preparation Tip:

Cook the onions and garlic over medium heat to keep the garlic from scorching.

Cook onion and garlic in a large skillet sprayed with nonfat cooking spray. Stir in the black beans, tomatoes, picanté sauce and seasonings. Bring to a boil. Reduce heat, cover and simmer 15 minutes, stirring occasionally.

In the meantime, cook the pasta to the desired doneness. Drain and add the pasta and parsley to the tomato and bean mixture and place in a 2-qt. casserole dish sprayed with nonfat cooking spray. Bake at 350° until hot and bubbly, approximately 30 minutes. Top with shredded cheese and return to the oven until cheese has melted. Top each serving with additional picanté sauce and a tablespoon of sour cream.

NUTRITION INFORMATION
PER SERVING

Serving Size: approximately 1 cup

Calories: 218
Protein: ....10 g
Carbohydrate: ....38 g
Fat: ....1.5 g
Cholesterol: ....0 mg
Sodium: ....766 mg
Fiber: ....8 g

Dietary Exchanges:
  2 starch and 2 vegetable

Quick and Easy Baked Beans

*Mixed together the night before and placed in an automatic oven the day you want to serve them, dinner will be ready and waiting when you get home. Serve with **Boston Brown Bread** and a tossed salad.*

8 PORTIONS

3 16-oz. cans (6 cups) nonfat, vegetarian baked beans (such as Bush's)
1 cup chopped onions
½ cup diced green pepper
2 tablespoons molasses or packed brown sugar
3 teaspoons dry mustard
3 tablespoons imitation bacon bits

Place all ingredients except the imitation bacon bits in a 2-qt. casserole dish. Stir to mix. Sprinkle with imitation bacon bits and bake covered 1½ to 2 hours at 325°. Uncover the last 30 minutes of baking time if beans are too juicy.

Refried Beans

This recipe is very versatile and well worth your time. Freeze in 1 or 2-cup portions for use as a dip, a spread on corn tortillas, or as a filling for crêpes.

6 CUPS; 12 SERVINGS

    1 lb. dry pinto beans
    2 cups diced onion
 1½ cups medium salsa or picanté sauce
    2 tablespoons chili powder
  ½ tablespoon cumin
    2 cloves garlic, minced, or to taste
    2 tablespoons sugar

NUTRITION INFORMATION PER SERVING

Serving Size: ½ cup

Calories:	153
Protein:	8 g
Carbohydrate:	30 g
Fat:	1 g
Cholesterol:	0 mg
Sodium:	234 mg
Fiber:	3 g

Dietary Exchanges:
  1 starch and 2 vegetable

Wash and pick over the pinto beans. Cover with water and soak overnight. The next day, drain and rinse the beans.

Place all of the ingredients in a large pan, cover with water and bring to a boil. Reduce heat and simmer uncovered for about 3 hours or until beans are done and can be mashed. Add water as needed - approximately 3 cups. Exact amount will depend on altitude, your cooking conditions and desired consistency. Mash beans leaving some whole.

Superbowl Beans

ADM Midland Harvest Herb 'n Spice Mix® is a soy product that is all vegetable, cholesterol-free and a low-fat alternative to meat.

Tips:

Please see page 249 to order the ADM Midland Harvest Herb 'n Spice Mix®.

Campbell's Healthy Request® soup works very well in this recipe.

If sodium is a concern, look for salt-free varieties of tomato paste, catsup, green beans and lima beans.

25 PORTIONS

1   package ADM Midland Harvest Herb 'n Spice Mix®
2   cups chopped onion
1   cup diced celery
1   10 fl.-oz. can tomato soup
1   6-oz. can tomato paste
½   cup catsup
2   16-oz. cans green beans, drained and rinsed
1   16-oz. can lima beans, drained and rinsed
1   16-oz. can chili hot beans
1   16-oz. can nonfat, vegetarian baked beans
2   teaspoons prepared mustard
    Nonfat cooking spray

Reconstitute herb 'n spice mix according to the package directions. Brown as you would ground beef in a skillet sprayed with nonfat cooking spray. Add onion and celery and cook until tender. Stir in soup, tomato paste and catsup. Simmer 15 to 20 minutes. Place in a large crock pot or dutch oven. Add remaining ingredients. Mix well. Bake uncovered 1 hour at 350°.

Three Bean Casserole

These beans rank among the quick and easy if planned ahead and prepared in stages. If beans soak overnight, the casserole can be put together the next morning and baked in a timed oven. Add a tossed salad and a cooked vegetable when you get home and dinner's ready! Double the recipe and freeze half for future meals.

8 PORTIONS

1 cup dry white beans
½ cup dry kidney or pinto beans
½ cup dry lima beans
1 cup chopped onion
⅓ cup firmly packed brown sugar
½ cup chili sauce
1 teaspoon dry mustard
1 teaspoon salt
2 tablespoons imitation bacon bits

Mix and soak beans 12 hours or overnight. Partially cook beans a few minutes, pour off water and rinse.

Put onions in bottom of a crock pot or dutch oven and add beans and all other ingredients. Cover with boiling water 1½ to 2 inches above the beans. Bake covered for 4 hours at 350°. Bake uncovered the last hour if the beans haven't cooked down enough.

NUTRITION INFORMATION PER SERVING

Serving Size: 1 portion

Calories: 147
Protein: ....6.5 g
Carbohydrate: ....29 g
Fat: ....0.5 g
Cholesterol: ....0 mg
Sodium: ....502 mg
Fiber: ....4.5 g

Dietary Exchanges:
1 starch and 2 vegetable

Tofu Stuffed Shells

Tofu, a soybean product, is a high protein food, low in calories and saturated fat and free of cholesterol. It can be found in the produce department of most supermarkets. For most recipes it's necessary to press the moisture out of the tofu by using a paper towel.

14 STUFFED SHELLS

14　jumbo pasta shells
3　medium onions, chopped
3　cloves garlic, minced
½　cup coarsely grated carrots
1　lb. firm tofu, pressed dry and mashed
1　cup nonfat, low-cholesterol ricotta cheese
1　egg white
1　tablespoon dried parsley or ¼ cup fresh parsley
2　teaspoons dried basil
2　tablespoons light soy sauce
1　10-oz. pkg. frozen chopped spinach, well drained
1　26-oz. can (about 3 cups) spaghetti sauce
　　Nonfat cooking spray

Cook pasta shells to al denté (firm to the tooth, not tender), rinse carefully and set aside.

Sauté onions, garlic and carrots in skillet sprayed with nonfat cooking spray. Mix mashed tofu with ricotta cheese, egg white, parsley, basil and soy sauce. Add onion mixture and spinach. Mix well.

Stuff shells with filling and place in a shallow baking dish that has ½ cup spaghetti sauce in the bottom to prevent sticking. Spoon spaghetti sauce over the top of each shell. Bake at 350° for ½ hour or until heated through.

NUTRITION INFORMATION
PER SERVING

Serving Size: 1 stuffed shell

Calories: 106
Protein: ....8.5 g
Carbohydrate: ....16 g
Fat: ....1 g
Cholesterol: .....less than 1 mg
Sodium: ....302 mg
Fiber: ....1.5 g

Dietary Exchanges:
1 starch and 1 very lean meat

Preparation Tip:

If jumbo pasta shells are not available substitute 10 pieces of manicotti.

Note:

Poly-O® ricotta cheese works very well in this recipe. Look for a spaghetti sauce with less than 1g fat per ½ cup. See **Appendix D** for specific-brand names.

Tortilla Black Bean Casserole

This recipe is featured on the front cover!

An excellent choice when you're having guests. It can be prepared ahead of time and popped into the oven as your guests arrive. The garnish creates a very attractive entrée. If you wish, add a diced black olive on each serving, however, don't over do it as olives are high in fat.

9 X 13" BAKING DISH; 8 PORTIONS

2 cups chopped onions
1½ cups chopped green peppers
1 14½-oz. can (about 2 cups) tomatoes, cut up
1 cup mild or medium picanté sauce
3 or 4 cloves garlic, minced
2½ teaspoons cumin
2 15-oz. cans (about 4 cups) black beans, drained and rinsed
8 6-inch corn tortillas, made without oil
2 cups shredded, nonfat Mozzarella cheese
garnish: sliced tomatoes, shredded lettuce, green onions and nonfat, cholesterol-free sour cream

In large skillet, combine onions, green peppers, undrained tomatoes, picanté sauce, garlic and cumin. Bring to a boil, reduce heat and simmer uncovered for 10 minutes. Stir in beans.

Spread ⅓ of the vegetable bean mixture over the bottom of a 9 x 13-inch baking dish. Top with half of the tortillas, overlapping as necessary (see diagram on side) and ½ of the cheese. Add another ⅓ of the bean mixture, then the remaining tortillas and bean mixture. Cover and bake at 350° for 40 minutes or until heated through. Sprinkle with remaining cheese and return to the oven for cheese to melt. Let stand for 10 minutes before serving.

Top each serving with a tomato slice, shredded lettuce, sliced green onions, and 2 tablespoons of nonfat, cholesterol-free sour cream.

NUTRITION INFORMATION PER SERVING
Serving Size: 1 portion
Calories: 295
Protein: ....22.5 g
Carbohydrate: ....49.5 g
Fat:..................................3 g
Cholesterol: ....4 mg
Sodium: ....443 mg
Fiber: ....6.5 g
Dietary Exchanges:
3 starch, 1 vegetable and 1 lean meat

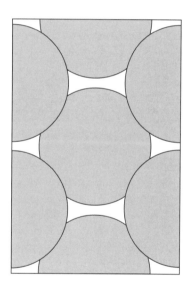

Tostadas

A wonderful Mexican-style tostada without all the fat. We enjoy serving these to friends. Prepare toppings in separate bowls and let your guests assemble their own.

6 SERVINGS

6 corn tortillas (no oil added)
1 cup nonfat refried beans (such as Old El Paso)
1 cup ADM Midland Harvest Taco Mix®
2 cups shredded lettuce
1 medium tomato, chopped
6 green onions, thinly sliced
½ cup nonfat, cholesterol-free sour cream
½ cup nonfat pizza cheese, grated (optional)
6 tablespoons medium salsa or picanté sauce

Bake tortillas for 8 to 10 minutes at 350°. Cool.

Make taco mix according to the package directions. Spread each tortilla with proportionate amounts of refried beans and taco mix. Add shredded lettuce, tomatoes, onions, sour cream and cheese if desired. Pass salsa or picanté sauce.

NUTRITION INFORMATION PER SERVING

Serving Size: 1 tostada

Calories: 248
Protein: ....14.5 g
Carbohydrate: ....41.5 g
Fat: ....1.5 g
Cholesterol: ....1 mg
Sodium: ....906 mg
Fiber: ....4 g

Dietary Exchanges:
2 starch, 2 vegetable and
1 very lean meat

N o t e :

I like to order the ADM Midland Harvest Taco Mix® from the Mail Order Catalog (see page 249).

Chapter 5

Fabulously Fit Main Dishes: Grains and Pasta

Rice and pasta make simple dishes, yet go beyond being plain. Pasta, rice, couscous, barley, and other grains make a great base for entrées. Try wild and brown rices, which are higher in fiber than white rice. Experiment with flavored pastas like lemon basil, garlic, artichoke or tomato (whole-wheat pasta is a great choice as it's highest in fiber). For flavor, cook pasta or grains in a fat-free vegetable or chicken broth, use fresh herbs or spices, and maybe even some dried or cooked fruit or sautéed vegetables.

Don't stop at rice and pasta. Experiment with other grains like quinoa, bulgur and couscous. Couscous is great cooked in broth with added vegetables, or in fruit juice with added fruits. Either one of these grains is just as good cold or hot. And don't overlook the boxed grain dishes available at the supermarket. Just be sure to make them without added butter or oil. Read labels to help you avoid those that are high in sodium (See **Appendix C** for more information on label reading).

Be creative with your toppings. Try canned creamed corn, mild chilies, and onions over rice. The **Creamy Fettuccine** recipe (see page 89) is a good starting point for pasta dishes. Add fresh steamed or sautéed vegetables and kidney beans for a creamy pasta primavera. Or, cook a variety of vegetables in fat-free broth thickened with a little cornstarch to serve over a favorite grain or pasta. Fresh tomatoes, chopped and cooked with okra, celery and onion, and seasoned with hot sauce and thyme, make a quick Cajun dish when served over rice.

Grains

Glossary of Grains

- **Amaranth** - A highly nutritious grain that was used by the Aztecs. It is not a true grain, but related to a family of weeds. Unlike true grains, it contains the amino acid lysine, so offers a higher quality protein than most grains. It is very tiny, like a poppy seed, growing in a range of colors but most commonly found in the market as a creamy yellow grain.It has a sweet, somewhat earthy taste like corn and is best prepared with other grains like brown rice or buckwheat.

- **Barley** - An ancient grain that is grown as hundreds of species, its most common forms are as flakes, grits, hulled (Scotch), and pearl barley. Hulled barley is the whole grain, including the bran, and is the most nutritious form. The grains are oval, brown and offer a very hearty flavor. Pearled barley is an ivory colored grain that has had the bran, and many nutrients, removed during processing. It has a delicate flavor that lends itself to soups and side dishes.

- **Buckwheat** - This is neither a true grain nor related to wheat, but is the berry-like fruit of a leafy plant related to sorrel that look like tiny beechnuts. Like amaranth, it also contains lysine so offers a higher quality protein than most grains. It can be purchased as flour, grits, whole groats, and kasha. Groats are raw kernels that are either mild-flavored white, which can be substituted in rice dishes, or the more strongly flavored roasted brown kernels. Kasha is toasted, hulled buckwheat kernels cracked into granules. Its assertive flavor mixes well in a number of side or main dishes with other vegetables.

- **Corn** - The edible kernels grow in rows on large ears covered with husk in many colors and varieties. Although it is a grain, it is most often eaten as a vegetable in the United States. The most common is sweet or green corn, ranging in color from ivory to yellow and typically eaten as corn on the cob. Kernels are also ground into cornmeal, which may be used for hominy, grits, polenta, and cornbread. Tortillas are made from boiled mashed kernels.

- **Couscous** - A product of wheat, it is a quick-cooking grain used widely in North Africa, but gaining popularity in the United States. A very tiny, round grain, it may be purchased as a refined grain or as a more nutritious whole-wheat variety.

- **Millet** - A very nutritious tiny, round, golden grain used widely in Asia and Africa, it is actually the very small seed of a grass. It is most often found in health food stores, usually as whole grain pearl millet. It has a mild, delicate flavor that lends itself to a variety of flavorings, and its versatility allows it to substitute for rice. It can be served as a hot cereal, or added to soups and stews.

- **Oats** - A creamy, light brown and nutritious grain, oats are higher in protein and fat than most other grains. The fat is largely unsaturated, however, and all forms of oats are a good source of primarily soluble fiber, which has been found to help lower blood cholesterol levels when substantial amounts are eaten regularly. Oats are available as groats, rolled oats, and steel-cut oats, as well as oat flour and oat bran. Groats are the whole oat kernels and can be cooked and served like other grains as a side dish. Rolled oats are the most common form, have been pressed flat with rollers and cook more quickly. They are most commonly eaten as a hot cereal but are great additions to cookies, breads, and muffins.

- **Quinoa** - (keen-wah) - Not a true grain, but related to leafy green vegetables like spinach, it is highly nutritious, providing more iron and protein than most grains. A tiny, flattened, oval-shaped grain, it may be yellow, red, or brown, but is most often pale yellow in color. When cooked, the grain is soft and tender with a crunchy "tail" and offers delicate flavor. It can be combined with other grains, or makes a good side dish, cold salad, or addition to soups.

- **Rye** - A bluish-grey grain, it is closely related and appears very similar to wheat, but has a higher nutrient content. Its flavor is distinctive and hearty, and it is most nutritious in its whole forms (as opposed to the highly refined rye flour breads consumed in the United States) as cracked rye, flake, or whole rye berries. Whole rye berries resemble wheat berries and are the whole kernel groats of the plant. Flakes resemble rolled oats and can be eaten as a hot breakfast cereal or added to baked goods. Because of its strong flavor, rye is best when combined and cooked with other grains.

- **Triticale** - (tri-ti-kay-lee) - A hybrid of wheat and rye, it has a higher quality protein than wheat, and a nutty flavor that is much milder than rye. It may be purchased as berries, flakes that have been flattened like rolled oats, or cracked triticale. Triticale berries are twice the size of wheat berries, retain the high fiber bran and nutritious germ, and may be substituted for bulgar or wheat berries in recipes or served as a pilaf or side dish. May also be used as a thickener in soups and stews.

- **Wheat** - The most important grain crop in the world, wheat is a highly nutritious grain grown as thousands of varieties. Most wheat is ground into flour which is then used for bread, pasta, and other baked goods. There are a variety of other wheat products, some described below. Whole-wheat products are the most nutritious, a good source of protein, B vitamins, and some minerals.

- **Wheat berries** are the whole kernel, or groat, of the wheat and have not been milled. Brown, round in shape, and with a nutty, robust flavor and chewy texture, they are often mixed with other grains or used as the base for a main dish. Wheat berries are ground to produce whole-wheat flour.

- **Wheat bran**, the high-fiber bran covering of the wheat berry, is an excellent addition to cereals and baked goods, boosting fiber and enhancing texture.

- **Wheat germ** is the highly nutritious germ of the wheat kernel, with 25% of its calories coming from polyunsaturated fat. Defatted versions are also available. It adds a nice crunch as a topping for cereal, yogurt, and as an addition to baked goods.

- **Bulgar** is whole-wheat that has been precooked and dried, a processed form of cracked wheat. With a notable flavor, it is popular in Middle Eastern cuisine and is good in cold salads like tabbouleh.

- **Cracked wheat** is coarsely crushed, minimally processed wheat   kernels that offer a light wheaty flavor. The can be substituted in recipes for rice and other grains.
- **Rolled wheat,** also called wheat flakes, are whole-wheat berries that have been flattened like rolled oats, though thicker and firmer. They may be cooked as hot cereal or added to baked goods.

Grains: Guide for Cooking Times and Yields

Amounts are for dry, uncooked grains

GRAIN	LIQUID (Cups)	COOKING TIME	YIELD (Cups)
Amaranth-1 cup	2½	25 minutes	3
Barley (hulled)-1 cup	3	1½ hours*	3½ to 4
Barley (pearl)-1 cup	3	50 minutes	3½
Barley flakes-½ cup	1½	30 minutes	1
Buckwheat groats-½ cup	1	15 minutes	1¾
Buckwheat (kasha)-½ cup	2½	12 minutes	2
Bulgur-1 cup	2	20 minutes	3
Couscous-1 cup	2	5 minutes	3
Cracked wheat-½ cup	1	15 minutes	1
Millet-1 cup	2	25 minutes	3
Oats(grouts)-½ cup stand 45 mins.	1	6 minutes	1¼
Oats(rolled, quick)-½ cup stand 4 mins.	1	1 minute	1
Oat bran-½ cup	1	6 minutes	1
Quinoa-1 cup	2	15 minutes	3
Rye berries-½ cup	1½	1 hr, 55 mins*	1½
Rye flakes-½ cup	1½	1 hr, 5 mins*	1¼
Triticale-1 cup	3	2 hours*	2½
Wheat berries-1 cup	3	2 hours*	3
Wheat flakes-½ cup	2	53 minutes	1

Cooking time can be decreased by soaking in water in the refrigerator overnight.

Rice

Rice may be the world's most important food as it is the staple food of half the world's population. Rice contains high quality protein and comes in three basic varieties according to grain length:

Long grain separates when cooked and produces fluffy rice that is good for side dishes and pilafs.

Medium grain is more moist and tender than long grain but tends to become sticky when cooled.

Short grain is more oval in shape, higher in starch, and generally more moist and sticky. It is the traditional rice used in Oriental cooking and is good for rice pudding or risotto.

Glossary of Rice

- **Arborio rice** is a high-starch, short, almost round-grained rice that absorbs a high volume of liquid and produces very creamy grains. It is grown primarily in Italy and is used to make risotto.

- **Basmati rice** is an aromatic long grain rice grown in India and Pakistan. It has a very delicate, buttery flavor that makes a very tasty side dish, or it can be substituted for regular long grain rice in recipes. Similar to basmati, Texmati rice, grown in Texas, is a firm-textured popcorn rice which has a pecan-like flavor.

- **Brown rice** is the whole rice kernel with intact bran, thus retaining more fiber and nutrients than white rice. It takes longer to cook (though quick varieties are now available) but has a rich, nutty flavor and chewier texture than white rice.

- **Jamine rice** is a long grain aromatic rice grown in the United States and Thailand. Similar in flavor to basmati rice, it is good in cold dishes as it stays fluffy when cooled.

- **White rice,** the most commonly consumed rice, is polished or milled rice with the bran and most of the germ removed, thus removing many nutrients. In the United States it is usually enriched to replace the lost nutrients, though it is still low in fiber. It is more tender than brown rice, milder in flavor and cooks more quickly.

• **Wild Rice** - Not a true rice but a grey and brown grass seed native to North America, it is highly nutritious with twice the protein of other rices and a higher content of B vitamins. Its long grain shape has a rich, nutty flavor and somewhat chewy texture.

Rice: Cooking Times and Yields

Per ½ cup uncooked rice

RICE	LIQUID (cups)	COOKING TIME	Yield (cups)
Arborio	¾	15 minutes	1½
Basmati, white	½	15 minutes	2
Brown, long grain	1	25–30 minutes	1½
Brown, short grain	1	40 minutes	1½
Brown, quick	¾	10 minutes	1
Jasmine	1	15–20 minutes	1¾
Texmati, brown	1+2 Tbsp.	40 minutes	2
Texmati, white	¾+2 Tbsp.	15 minutes	1¼
White, long grain	1	15–20 minutes	1¾
Wild rice	2	50 minutes	2
Wild pecan	1	20 minutes	1½

Pasta

Pasta is a wonderful, basic food for a low-fat lifestyle. If you feel ambitious, the new pasta machines make it easy to make your own fresh pasta which can then be frozen for later use. There are also many wonderful flavors and varieties of fresh and dried pasta on the market. Check the label to be sure that no eggs are in the pasta ingredients, and be sure to buy only the eggless, or cholesterol-free noodles. Remember that whole-wheat pasta is the best nutritional choice for a higher fiber and nutrient content.

When preparing dried pasta, approximately two ounces of dry will equal one cup when cooked. (Use the following guide for more specific cooking information on yields). Contrary to popular belief, you don't need to use oil when boiling pasta. Stirring briskly with a fork while cooking will separate the pieces. Once the pasta is cooked and drained, try spraying with nonstick cooking spray to add moisture and prevent clumping and sticking. For the best texture, cook only until al denté, which is Italian for "to the tooth", meaning that the pasta is tender and firm, not mushy.

Pasta Yields

PASTA	DRY MEASURE	YIELD	COOKING TIME
Eggless noodles	1⅓ cups (2 ounces)	1½ cups	6–8 minutes
Fresh pasta	3 ounces	1 cup	2–3 minutes
Macaroni	½ cup (2 ounces)	1 cup	10 minutes
	1 cup (3½ ounces)	1¾ cups	
Spaghetti	2 ounces	1 cup	10–12 minutes
	1 pound	8 cups	

Basmati Rice

Basmati rice has an aroma much like lightly buttered popcorn. It is best if rinsed a couple of times and then soaked before cooking.

8 SERVINGS

2 cups basmati rice, rinsed twice, soaked for ½ hour and well drained
2 tablespoons lemon juice
4 cups nonfat chicken broth
2 pinches of saffron threads, crushed
½ teaspoon salt
½ tablespoon imitation butter sprinkles

Rinse and soak rice. Put all ingredients together in a large baking dish and bake at 350° for 1 hour or until the liquid has been absorbed.

NUTRITION INFORMATION PER SERVING
Serving Size: approximately ⅔ cup
Calories: 161
Protein: ....5 g
Carbohydrate: ....35 g
Fat: ....less than 1 g
Cholesterol: ....0 mg
Sodium: ....278 mg
Fiber: ....less than 0.5 g
Dietary Exchanges: 2 starch

Broccoli and Mostaccioli

This recipe cuts in half very easily. However, you might not want to because it's particularly good the next day as a leftover!

9 X 13" BAKING PAN; 9 PORTIONS

3   cloves garlic, minced
1   cup chopped onion
¼   teaspoon nutmeg
1   teaspoon dried basil
2   cups nonfat, low-cholesterol ricotta cheese
1½ lbs. broccoli, cut in spears and steamed
¼   teaspoon black pepper
1   28-oz. jar (about 3½ cups) spaghetti sauce, divided
8   oz. dry mostaccioli, cooked according to directions (3½–4 cups cooked)
2   tablespoons nonfat Parmesan cheese, divided
¼   cup seasoned bread crumbs or stuffing mix
2   tablespoons wheat germ
    Nonfat cooking spray

Sauté garlic, onion and nutmeg in a pan sprayed with nonfat cooking spray. Add the onion mixture and basil to the ricotta cheese and set aside.

Spray a 9 x 13-inch pan with nonfat cooking spray. Place ingredients in the pan in the following order: half of the spaghetti sauce, half of the mostaccioli, half of the Parmesan cheese, all of the broccoli, black pepper, and ricotta cheese, then the remainder of the mostaccioli and sauce. Sprinkle the top with a mixture of bread crumbs, wheat germ and remaining Parmesan cheese.

Cover and bake for 35 minutes at 350°. Bake uncovered the last few minutes. Sauce should be bubbly and the top browned.

NUTRITION INFORMATION PER SERVING

Serving Size: 1 portion

Calories: 215
Protein: ....16 g
Carbohydrate: ....36.5 g
Fat: ....1 g
Cholesterol: ....3 mg
Sodium: ....376 mg
Fiber: ....2 g

Dietary Exchanges:
1 starch, 4 vegetable and
1 very lean meat

N o t e :

Look for a Spaghetti sauce with 1 g fat or less per serving. See **Appendix D** for brand names.

Cabbage and Noodles

It takes only a few minutes to transform these simple ingredients into a very tasty main dish and clean up is easy. For variety, top with crushed fat-free crackers or corn flakes before baking.

10 PORTIONS

- 1   pkg. ADM Midland Harvest Herb 'n Spice Mix®
- 6   oz. uncooked eggless noodles (about 3 cups cooked)
- 1   large onion, chopped
- 1¼ teaspoons fennel seeds
- ½   small head of cabbage, shredded, (about 4 cups)
- 1   cup nonfat chicken broth
- 1   10 fl.-oz. can Campbell's Healthy Request® tomato soup
- 2   teaspoons imitation butter sprinkles
     Pepper to taste
     Nonfat cooking spray

Reconstitute the herb 'n spice mix according to the directions on the package and set aside.

In large saucepan, cook noodles to desired doneness, drain and set aside.

Cook the onion and fennel seeds with the herb 'n spice mix in a saucepan that has been sprayed with a nonfat cooking spray. Add cabbage and broth, reduce heat and steam until tender. When cabbage is done add noodles, soup, imitation butter sprinkles and pepper. Place in a 3-qt. baking dish. Heat in a 350° oven for 30 minutes or until hot.

NUTRITION INFORMATION PER SERVING

Serving Size: 1 portion

Calories: 169
Protein: ....11.5 g
Carbohydrate: ....23.5 g
Fat:.....................................3 g
Cholesterol: ....0 mg
Sodium: ....263 mg
Fiber: ....3.5 g

Dietary Exchanges:
1 starch, 2 vegetable and
1 very lean meat

N o t e :

Two suggested brand names of imitation butter sprinkles are Butter Buds® or Molly McButter®.

Preparation Tip:

If you're not planning on serving a large group, place in two 1½-qt. baking dishes and freeze one.

Cornbread Hot Tamale Pie

Cornbread cooked atop this Tamale Pie makes a very attractive, tasty entrée – a favorite with our family. Don't be deterred by the list of ingredients. This recipe can be made very easily in 30 minutes.

6 PORTIONS

Tamale Pie:
1 cup unflavored TVP® beef granules
¾ cup boiling water
½ cup diced green peppers
¾ cup diced onion
3 cloves garlic, minced
1 10 fl.-oz. can Campbell's Healthy Request tomato soup
1 cup water
1½ cups frozen corn
2 teaspoons jalapeño pepper, chopped fine
1 teaspoon chili powder
½ teaspoon cumin
Nonfat cooking spray

Topping:
¾ cup yellow corn meal
1 tablespoon flour
½ teaspoon salt
1 tablespoon sugar
1½ teaspoons baking powder
2 egg whites
⅓ cup skim milk
1 tablespoon extra-light margarine, melted

Pie: Reconstitute TVP® granules with the boiling water. In large skillet sprayed with nonfat cooking spray, sauté green peppers, onion and garlic. Add reconstituted TVP®, soup, water, corn, jalapeño pepper, chili powder and cumin. Simmer 10 minutes to blend flavors. Pour into a 2-qt. casserole dish sprayed with nonfat cooking spray.

Topping: In small mixing bowl, combine dry ingredients and set aside. In a separate bowl, add egg whites to the skim milk and 1 tablespoon extra-light stick margarine and beat with a fork.

Add liquid ingredients to the dry ingredients and mix thoroughly. Spread topping over the TVP mixture. Bake at 425° for 20 minutes or until cornbread is done.

NUTRITION INFORMATION PER SERVING

Serving Size: 1 portion

Calories: 215
Protein: ....14 g
Carbohydrates: ....39.5 g
Fat: ....3 g
Cholesterol: ....0 mg
Sodium: ....506 mg
Fiber: ....7 g

Dietary Exchanges:
2 starch, 1 vegetable and 1 lean meat

N o t e :

When looking for an acceptable low-fat margarine, select one with 6 g of fat or less per tablespoon. See **Appendix D** for specific brand names.

Creamy Fettuccine

A delectable dish that can be made in a jiffy and better yet, all in one pan. This ultra low-fat entrée uses nonfat yogurt and nonfat Parmesan cheese to achieve its creamy sauce. The flavor is enhanced the second day.

4 PORTIONS

- 8 oz. eggless fettuccine noodles, cooked (about 4 cups cooked)
- 2 tablespoons tub margarine
- 2 tablespoons imitation butter sprinkles*
- 1 cup plain nonfat yogurt
- 4 tablespoons nonfat Parmesan cheese
- 1 cup grated carrots
- 1 cup fresh or frozen peas
- ¼ cup fresh parsley, snipped
- ¾ teaspoon garlic powder or to taste
  Freshly ground black pepper to taste

Cook fettuccine noodles according to package directions. Drain. Return to saucepan and add remaining ingredients in order given. Heat over medium heat, stirring to blend flavors.

Variation: Steamed broccoli flowerets would be a fine substitute for the peas.

NUTRITION INFORMATION PER SERVING

Serving Size: 1 portion

Calories:	307
Protein:	14 g
Carbohydrate:	56 g
Fat:	2.5 g
Cholesterol:	6 mg
Sodium:	180 mg
Fiber:	1 g

Dietary Exchanges:
2 starch, 2 vegetable and 1 skim milk

T i p s :

Look for acceptable tub margarines with 4 grams of fat per tablespoon. Imitation butter sprinkles, Butter Buds® or Molly McButter®, work equally well in this recipe.

"Ground Beef" Casserole

Using the ADM Midland Harvest Herb 'n Spice Mix®, I've been able to adapt a popular family recipe. Make it ahead to pop into the oven as you're preparing the rest of the meal.

8 PORTIONS

¾ package ADM Midland Harvest Herb 'n Spice Mix®
½ cup uncooked white rice
2 cups canned corn, undrained
2 cups tomato sauce
¾ cup water
1 cup chopped onion
½ cup diced green pepper
   Pepper to taste
   Nonfat cooking spray

Reconstitute the herb and spice mix as directed on the package using either olive or canola oil. One package makes approximately 1 pound. Three quarters of a pound will be used for this recipe. Save the remainder and add it to soup or chili. When reconstituted it has a keeping quality much like meat.

Spray a skillet with a nonfat cooking spray and cook the mix as if you were browning ground beef. Place remaining ingredients in a 2-qt. baking dish in the order listed. Cover and bake 1 hour at 350°.

NUTRITION INFORMATION PER SERVING

Serving Size: 1 portion

Calories: 169
Protein: ....10.5 g
Carbohydrate ....27 g
Fat: ....2.5 g
Cholesterol: ....0 mg
Sodium: ....297 mg
Fiber: ....5 g

Dietary Exchanges:
1 starch, 2 vegetable and 1 very lean meat

N o t e :

I like to order the ADM Midland Harvest Herb 'n Spice Mix® from the Mail Order Catalog (see page 249) because it cooks up like ground beef, retaining its chunk-like quality.

Jackpot Casserole

This "can opener" dinner turns into a fabulous feast. A low cost and hearty meal that will have your family asking for seconds.

6 PORTIONS

1 large onion, chopped
1 green pepper, chopped
3 cloves garlic, minced
2 cups cream-style corn
4 cups cooked macaroni (2 cups whole wheat
    macaroni and 2 cups regular macaroni)
½ can (5 fl.-oz.) Campbell's Healthy Request®
    tomato soup
1 cup nonfat Cheddar cheese, shredded
    Black pepper to taste

Sauté onion, green pepper and garlic in a large skillet sprayed with nonfat cooking spray. Mix the remaining ingredients together in a large mixing bowl and add the onion mixture. Place in a 2-qt. baking dish that has been sprayed with a nonfat cooking spray. Bake 30 minutes at 350°.

Variation: Substitute 1 cup of reconstituted unflavored TVP® granules for 1 cup of the cooked macaroni.

NUTRITION INFORMATION PER SERVING

Serving Size: 1 portion

Calories: 239
Protein: ....13 g
Carbohydrate: ....47 g
Fat: ....1.5 g
Cholesterol: ....2.5 mg
Sodium: ....234 mg
Fiber: ....3.5 g

Dietary Exchanges:
  2 starch and 3 vegetable

N o t e :

Whole-wheat pastas are available in health food stores and some bulk food stores. Many supermarkets now carry whole-wheat pasta varieties.

NUTRITION INFORMATION
PER SERVING

Serving Size: 1 portion

Calories: 310
Protein: ....9 g
Carbohydrate: ....66.5 g
Fat: ....1.5 g
Cholesterol: ....0 mg
Sodium: ....201 mg
Fiber: ....1 g

Dietary Exchanges:
2½ starch, 2 vegetable and
1 fruit

Linguini with Pineapple Salsa

A wonderful adaptation of the ever-so-popular salsas and a nice change from the usual marinara sauces. This meal can be ready in almost the time it takes to cook the linguini.

6 PORTIONS

⅔ cup chopped red onions
3 cloves garlic, minced
1 red pepper, cut in chunks
1 green pepper, cut into chunks
2 large tomatoes, chopped
½ jalapeño pepper, finely chopped
1 teaspoon dried basil
¼ cup fresh parsley, snipped
1 teaspoon dry mint
2 tablespoons white wine
½ teaspoon salt
1 tablespoon cornstarch
1 20-oz. can pineapple tidbits packed in juice, drained; reserve juice
12 oz. dry linguini, cooked (about 6 cups cooked)
   Nonfat cooking spray

Spray large skillet with a nonfat cooking spray. Sauté the onions, garlic, red and green peppers until crisp-tender. Add tomato, jalapeño pepper, basil, parsley, mint, wine and salt.

Dissolve cornstarch in reserved pineapple juice and add to the vegetables. Add pineapple. Heat mixture to boiling, reduce heat and simmer until sauce thickens and becomes clear. Cook 1 minute longer. Serve over cooked linguini noodles.

Orange Rice

3 CUPS; 6 PORTIONS

1½ cups water
½ cup orange juice
1 cup uncooked rice, white or brown

Combine water and juice in saucepan and bring to a boil. Add rice and stir. Cover and cook over low heat 15 to 20 minutes or until tender and liquid is absorbed. (Brown rice will take 40 to 45 minutes to cook).

NUTRITION INFORMATION PER SERVING

Serving Size: ½ cup

Calories: 49
Protein: ....1 g
Carbohydrate: ....10.5 g
Fat: ....less than 0.5 g
Cholesterol: ....0 mg
Sodium: ....3.5 mg
Fiber: ....0.5 g

Dietary Exchanges:
½ starch

Rice Pilaf

3 CUPS; 6 PORTIONS

2 cups nonfat chicken broth
1 cup uncooked white rice
1 bay leaf
¼ cup minced onion
2 teaspoons imitation butter sprinkles

Bring chicken broth to a boil in a medium saucepan. Add the remaining ingredients, stir well. Reduce heat, cover and cook about 15 to 20 minutes or until rice is tender. Remove bay leaf and serve.

NUTRITION INFORMATION PER SERVING

Serving Size: ½ cup

Calories: 81
Protein: ....3 g
Carbohydrate: ....16 g
Fat: ....less than 0.5 g
Cholesterol: ....0 mg
Sodium: ....113 mg
Fiber: ....0.5 g

Dietary Exchanges:
1 starch

N o t e :

Two examples of imitation butter sprinkles are Molly McButter® and Butter Buds®.

Penne with Artichokes and Leeks

6 PORTIONS

NUTRITION INFORMATION
PER SERVING

Serving Size: 1 portion

Calories: 251
Protein: ....11 g
Carbohydrate: ....51.5 g
Fat:................................1.5 g
Cholesterol: ....1.5 mg
Sodium: ....673 mg
Fiber: ....6 g

Dietary Exchanges:
2 starch and 4 vegetable

4 cups cooked penne or ziti (about 8 oz. dry)
¼ cup dry white wine or nonfat chicken broth
1 teaspoon dried basil
1 teaspoon dried oregano
2 bay leaves
4 large cloves garlic, minced
10 oz. nonfat chicken broth (1¼ cups)
1 cup sliced mushrooms
2 cups julienned leeks, using some green stalks
1 tablespoon whole-wheat flour
1 14-oz. can (about 2 cups) artichoke hearts, drained, rinsed and quartered
2½ cups canned stewed tomatoes, undrained
½ teaspoon pepper
½ teaspoon salt
    garnish: nonfat Parmesan cheese
    fresh basil leaves, chopped fine

Cook pasta to al denté stage, rinse and set aside.

Combine wine, seasonings and chicken broth. Bring to a boil and simmer for 15 minutes. Remove bay leaves and set aside.

In large skillet or saucepan, sauté the mushrooms and leeks until just transparent, taking care not to overcook. Sprinkle the leeks with the whole-wheat flour. Gradually add approximately 1¼ cups of the wine-broth mixture and stir well. Cover and cook for 3 minutes.

Add pasta, artichokes, tomatoes, salt and pepper. Heat and serve, sprinkling each serving with 1 teaspoon nonfat Parmesan cheese and chopped fresh basil.

Spanish Rice and Beans

Rice and beans make a substantial contribution to a vegetarian mealplan. Consider adding imitation bacon bits for enhanced flavor and frozen corn for variety and color.

6 PORTIONS

1 large onion, minced
3 stalks celery, diced
1 green pepper, chopped
1 red pepper, chopped
3 cloves garlic, minced
1 teaspoon chili powder
1 teaspoon cumin
½ teaspoon dried basil
½ teaspoon dried thyme
½ teaspoon salt
¼ teaspoon black pepper
1 cup chopped tomatoes
1 cup tomato sauce
1 16-oz. can (2 cups) garbanzo beans, drained and rinsed
3 cups cooked rice
  Nonfat cooking spray

NUTRITION INFORMATION PER SERVING

Serving Size: 1 portion

Calories: 243
Protein: ....8 g
Carbohydrate: ....49 g
Fat: ....2 g
Cholesterol: ....0 mg
Sodium: ....575 mg
Fiber: ....6.5 g

Dietary Exchanges:
  2 starch and 3 vegetable

Sauté onion, celery, peppers and garlic in skillet sprayed with nonfat cooking spray. Add spices and continue cooking until fragrant. Add tomatoes, tomato sauce, beans and rice and cook until thoroughly heated.

Note:

Sesame oil, fresh ginger and crushed red pepper give this recipe its distinctive flavor. The crushed red pepper and the ginger root make it hot and spicy so consider your personal preference when deciding how much to use.

Szechuan Asparagus with Vermicelli

This recipe is featured on the front cover!

Asparagus and pasta lovers will certainly want to make this dish often when asparagus is in season. It's equally good served hot or cold.

4 PORTIONS

1½ lbs. asparagus, trimmed and broken into 2" pieces
1 cup sliced green onions, using some tops
1 large red pepper, cut into julienne strips or rings
1 clove garlic, minced
1 tablespoon minced fresh ginger root
¼ to ½ teaspoon crushed red pepper or cayenne pepper
½ tablespoon sesame oil
2 tablespoons light soy sauce
2 tablespoons rice vinegar
3 tablespoons white wine
1 teaspoon sugar
1 8-oz. pkg. uncooked vermicelli

Prepare the asparagus and set aside.

Sauté onions, red pepper strips, garlic, ginger root and crushed red pepper in sesame oil just until flavors are blended taking care not to overcook the onions and peppers.

In another pan, bring to a boil the soy sauce, rice vinegar, wine and sugar. Add to the onion mixture; set aside and keep warm.

In the meantime, cook the vermicelli to the desired doneness. While the vermicelli is cooking, steam the asparagus for about 5 minutes. Drain and rinse the pasta and place it in a large serving bowl. Add asparagus and top with the onion mixture. Toss and serve.

Tomato Lasagna Rollups

Pasta lovers will find this a very tasty and satisfying dish.
Tomatoes with Italian seasonings give this sauce its appeal.

9 X 13" BAKING PAN; 8 PORTIONS

8 pieces uncooked lasagna noodles
1 cup chopped onions
3 cloves garlic, minced
2 cups stewed tomatoes
1 6-oz. can tomato paste
1 teaspoon dried basil
1 teaspoon dried oregano
½ teaspoon Italian seasoning
2 tablespoons red wine
1 15-oz. carton nonfat, low-cholesterol Poly-O®
  ricotta cheese
1 10-oz. pkg. frozen spinach, well drained
1 cup nonfat Mozzarella cheese
2 egg whites
¼ teaspoon nutmeg
¼ teaspoon black pepper
  Nonfat cooking spray
  garnish: chopped fresh basil

NUTRITION INFORMATION PER SERVING

Serving Size: 1 rollup

Calories: 228
Protein: ....20 g
Carbohydrate: ....35.5 g
Fat: ....1 g
Cholesterol: ....4.5 mg
Sodium: ....364 mg
Fiber: ....3 g

Dietary Exchanges:
1 starch, 2 vegetable and
2 very lean meat

Serving Tip:

Cut each rollup in half and place cut side down in the baking dish for a very attractive addition to a buffet table. You may need to secure them with toothpicks.

Cook pasta to al denté stage. Drain and lay out on foil.

Sauté onions and garlic in skillet sprayed with vegetable cooking spray. Add tomatoes, tomato paste, spices and wine. Cover and simmer 5 to 10 minutes. In separate bowl, mix ricotta cheese, spinach, Mozzarella cheese, egg white, nutmeg and pepper.

Spread a small amount of the tomato sauce in bottom of a 9 x 13-inch baking pan sprayed with nonfat cooking spray. Spread ⅓ cup of cheese mixture on each piece of lasagna noodle, roll up and place in the baking dish. Top with remaining tomato sauce, cover and bake for 35 minutes at 350°. Garnish with fresh basil.

Vegetable Lasagna

The beauty of this lasagna is that the noodles cook as the lasagna is baking, eliminating the need to handle the hot noodles which shortens the preparation time.

9 X 13" BAKING PAN; 12 PORTIONS

1½ cups diced onions
3 large cloves garlic, minced
4 cups cooked and drained broccoli, cut in small pieces
4 cups spaghetti sauce
1½ cups water, divided
1 teaspoon dried basil
½ teaspoon dried oregano
½ teaspoon fennel seeds
¼ cup chopped fresh parsley
9 uncooked lasagna noodles
1 15-oz. carton nonfat, low-cholesterol Poly-O® ricotta cheese
1 cup nonfat Mozzarella cheese
  Nonfat cooking spray

Sauté onions and garlic in skillet sprayed with nonfat cooking spray. Add broccoli and about 3 tablespoons of water. Steam covered to partially cook. Cook out excess water, if any.

In separate bowl, mix spaghetti sauce, remaining water, basil, oregano, fennel seed and parsley.

Layering: Pour 1 cup of sauce in bottom of a 9 x 13-inch baking pan. Place 3 noodles on the sauce, spread with ½ of ricotta cheese. Cover with broccoli and onion mixture. Add another layer of sauce. Add 3 more noodles, the rest of the ricotta, all of the Mozzarella and more sauce, then the 3 remaining noodles and the remainder of the sauce. Cover tightly and bake at 350° for 1 to 1½ hours or until noodles are done. Uncover for the last 20 minutes of baking. Let sit 10 minutes before serving.

NUTRITION INFORMATION PER SERVING

Serving Size: 1 portion

Calories: 170
Protein: ....13.5 g
Carbohydrate: ....27.5 g
Fat: ....less than 1 g
Cholesterol: ....3 mg
Sodium: ....347 mg
Fiber: ....2 g

Dietary Exchanges:
1 starch, 2 vegetable and
1 very lean meat

Note:

Select a spaghetti sauce with less than 1 g fat per ½ cup. Please refer to **Appendix D** for specific brands.

Lemony Vegetable Pasta, page 161

Crêpes with Hearty Bean Filling, page 63, **Whole Wheat Crêpes,** page 193,
Boston Brown Bread, page 184 and **Sweet and Spicy Tomato Sauce,** page 123

Chapter 6

Fabulously Fit Main Dishes: Vegetables—Main Dish and on the Side

The myriad colors of vegetables lets you put together a meal with lots of eye appeal, something that is as important as the taste of the food. Steamed vegetables are a wonderful addition to any meal, and the method of steaming retains nutrients while enhancing the bright color of the vegetables. When steaming, add herbs or spices to enhance the flavor (suggested flavor combinations are given on page 47).

As for toppings, you can add butter flavor by sprinkling with a butter substitute. Some of our favorite substitutes are Molly McButter® and Butter Buds®. Better yet, by liquefying the substitute according to package directions, you can add moisture and butter flavor without the fat. Or, make a creamy topping by mixing plain nonfat yogurt with your favorite herb. Fat-free salsas make fabulous toppings as well.

Baked Vegetable Packets

We take these packets with us to potlucks. They stay hot and we have a main dish to build a meal around.

4 SERVINGS

4 medium potatoes, unpeeled and thinly sliced
4 small summer squash, sliced
4 medium carrots, sliced
1 large onion, sliced
½ cup sliced fresh mushrooms
1 cup broccoli flowerets
1 teaspoon dried basil
1 teaspoon dried dill weed
½ teaspoon salt
¼ teaspoon pepper
1 tablespoon imitation butter sprinkles
½ teaspoon garlic powder
1 large tomato, cut into 8 wedges

Combine first 6 ingredients in a large bowl; sprinkle with seasonings and toss to coat. Divide vegetables evenly onto 4 (18-inch) squares of heavy duty foil. Top each serving with 2 tomato wedges. Seal each packet and bake at 350° for 30 minutes or until vegetables are done.

NUTRITION INFORMATION PER SERVING

Serving Size: 1 packet

Calories: 207
Protein: ....6.5 g
Carbohydrate: ....47 g
Fat: ....less than 1 g
Cholesterol: ....0 mg
Sodium: ....340 mg
Fiber: ....5 g

Dietary Exchanges:
2 starch and 2 vegetable

Broccoli Ricotta Crêpes

10 CRÊPES

1 15-oz. carton (about 2 cups) nonfat, low-cholesterol ricotta cheese
2 egg whites, beaten lightly
1 cup nonfat shredded Mozzarella cheese
1 10-oz. pkg. frozen chopped broccoli, cooked, drained and slightly mashed
¼ cup diced green onions, using some tops
¼ teaspoon nutmeg
2 tablespoons fresh parsley, snipped
10 **Whole Wheat Crêpes** (page 193)
   Sweet and Spicy Tomato Sauce (page 123)

Beat ricotta with egg whites until light. Add remaining ingredients and thoroughly combine.

Fill each crêpe with about ⅓ cup filling. Roll and place seam side down in a shallow baking dish. Cover and bake at 350° for about 20 minutes or until heated through. Serve with **Sweet and Spicy Tomato Sauce** (see page 123) Makes filling for 10 crêpes.

NUTRITION INFORMATION PER SERVING

Serving Size: 1 crêpe, ½ cup sauce

Calories: 198
Protein: ....18 g
Carbohydrate: ....32 g
Fat: ....less than 1 g
Cholesterol: ....4.5 mg
Sodium: ....446 mg
Fiber: ....3 g

Dietary Exchanges:
1 starch, 1 skim milk and
1 vegetable

Calzones

Calzones take about an hour to make and they're well worth the effort. Bake and wrap them for freezing in dinner-size portions and you have quick meals for evenings when you're hurried and don't have time to cook.

8 CALZONES

1   cup chopped onions
3   cloves garlic, minced—more if desired
2   cups nonfat, low-cholesterol ricotta cheese
1   10-oz. pkg. frozen chopped broccoli or steamed
    fresh, cooked, drained and slightly mashed
1   cup nonfat Mozzarella cheese, shredded
1   egg white
1¼ teaspoons dried basil
½   teaspoon dried oregano
½   teaspoon dried thyme
¼   teaspoon black pepper

1   loaf frozen Honey Wheat bread dough (page 240)
    Marinara or spaghetti sauce, if desired
    Nonfat cooking spray

Sauté onions and garlic in a skillet sprayed with nonfat cooking spray. Take care not to scorch the garlic. Mix onions and garlic with the next 8 ingredients in medium-size mixing bowl. Set aside.

Divide the thawed bread dough into 8 pieces and roll into circles on a floured board. Place filling on each circle, fold dough over the filling and seal edges. Place on a large cookie sheet sprayed with vegetable cooking spray. Bake at 350° for 20 minutes or until puffed and golden brown. You may serve with marinara or spaghetti sauce.

NUTRITION INFORMATION
PER SERVING

Serving Size: 1 calzone

Calories: 228
Protein: ....20 g
Carbohydrate: ....35.5 g
Fat:.................................3 g
Cholesterol: ....4.5 mg
Sodium: ....446 mg
Fiber:............................3.5 g

Dietary Exchanges:
1 starch, 1 vegetable, 1 skim milk and 1 lean meat

Preparation Tips:

A 10-oz. package of frozen spinach can be substituted for the broccoli. Drain it well before adding it to the rest of the ingredients.

When selecting an ultra low-fat spaghetti or marinara sauce, choose one with 1 g fat or less per ½ cup

To shorten preparation time, place the filling in pita bread and bake them.

Corn, Bean and Rice Goulash

Using packets of previously prepared and frozen rice, this recipe can be prepared and baked in less than an hour. Stuff any leftovers into pita bread and heat for a very delicious hot lunch.

8 PORTIONS

1   cup diced onions
3   cloves garlic, minced
2   cups tomato sauce
2   tablespoons brown sugar
2   tablespoons sweet relish
2   teaspoons dry mustard
1   tablespoon vinegar
2   cups cooked rice (1 cup brown and 1 cup white rice)
1½ cups frozen corn
1   16-oz. can (2 cups) pinto beans, drained and rinsed
1   16-oz. can (2 cups) baby lima beans, drained and rinsed
1   cup nonfat Mozzarella cheese
    Nonfat cooking spray

Sauté onions and garlic in a pan sprayed with nonfat cooking spray. Mix all ingredients together except cheese and place in a 2-qt. baking dish. Bake at 350° about 30 minutes or until bubbly. Add cheese and return to oven to melt cheese.

NUTRITION INFORMATION PER SERVING
Serving Size: 1 portion
Calories: 225
Protein: ....12.5 g
Carbohydrate: ....43.5 g
Fat: ....less than 1 g
Cholesterol: ....2 mg
Sodium: ....363 mg
Fiber: ....4 g
Dietary Exchanges: 2 starch and 2 vegetable

Cabbage Rolls

These cabbage rolls freeze well and the recipe makes enough for several meals.

9 X 13" BAKING PAN; 15 CABBAGE ROLLS

Rolls:

1 large head cabbage
2½ cups nonfat chicken broth
1 8-ounce package Indian Harvest® rice
1 Garden Vegetable seasoning packet
4 spicy bean burger patties to equal 12 ounces (such as Morningstar Farms® brand)
¾ cup grated carrots
1 cup golden raisins
¼ cup chopped walnuts
¼ cup chili sauce

Sauce:

1 28-ounce can (3½ cups) diced tomatoes
2 tablespoons vinegar
2 tablespoons brown sugar
½ tablespoon Worchestershire sauce
½ teaspoon black pepper
garnish: basil, chopped

Rolls: Steam cabbage in a steamer or saucepan until outside leaves are wilted and will remove easily. Remove leaves and set aside. Keep steaming the cabbage and removing leaves until you have enough. Place all cabbage leaves in kettle with a small amount of water and cook 5 to 8 minutes longer. Remove from the water and set aside to cool.

Pour the nonfat chicken broth into a medium-size saucepan, bring to a boil and add rice and seasoning packet. Cook over low heat according to the directions on the rice package you choose. Remove from heat and cool.

NUTRITION INFORMATION PER SERVING

Serving Size: 1 cabbage roll

Calories: 134
Protein: ....6 g
Carbohydrate: ....25 g
Fat: ....1.5 g
Cholesterol: ....0 mg
Sodium: ....407 mg
Fiber: ....4 g

Dietary Exchanges:
1 starch and 2 vegetable

N o t e :

Indian Harvest (see page 247) offers a wide array of rice, grains and seasonings. For this recipe, I use their Black Pearl Medley, a blend of black barley, brown rice and Daikon radish seeds and cook it with the Garden Vegetable seasoning packet, minus the butter. If you do not have Indian Harvest® any of the rice pilaf products (minus the butter) available in most supermarkets are acceptable.

In large mixing bowl, mash the bean burgers. Mix beans, carrots, cooked rice, raisins, walnuts and chili sauce together.

Place ½ cup of the bean and rice mixture on a cabbage leaf, roll up and secure with two toothpicks. Place in a 9 x 13-inch (or larger) baking pan. Make tomato sauce.

Sauce: Combine all ingredients in a medium-size saucepan, heat and pour the tomato sauce over the cabbage rolls. Cover tightly and bake at 350° for 45 to 50 minutes or until cabbage is tender. At serving time garnish with chopped basil.

N o t e s :

I like to use three spicy bean burgers from Chili's restaurant (4 ounces each). I've substituted the Morningstar Farms brand in this recipe as they are more widely available in supermarkets.

Sodium in this recipe may be further reduced by using "no salt added" canned tomatoes, or fresh tomatoes and by using low-sodium chili sauce.

Gratin of Vegetables

Can be served as an entrée or as a side dish.

9 X 13" BAKING DISH; 8 PORTIONS

½ cup sliced green onions, using some tops
1 tablespoon imitation butter sprinkles
¼ teaspoon garlic powder
2 cups nonfat, cholesterol-free sour cream
10 medium red-skinned potatoes, scrubbed and unpeeled
2 cups cauliflower, large pieces
2 cups broccoli, large flowerets
1 cup sliced carrots
8 small onions, cooked in small amount of water and drained
¾ cup nonfat Mozzarella cheese, grated
Nonfat cooking spray

Mix green onions, imitation butter sprinkles and garlic powder with sour cream and let set for an hour or so to blend flavors.

Scrub potatoes and boil in small amount of water until tender. Quarter potatoes and place in 9 x 13-inch baking dish that has been lightly sprayed with nonfat cooking spray. Lightly steam cauliflower, broccoli and carrots and arrange with the potatoes in the serving dish. Add the drained onions.

Spoon the sour cream mixture over the vegetables. Sprinkle with cheese and bake at 350° until bubbly hot and the cheese has melted.

NUTRITION INFORMATION PER SERVING

Serving Size: 1 portion

Calories: 263
Protein: ....15.5 g
Carbohydrate: ....53 g
Fat: ....0.5 g
Cholesterol: ....3 mg
Sodium: ....226 mg
Fiber: ....6 g

Dietary Exchanges:
2 starch, 3 vegetable and ½ skim milk

Mashed Potato Pie

This crowd pleaser is an adaptation of the meat and potato pie our mothers used to make when they had left over pot roast and mashed potatoes.

8 PORTIONS

1 cup unflavored TVP® beef granules
¾ cup hot water
1 medium onion, diced
¾ cup catsup
1 tablespoon brown sugar
1 tablespoon yellow mustard
1 tablespoon vinegar
1 16-oz. pkg. frozen peas and carrots, cooked and drained
1 teaspoon salt-free herb and spice mix
3 cups cooked potatoes, mashed
½ cup skim milk, warmed
1 tablespoon imitation butter sprinkles
2 tablespoons dried minced onions or chives
  Onion powder to taste
⅓ to ½ cup nonfat, cholesterol-free sour cream
2 tablespoons snipped fresh parsley
  Pepper to taste
  Paprika
  Nonfat cooking spray

NUTRITION INFORMATION PER SERVING
Serving Size: 1 portion
Calories: 158
Protein: ....11 g
Carbohydrate: ....31.5 g
Fat: ....0.5 g
Cholesterol: ..less than 0.5 mg
Sodium: ....324 mg
Fiber: ....5.5 g
Dietary Exchanges:
2 starch

Notes:

Please see **Appendix D** for brand-specific soybean products.

Mrs. Dash® works well in this recipe as the salt-free herb and spice mix.

Reconstitute TVP® granules with the hot water. Stir until completely moistened. Spray a skillet with nonfat cooking spray and cook reconstituted TVP® granules with chopped onion until onion is translucent. Add catsup, brown sugar, mustard and vinegar and simmer 5 minutes to blend flavors. Place mixture in the bottom of a 2-qt. casserole dish that has been sprayed lightly with a nonfat cooking spray.

Place the drained peas and carrots on top of the TVP mixture. Season them with the herb and spice seasoning.

Add the butter sprinkles and minced onion to the warmed skim milk and set aside. Mash the potatoes thoroughly, adding milk mixture, sour cream, parsley, pepper and onion powder. Spread potatoes over the top of vegetables. Sprinkle with paprika. Cover and bake at 350° for 30 minutes or until hot.

Vegetable Kabobs Over Rice

Serve these kabobs over rice pilaf.

8 SKEWERS; 4 SERVINGS

½ cup nonfat Italian dressing
1 tablespoon fresh parsley, snipped
1 teaspoon dried dill weed
1 teaspoon dried basil

1 medium zucchini, cut into 1½" chunks
2 medium yellow squash, cut into 1½" chunks
8 small onions, or 1 large onion, quartered and separated
8 fresh mushrooms
8 cherry tomatoes
2 cups cooked rice
  Nonfat cooking spray

Mix Italian dressing with the herbs and chill.

Place vegetables on 8 skewers alternating zucchini, squash, onions, mushrooms and tomatoes. Spray the grill with vegetable cooking spray. Place the kabobs on a medium hot grill and baste frequently with the dressing mixture. Cook approximately 15 minutes or until vegetables have reached the desired doneness.

Each serving consists of ½ cup rice and 2 vegetable kabobs.

NUTRITION INFORMATION PER SERVINGS

Serving Size: 2 skewers and ½ cup rice

Calories: 205
Protein: ....5.5 g
Carbohydrate: ....44 g
Fat: ....1 g
Cholesterol: ....0 mg
Sodium: ....462 mg
Fiber: ....3 g

Dietary Exchanges:
2 starch and 2 vegetable

Vegetable Stir-fry

Stir-frys can be prepared in very little time if you plan ahead. In little more than a half hour this scrumptious stir-fry will be ready to eat.

6 PORTIONS

2   cups nonfat chicken broth, divided
1   tablespoon lite soy sauce
2   tablespoons cornstarch
2   teaspoons grated or minced fresh ginger
4   cups fresh vegetables, cut up (1 cup of each-carrots, broccoli flowerets, red pepper, green onions)
1   14-oz. can baby corn, well drained
3   cloves garlic, minced
½   teaspoon herb and spice mix (such as Mrs. Dash®)
1   6-oz. can water chestnuts, drained
6   cups cooked rice (3 cups brown rice and 3 cups white rice)
4   tablespoons liquefied artificial butter sprinkles
    Nonfat cooking spray

In small saucepan, stir together 1¾ cups broth, soy sauce, cornstarch and ginger. Bring to a boil and cook until the mixture thickens and becomes clear. Set aside and keep warm.

In large skillet sprayed with nonfat cooking spray, sauté in this order: carrots, broccoli flowerets, pepper chunks, green onion, corn and garlic until vegetables are tender crisp. Add additional broth, 1 tablespoon at a time, to aid in cooking; do not overcook. Add herb and spice mix.

Add the thickened broth and drained water chestnuts. Heat and spoon over individual portions of steaming hot rice that has been moistened with liquefied imitation butter sprinkles.

NUTRITION INFORMATION PER SERVING

Serving Size: 1 portion

Calories: 336
Protein: ....9.5 g
Carbohydrate: ....71.5 g
Fat:....................................2 g
Cholesterol: ....0 mg
Sodium: ....234 mg
Fiber: ....3.5 g

Dietary Exchanges:
  4 starch and 2 vegetable

Preparation Tip:

To shorten preparation time, prepare vegetables in advance. Have frozen packets of rice ready to thaw. If the broth you're using is too high in sodium, dilute it half and half with water and save the remainder for future use.

Liquefy artificial butter sprinkles, Butter Buds® or Molly McButter®, according to package directions.

Vegetable Masala

The spices in this recipe create a very flavorful curry. For ease in preparation, measure the ingredients ahead of time. Mango chutney is a nice accompaniment to this meal.

6 PORTIONS

1¼ lb. red-skinned potatoes, cut into 1-inch chunks (6 or 7 medium-size potatoes)
3 cups cauliflower pieces
Nonfat cooking spray
2 teaspoons turmeric powder, divided
1 teaspoon salt
6 tablespoons fat-free chicken broth, divided
½ tablespoon olive oil
2 teaspoons ground cumin
¼ teaspoon cayenne or red pepper flakes (use more, if desired)
1 tablespoon finely chopped fresh ginger
2 large garlic cloves, minced
⅛ teaspoon asifiteda
2 teaspoons sugar
1½ cups frozen peas
3 small tomatoes, peeled and quartered
garnish: cilantro leaves, chopped

Prepare and cook potatoes in a small amount of water. Do not overcook. When they are cool, remove the skins and set aside.

In large saucepan sprayed with a nonfat cooking spray, cook cauliflower with 1 teaspoon of the turmeric, salt and half the chicken broth. Cover and steam until just tender. Set aside.

In separate skillet, add oil and the remaining spices including the remaining 1 teaspoon of turmeric and cook for about 15 seconds, stirring so they don't burn. Add remaining broth and mix until smooth. Add potatoes, peas and tomatoes stirring to mix well with spices. When well heated, add to the cauliflower and continue on low heat until all vegetables are warm. Can add a bit more broth at this point, if desired. Garnish with chopped cilantro. Serve with **Basmati Rice** (see page 85).

NUTRITION INFORMATION PER SERVING

Serving Size: approximately 1½ cups

Calories: 146
Protein: ....5 g
Carbohydrate: ....30 g
Fat: ....less than 2 g
Cholesterol: ....0 mg
Sodium: ....408 mg
Fiber: ....2.5 g

Dietary Exchanges:
1 starch and 2 vegetable

Preparation Tip:

Asifiteda is available in ethnic food stores. If you can't get it, double the garlic in the recipe.

Asparagus with Lemon Sauce

8 X 8" BAKING DISH; 4 PORTIONS

1 lb. asparagus spears, washed and trimmed
⅓ cup nonfat, cholesterol-free mayonnaise
1 tablespoon nonfat plain yogurt
2 teaspoons imitation butter sprinkles
⅛ teaspoon white pepper
½ teaspoon dry mustard
1 tablespoon lemon juice
⅓ cup nonfat cracker or bread crumbs
    Nonfat cooking spray
    garnish: red pepper strips

NUTRITION INFORMATION PER SERVING

Serving Size: 1 portion

Calories: 92
Protein: ....4 g
Carbohydrate: ....17.5 g
Fat: ....less than 1 g
Cholesterol: ....0 mg
Sodium: ....146 mg
Fiber: ....0.5 g

Dietary Exchanges:
  1 starch and 1 vegetable

Cook asparagus spears in small amount of water in microwave for 8 minutes. Drain and place asparagus spears side by side in an 8 x 8-inch baking dish. Blend mayonnaise with yogurt, imitation butter sprinkles, pepper, dry mustard and lemon juice. Spoon sauce over the middle of the asparagus and sprinkle crumbs over the dressing. Add the red pepper strips. Bake at 375° for 15 minutes or broil until bubbly and browned.

Black-eyed Peas and Corn

Black-eyed peas are supposed to bring good luck if eaten on New Year's day, however don't wait until then to eat them. These are so good they'll soon become a staple in your kitchen.

6 PORTIONS

1 16-oz. can (2 cups) black-eyed peas, drained and rinsed
1 16-oz. can (2 cups) corn, drained
1 stalk celery, finely chopped
¼ cup finely diced red pepper
1½ teaspoons dried parsley or ¼ cup fresh parsley, snipped
⅓ cup finely diced onion
¼ cup nonfat chicken broth
4 tablespoons medium salsa or to taste
Pepper to taste

Combine all ingredients together, mix well and chill.

NUTRITION INFORMATION PER SERVING

Serving Size: 1 portion

Calories: 140
Protein: ....5 g
Carbohydrate: ....30.5 g
Fat: ....1 g
Cholesterol: ....0 mg
Sodium: ....318 mg
Fiber: ....6.5 g

Dietary Exchanges:
2 starch

Buttercup Squash with Peas and Onions

This is my favorite squash. It has a slightly sweet, nutty flavor and a smooth, almost creamy texture. Best if purchased in the fall.

6 PORTIONS

1 medium-size buttercup squash
¼ teaspoon salt
1 10-oz. package frozen peas and onions
1 tablespoon imitation butter sprinkles

With a sharp knife remove the knot from one end of the squash (opposite the stem end). Scrape the inside, removing all of the seeds and the stringy membrane. Rub the inside with salt. Bake in a pan with ½-inch of water at 375° for 1 hour or until squash is soft and well cooked. Be sure to test the thick end.

Just prior to serving, prepare the peas and onions, omitting the butter. Drain well, toss with the imitation butter sprinkles and place them in the squash cavity. To serve, cut as you would an angel food cake and spoon peas and onions onto the plate.

NUTRITION INFORMATION PER SERVING

Serving Size: 1 portion

Calories: 62
Protein: ....2 g
Carbohydrate: ....14.5 g
Fat: ....less than 0.5 g
Cholesterol: ....0 mg
Sodium: ....110 mg
Fiber: ....2 g

Dietary Exchanges:
1 starch

N o t e :

Buttercup squash is also good seasoned with salt and pepper, imitation butter sprinkles, brown sugar or honey.

Carrots and Grapes

8 PORTIONS

1 lb. fresh baby carrots
3 tablespoons liquefied imitation butter sprinkles
1½ tablespoons brown sugar, packed
1 teaspoon cornstarch
2 tablespoons white wine
2 drops imitation butter flavoring
3 tablespoons fresh parsley, snipped
1½ cups seedless green grapes

Steam carrots until just tender.

Make sauce of liquid butter sprinkles, brown sugar, cornstarch and white wine. Cook over medium heat until mixture thickens. Add butter flavoring. Spoon over carrots; add parsley and grapes. Heat gently and serve.

NUTRITION INFORMATION PER SERVING

Serving Size: 1 portion

Calories: 50
Protein: ....1 g
Carbohydrate: ....12 g
Fat: ....less than 0.5 g
Cholesterol: ....0 mg
Sodium: ....22 mg
Fiber: ....2 g

Dietary Exchanges:
½ vegetable and ½ fruit

Note:

Liquefy Butter Buds® or Molly McButter® according to the packaged directions. Keep a jar handy in the refrigerator for immediate use.

Green and Yellow Mixit

Experiment with these seasonings according to your personal preference.

6 PORTIONS

4 small zucchini, cut in chunks
4 medium yellow squash, cut in chunks
1 large onion, cut in wedges
   Nonfat cooking spray
   Dill weed, thyme, basil, oregano, onion
   and garlic powder
   Black pepper.

Sauté the vegetables in a large skillet sprayed with nonfat cooking spray. Add suggested herbs according to your personal preference and cook a couple of minutes to desired doneness.

NUTRITION INFORMATION PER SERVING

Serving Size: 1 portion

Calories: 24
Protein: ....1 g
Carbohydrate: ....5.5 g
Fat: ....less than 0.5 g
Cholesterol: ....0 mg
Sodium: ....3 mg
Fiber: ....less than 1 g

Dietary Exchanges:
   1 vegetable

Green Beans in Creamy Tomato Sauce

8 PORTIONS

1 cup chopped onion
2 cloves garlic, minced
1 lb. green beans, trimmed and cut
2 cups stewed tomatoes
1 tablespoon nonfat dry milk powder
¼ teaspoon salt
⅛ teaspoon black pepper
⅛ teaspoon dried dill weed
   Nonfat cooking spray

Sauté the onion and garlic in a large skillet sprayed with nonfat cooking spray. Add the remaining ingredients, cover and simmer for 15 to 20 minutes or until beans are tender and the sauce has thickened a bit.

NUTRITION INFORMATION PER SERVING

Serving Size: 1 portion

Calories: 43
Protein: ....2 g
Carbohydrate: ....10 g
Fat: ....less than 0.5 g
Cholesterol: ....0 mg
Sodium: ....216 mg
Fiber: ....1.5 g

Dietary Exchanges:
   2 vegetable

Oven Fried Potatoes

9 X 13" BAKING DISH; 8 PORTIONS

14 medium red-skinned potatoes
   (approximately 2" in diameter, each)
2 large onions, cut in large chunks
   Nonfat cooking spray
2 tablespoons imitation butter sprinkles
   Basil, dill weed, garlic powder, fresh parsley,
   paprika

Scrub and slice each potato into 6 to 8 wedges and place with onions in a 9 x 13-inch baking dish. Spray lightly with nonfat cooking spray and sprinkle with imitation butter sprinkles and suggested herbs according to your personal preference. Cover and bake for 30 minutes at 350°. Uncover, stir potatoes and continue baking uncovered until they are done.

NUTRITION INFORMATION PER SERVING

Serving Size: 1 portion

Calories: 210
Protein: ....4.5 g
Carbohydrate: ....48 g
Fat: ....0.5 g
Cholesterol: ....0 mg
Sodium: ....16 mg
Fiber: ....5 g

Dietary Exchanges:
3 starch

Variations:

Coat potatoes and onions with 2 tablespoons of malt vinegar before adding seasonings. Or, spray potatoes and onions with nonfat cooking spray, place in a plastic bag, and add 2 tablespoons of Lipton Onion Soup® mix. Shake to coat potatoes. Bake as directed.

Stuffed Zucchini

This recipe makes ample filling to heap on the zucchini. Any filling that's left, wrap in foil and bake with the zucchini. Make ahead to pop into the oven while preparing the rest of the dinner.

4 PORTIONS

2 medium zucchini
1 medium onion, chopped
2 cloves garlic, minced
1 red pepper, seeded and diced
½ cup chopped zucchini pulp
½ cup chopped mushrooms
1 teaspoon Italian seasoning
¼ teaspoon salt
   Dash cayenne pepper
¼ teaspoon pepper
¼ cup fresh parsley, snipped
1 tomato, chopped
1 cup cooked rice
   Nonfat cooking spray

NUTRITION INFORMATION PER SERVING

Serving Size: 1 portion

Calories: 104
Protein: ....3 g
Carbohydrate: ....22.5 g
Fat: ....less than 1 g
Cholesterol: ....0 mg
Sodium: ....143 mg
Fiber: ....1 g

Dietary Exchanges:
1 starch and 1 vegetable

Wash zucchini, trim ends and slice in half lengthwise. Scoop out the pulp leaving a thin shell, approximately ⅛ to ¼-inch thick.

To prepare the filling, sauté onion, garlic and red peppers until soft in a skillet sprayed with nonfat cooking spray. Add chopped zucchini, mushrooms, Italian seasoning, salt, cayenne and black pepper and parsley; cook until tender. Remove from heat and add tomato and rice. Mix well.

Pack the mixture into the zucchini shells. Place in a baking dish which has ¼-inch of water in the bottom. Cover and bake for 20 minutes at 375°. Place remaining filling in foil and bake alongside the zucchini. Uncover zucchini and bake an additional 20 minutes or until zucchini is tender. Spoon on additional filling and serve.

Sweet and Sour Cabbage with Apples

An adaptation of the cabbage my Grandma used to serve with sauerbraten.

6 PORTIONS

1 onion, chopped
1 teaspoon caraway seeds
4 cups of coarsely shredded cabbage
2 baking apples, like Granny Smith, unpeeled and sliced
½ teaspoon allspice
½ cup raisins
¾ cup nonfat chicken broth
⅓ cup brown sugar, packed
2 teaspoons cornstarch
⅓ cup cider vinegar
2 tablespoons imitation butter sprinkles
  Herb and spice blend seasonings to taste
¼ teaspoon pepper
  Nonfat cooking spray

Sauté onion and caraway seed in a large skillet sprayed with vegetable cooking spray. Add cabbage, apple, allspice, raisins and broth. Cover and steam over low heat for 20 minutes. When the cabbage is wilted and tender, add the brown sugar, and cornstarch that has been mixed with the vinegar. Cook another couple of minutes. Just before serving add the butter sprinkles, herb and spice seasonings and pepper.

NUTRITION INFORMATION PER SERVING

Serving Size: 1 portion

Calories: 133
Protein: ....2 g
Carbohydrate: ....34 g
Fat: ....0.5 g
Cholesterol: ....0 mg
Sodium: ....61 mg
Fiber: ....1.5 g

Dietary Exchanges:
  2 vegetable and 1½ fruit

Note:

Either Mrs. Dash® or salt-free Spike® works well as the herb and spice blend in this recipe

Sweet Potato Pone

A great recipe for your Thanksgiving dinner.

5 PORTIONS

- 1 lb. raw sweet potatoes, peeled, shredded (to equal 3 cups)
- ½ cup nonfat, cholesterol-free egg substitute
- 1 cup evaporated skim milk
- ¼ cup packed brown sugar
- ¼ cup molasses
- 2 tablespoons liquefied artificial butter sprinkles
- ½ teaspoon cinnamon
- ½ teaspoon nutmeg
- ¼ teaspoon salt
- 1 cup mini marshmallows (optional)

In large bowl, combine all ingredients and transfer to a 1-qt. baking dish. Bake covered for 45 minutes at 350°. Uncover and bake 1 hour more. Add marshmallows when baking is completed and place them under the broiler to brown marshmallows.

NUTRITION INFORMATION PER SERVING

Serving Size: 1 portion

Calories: 228
Protein: ....7 g
Carbohydrate: ....50 g
Fat: ....0 g
Cholesterol: ....0 mg
Sodium: ....226 mg
Fiber: ....less than 1 g

Dietary Exchanges:
1 starch, 1 skim milk and
1 fruit

Note:

Liquefy Butter Buds® or Molly McButter® according to package directions.

Tomato Chutney

This tomato chutney is also wonderful served on angel hair pasta.

NUTRITION INFORMATION
PER SERVING

Serving Size: ½ cup

Calories: 84
Protein: ....1.5 g
Carbohydrate: ....21 g
Fat: ....0.5 g
Cholesterol: ....0 mg
Sodium: ....152 mg
Fiber: ....1 g

Dietary Exchanges:
1 vegetable and 1 fruit

4   tomatoes, chopped
1   cup crushed pineapple, in juice, undrained
½   cup chopped onion
½   cup finely diced celery
3   small bay leaves
1   medium apple, unpeeled, chopped
½   cup raisins
¼   cup apple cider vinegar
½   teaspoon cinnamon
¼   teaspoon allspice
¼   teaspoon ginger
½   teaspoon salt

In a 2-qt. saucepan, combine tomatoes, pineapple, onions, celery and bay leaves. Simmer for 5 minutes. Add apple, raisins, vinegar and spices. Cover and simmer for 40 minutes. Uncover and continue simmering until mixture thickens a bit. Discard bay leaves and serve with **Lentil Patties** (see page 66).

Sweet and Spicy Tomato Sauce

*This sauce works well for the **Crêpes with Hearty Bean Filling** recipe on page 63 the **Broccoli Ricotta Crêpes** on page 103 and the **Calzones** on page 104.*

5 CUPS; 10 PORTIONS

2 medium onions, cut in thin slices and separated
4 cups stewed tomatoes
2 6-oz. cans (1½ cups) tomato paste
½ teaspoon black pepper
¼ teaspoon cayenne pepper or red pepper flakes
  Juice of 2 small lemons
2 teaspoons vinegar
⅓ cup packed dark brown sugar
  Nonfat cooking spray

Cook onions in sauce pan sprayed with nonfat cooking spray. Add the remaining ingredients and simmer 20 minutes to thicken and blend flavors. Serve over crêpes or calzones.

NUTRITION INFORMATION PER SERVING

Serving Size: ½ cup

Calories: 92
Protein: ....2.5 g
Carbohydrate: ....22.5 g
Fat: ....0.5 g
Cholesterol: ....0 mg
Sodium: ....256 mg
Fiber: ....2 g

Dietary Exchanges:
  1 vegetable and 1 fruit

Vegetable Spaghetti Sauce

This sauce can be made in about the time it takes to cook the spaghetti. An added bonus is that this recipe makes enough for 2 meals for a family of four. Cooked spaghetti keeps very well in the refrigerator. Heat and add sauce at serving time.

8 PORTIONS

½ cup chopped onion
3 cloves garlic, minced
½ cup diced green pepper
1 cup grated carrots
1 cup chopped fresh mushrooms
1 summer squash, diced
1 tomato, diced
1 tablespoon sugar
¼ cup fresh parsley, snipped
2 tablespoons dry red wine
1 28-oz. can (3½ cups) low-fat spaghetti sauce
4 tablespoons nonfat Parmesan cheese
  Nonfat cooking spray

In large pan sprayed with vegetable cooking spray, sauté the onion, garlic, green pepper, carrots, mushrooms and squash to desired doneness. Add tomato, sugar, parsley, wine, spaghetti sauce and Parmesan cheese. Simmer about 2 minutes or longer, if desired.

NUTRITION INFORMATION PER SERVING

Serving Size: 1 portion

Calories: 74
Protein: ....3.5 g
Carbohydrate: ....15 g
Fat: ....0.5 g
Cholesterol: ....2.5 mg
Sodium: ....343 mg
Fiber: ....1.5 g

Dietary Exchanges:
1 starch

Chapter 7

Hearty Sandwiches and Substantial Soups, Stews, Chilies and Chowder

Soups and sandwiches make great lunch, mid-afternoon or supper fare. Experiment with a variety of sandwich breads and toppings. For example, try a different bread such as an oatmeal or zucchini bread, escarole or bibb lettuce instead of iceberg, spicy sprouts instead of alfalfa. You can even vary the spread that you use by adding different herbs or spices to a nonfat, cholesterol-free mayonnaise, or try chopped cucumber mixed with plain nonfat yogurt or cottage cheese.

Vegetables used as fillings create wonderful sandwiches. Try combinations using grated carrots, tomatoes, cucumbers, radishes, onions, mushrooms (grilled portabellas are outstanding) and, oh yes, sprouts. Add one of the many mustards, your favorite vinegar, non-fat salad dressing or salsa.

Be sure to round out your meal with fruit such as a fruit salad or blenderized smoothie.

Soup can be a meal by itself or one of the healthiest additions to a meal. It is one of the "comfort foods" which picks you up and makes you feel a little better, particularly on a cold day or when you're feeling a little under the weather. And cold soups can be especially refreshing when served with a salad on a hot summer day.

Soups are so easy to make and one pot makes for easy cleanup! An added bonus is that a large batch can be frozen in small containers for a quick meal later. Just a cautious note, thawing frozen soups containing noodles can cause the noodles to become mushy and fall apart. You might want to add freshly cooked noodles when using a frozen soup stock.

A good soup can be prepared from just about anything. Start with canned fat-free broth, cut up fresh vegetables, add pasta or rice along with herbs and spices; simmer, and you've created a nutritious meal while cleaning out your refrigerator at the same time!

When making a cream soup, replace the cream or milk in the

recipe by substituting a combination of nonfat chicken broth, whole-wheat flour and nonfat, cholesterol-free sour cream. Simply mix 2 tablespoons of whole-wheat flour with ¼ cup sour cream and add slowly to 1 quart of broth. The result will be a nonfat substitute for a rich, creamy soup. A combination of evaporated skim milk and pureéd cooked potatoes also makes a good "cream" base.

Serve soup as an appetizer, a snack, or as an entrée along with a crisp salad and crusty bread.

Baco's®, Lettuce and Tomato Sandwich

Baco's® give this sandwich the flavor, aroma and crunch of bacon without all the fat and cholesterol. A slice of sweet onion or dill chips can be added, or serve with a bowl of steaming hot soup or a fruit salad.

1 SERVING

1 large hamburger bun or 2 slices of bread, preferably whole wheat
2 tablespoons nonfat, cholesterol-free mayonnaise
½ of a medium tomato, sliced thin
  Lettuce
½ tablespoon Baco's®

Layer ingredients in order as they appear onto whole-grain bun or bread. Sprinkle Baco's® on just before serving.

Variation: Prepare a basil mayonnaise by combining chopped basil leaves, and ½ teaspoon vinegar with ½ cup nonfat, cholesterol-free mayonnaise. This makes enough mayonnaise for 4 sandwiches.

NUTRITION INFORMATION PER SERVING

Serving Size: 1 sandwich

Calories: 190
Protein: ....8 g
Carbohydrate: ....34 g
Fat: ....2 g
Cholesterol: ....0 mg
Sodium: ....635 mg
Fiber: ....7.5 g

Dietary Exchanges:
  2 starch and 1 vegetable

Note:

Look for buns or bread that are fat-free. See **Appendix D** for specific brands. Fat-free breads have no fat or animal products added.

Cucumber Sandwich

1 SERVING

1 whole-grain bun
4 slices peeled cucumber
4 pieces spinach, deveined and trimmed
1 thin slice onion
  Alfalfa sprouts
2 tablespoons Philadelphia Free® cream cheese,
  Fat-free refried beans or hummus
  Red wine vinegar

Arrange slices of cucumber, spinach, onion and sprouts over bun half. Spread cream cheese over sprouts and sprinkle with red-wine vinegar. Replace top half of bun.

NUTRITION INFORMATION PER SERVING

Serving Size: 1 sandwich

Calories: 185
Protein: ....11.5 g
Carbohydrate: ....31 g
Fat: ....2 g
Cholesterol: ....3 mg
Sodium: ....532 mg
Fiber: ....7.5 g

Dietary Exchanges:
2 starch and 1 very lean meat

N o t e :

The **Hummus** on page 130 is a wonderful complement to this sandwich.

Egg Sandwich

Nothing beats a tasty egg sandwich and this one won't let you down. Serve with a pasta salad and fruit.

4 SERVINGS

- 1 cup nonfat, cholesterol-free egg substitute
- 1 tablespoon chopped mild green chiles
  Nonfat cooking spray
- ¼ cup nonfat, cholesterol-free mayonnaise
- 1 teaspoon spicy brown mustard or Dijon-style mustard
  Pepper
- 4 thin slices sweet onion
- 4 slices tomato
- 4 lettuce leaves
- 4 low-fat English muffins

NUTRITION INFORMATION PER SERVING

Serving Size: 1 sandwich

Calories: 202
Protein: ....11.5 g
Carbohydrate: ....30.5 g
Fat: ....3 g
Cholesterol: ....0.5 mg
Sodium: ....570 mg
Fiber: ....2 g

Dietary Exchanges:
2 starch and 1 lean meat

Blend green chiles with egg substitute. Pour the egg mixture into an 8-inch skillet that has been sprayed with a nonfat cooking spray and cook. As edges set, lift edges to allow the uncooked egg to flow to bottom of pan, tilting pan as necessary. Cook until mixture is set and top is dry. With spatula edge cut mixture into quarters. Set aside. Combine mayonnaise with mustard. Add a dash of pepper.

Prepare sandwiches by spreading each muffin half with 1 tablespoon mayonnaise mixture. Layer the cooked egg, tomato, onion and lettuce and top with the remaining muffin half. Serve either hot or cold.

Hummus

*Hummus is a good addition to the **Cucumber Sandwich**, used as a spread for crackers or chips, or served as a stand-alone filling in pita bread.*

NUTRITION INFORMATION
PER SERVING

Serving Size: ¼ cup

Calories: 47
Protein: ....2.5 g
Carbohydrate: ....8 g
Fat: ....less than 1 g
Cholesterol: ....0 mg
Sodium: ....300 mg
Fiber: ....2.5 g

Dietary Exchanges:
½ starch

MAKES 2½ CUPS, 10 SERVINGS

½ cup chopped green onions
1 clove garlic, minced
2 cups garbanzo beans, drained
1 tablespoon Dijon-style mustard
  Juice of 1 lemon (2–3 tablespoons)
½ teaspoon dried basil
½ teaspoon dried dillweed
½ teaspoon dried tarragon
⅛ teaspoon cayenne pepper
½ teaspoon salt or to taste
¼ cup nonfat chicken broth

Place all ingredients, except the chicken broth, in a blender or food processor and process until smooth. Add chicken broth a tablespoon at a time until you have a soft, spreadable consistency.

Pita Pizza

At this writing Boboli is making a nonfat pizza sauce. Each package contains 3 5-oz. pouches. Select the pita pockets that contain no fat.

6 SERVINGS

1 pkg. (22 ounces) of 6 whole-wheat pita bread
15 oz. nonfat pizza sauce
¾ cup nonfat pizza cheese
1 cup finely diced green pepper
1 cup finely diced red pepper
1 cup chopped mushrooms
⅔ cup chopped onions
⅔ cup crushed pineapple or pineapple tidbits, fresh or canned, drained
1 cup seeded and chopped tomato

Place pita pockets onto large baking sheets. Spread pizza sauce evenly over the pita pockets. Do not open them. Cover each pita with a proportional share of the remaining ingredients. Bake at 450° for 8 to 10 minutes or to desired doneness.

NUTRITION INFORMATION PER SERVING

Serving Size: 1 pita pocket pizza

Calories:	231
Protein:	13 g
Carbohydrate:	42 g
Fat:	2.5 g
Cholesterol:	2 mg
Sodium:	917 mg
Fiber:	8.5 g

Dietary Exchanges:
2 starch, 1 vegetable and 1 lean meat

Sloppy Joes

Would you believe that you can be a vegetarian and enjoy Sloppy Joes? This recipe uses TVP® (texturized vegetable protein) in place of beef.

12 SERVINGS

2 cups unflavored TVP® beef granules
1¾ cups hot water
3 cloves garlic, minced
1 large onion, chopped
1 green pepper, diced
2 stalks celery, diced
1 6-oz. can tomato paste
½ cup catsup
1 tablespoon prepared yellow mustard
⅔ cup water
1 teaspoon dried basil
½ teaspoon dried oregano
⅛ to ¼ teaspoon red pepper
2 tablespoons Worcestershire sauce
12 Hamburger buns split
   Herb and spice blend seasoning to taste
   Pickles, sweet onions and greens as toppings
   Nonfat cooking spray

In medium-size mixing bowl, reconstitute the TVP® with the hot water. Stir to moisten the TVP®.

In large kettle sprayed with nonfat cooking spray, sauté garlic, onion, green pepper and celery until soft. Add the TVP®, tomato paste, catsup, mustard, water and seasonings and mix well. Heat to blend flavors and simmer 5 minutes. Serve on hamburger buns with the condiments of your choice. This freezes well.

NUTRITION INFORMATION PER SERVING

Serving Size: 1 sandwich

Calories: 191
Protein: ....13 g
Carbohydrate: ....32 g
Fat: ....2.5 g
Cholesterol: ....0 mg
Sodium: ....376 mg
Fiber: ....4.5 g

Dietary Exchanges:
2 starch and 1 lean meat

N o t e s :

Low-sodium varieties of tomato paste, catsup and mustard work well in this recipe.

Choose whole-wheat buns to increase nutrient and fiber content

Herb and spice blend seasonings that work well in this recipe are Mrs. Dash® or Salt-free Spike®

Vegetable Pita Sandwich

8 SERVINGS

 1 medium onion, sliced
⅔ cup broccoli, chopped in small pieces
⅔ cup chopped summer squash
⅔ cup chopped mushrooms
1½ cups chopped tomato
 1 cup nonfat shredded Cheddar cheese
 1 teaspoon dried dill weed
 1 teaspoon dried basil
¼ cup fresh parsley, snipped
24 spinach leaves, trimmed and torn in pieces
 4 whole-wheat pita breads, cut in half
 1 cup nonfat Italian dressing or nonfat dressing of choice
1½ cups alfalfa sprouts, loosely packed

In medium bowl, combine onion, broccoli, squash, mushrooms, tomato, cheese and seasonings. Stuff vegetable-cheese mixture into pita halves that have been lined with spinach. Drizzle each sandwich with 2 tablespoons of dressing and top with a puff of sprouts.

Variation: Steam broccoli, squash and mushrooms until tender crisp before stuffing the pita pockets.

NUTRITION INFORMATION PER SERVING

Serving Size: 1 pita half

Calories: 118
Protein: ....8.5 g
Carbohydrate: ....20 g
Fat: ....0.5 g
Cholesterol: ....2 mg
Sodium: ....748 mg
Fiber: ....2 g

Dietary Exchanges:
 1 starch, 1 vegetable and
 ½ very lean meat

N o t e :

Choose pita bread that has no fat added.

Veggie Submarine Sandwich

This sandwich is equally good served hot or cold.

2 SERVINGS

¼ cup sliced onion
½ cup sliced zucchini
1 clove garlic, minced
½ cup seeded and chopped tomatoes
½ cup seeded and chopped green pepper
¼ teaspoon dried thyme
⅛ teaspoon freshly ground black pepper
⅓ cup nonfat Cheddar or Mozzarella cheese, shredded
2 6-inch whole-wheat submarine sandwich buns, split
   Herbal vinegar
2 teaspoons yellow mustard
2 tablespoons nonfat, cholesterol-free mayonnaise
   Nonfat cooking spray

Sauté the onion, zucchini and garlic over medium heat in a pan sprayed with vegetable cooking spray. When they are tender crisp remove from heat and add the tomatoes, green pepper, thyme and black pepper. Toss and fill the buns with the veggie mixture. Sprinkle cheese on top and place under the broiler until the cheese has melted. Top with a splash of vinegar, mustard and mayonnaise.

NUTRITION INFORMATION PER SERVING

Serving Size: 1 sandwich

Calories: 307
Protein: ....18.5 g
Carbohydrate: ....51.5 g
Fat: ....4 g
Cholesterol: ....4 mg
Sodium: ....1005 mg
Fiber: ....11 g

Dietary Exchanges:
2 starch, 3 vegetable and 1 lean meat

N o t e :

Cucumbers, mushrooms, sprouts, radishes and shredded lettuce are all good additions to this sandwich. Omit cheese and add more veggies to eliminate cholesterol.

Cabbage Soup

The pepperoncini peppers and Tabasco sauce give this soup its unique flavor.

12 SERVINGS

2 cups nonfat chicken broth
¾ medium head cabbage, shredded
2 large white onions, chopped
1 green pepper, diced
3 mild pepperoncini, chopped fine or to taste
½ cup chopped celery
4 cups water
3 cloves garlic, minced
½ teaspoon salt
2 dashes of Tabasco sauce, or more to taste
3 tablespoons brown sugar
1 28-oz. can (3½ cups) tomatoes, with juice, chopped

Place all ingredients except the canned tomatoes, into a large soup kettle and bring to a boil. Reduce heat and simmer until ingredients are tender, about 1½ hours. Add chopped canned tomatoes and cook another ½ hour or until hot. Add water if needed.

NUTRITION INFORMATION PER SERVING

Serving Size: 1 cup

Calories: 49
Protein: ....2 g
Carbohydrate: ....11 g
Fat: ....less than 0.5 g
Cholesterol: ....0 mg
Sodium: ....269 mg
Fiber: ....0.5 g

Dietary Exchanges:
2 vegetable

Corn and Potato Chowder

6 SERVINGS

1½ cups finely chopped onion
1 cup thinly sliced carrots
2 stalks celery with tender leaves, thinly sliced
1 bay leaf
2 cups cubed red-skin potatoes
2 cups nonfat chicken broth
1 cup skim milk
1 cup fresh or frozen corn
¼ teaspoon salt
   Cayenne pepper to taste
   Herb and spice blend seasoning to taste
   Nonfat cooking spray
   garnish: fresh parsley

In large saucepan sprayed lightly with a nonfat cooking spray, sauté the onions until tender. Add carrots, celery, bay leaf, potatoes and broth. Cover, bring to a boil and cook for 10 to 15 minutes or until potatoes are done. Add milk and corn and simmer another 3 or 4 minutes. Remove bay leaf. In a blender, purée 1 cup of the soup then return it to the pot.

Add salt and other seasonings to taste. Garnish with snipped fresh parsley if desired.

NUTRITION INFORMATION
PER SERVING

Serving Size: 1½ cups

Calories: 96
Protein: ....5 g
Carbohydrate: ....19.5 g
Fat: ....0.5 g
Cholesterol: .....less than 1 mg
Sodium: ....251 mg
Fiber: ....less than 1 g

Dietary Exchanges:
1 starch and 1 vegetable

Country Bean Soup

This super yet simple bean soup was adapted from the label of a jar of Randall mixed beans. In minutes you have soup for a crowd.

11 SERVINGS

1   48-oz. jar (6 cups) Randall mixed beans
6   cups water
6   packets low-sodium beef broth (like MBT)
1   28-oz. can (3⅓ cups) tomatoes, undrained and
    chopped
2   cups frozen corn
¼   cup fresh parsley, snipped
2   teaspoons dried thyme
2   teaspoons dried basil
½   teaspoon dried oregano
    Herb and spice blend seasoning to taste
    Ground black pepper to taste

Combine all ingredients in a large soup kettle and bring to a boil. Reduce heat and simmer for 10 minutes.

NUTRITION INFORMATION PER SERVING

Serving Size: 1½ cups

Calories:	153
Protein:	8 g
Carbohydrate:	29 g
Fat:	1 g
Cholesterol:	0 mg
Sodium:	562 mg
Fiber:	10.5 g

Dietary Exchanges:
2 starch

Note:

Randall mixed beans is a combination of navy beans, light red kidney beans, small red beans, black-eyed peas, great northern beans, green peas, and baby lime beans in liquid.

Please see **Appendix D** for more information.

Fruit Soup

10 SERVINGS

1 cup dried apricots
¾ cup dried apples
½ cup dried peaches
½ cup dried prunes (pits removed)
½ cup dark seedless raisins
2 qts. water
¼ cup sugar
¼ cup tapioca
1 3-inch stick of cinnamon
1 teaspoon lemon or orange zest
1 cup raspberry syrup

Rinse all fruit well and place in a large kettle with 2 quarts of water. Cover and soak 2 to 3 hours or overnight. Add to the fruit: sugar, tapioca, cinnamon and orange or lemon zest.

Bring to a boil, reduce heat, cover tightly and simmer 1 hour or until fruit is tender. Remove from heat and stir in 1 cup raspberry syrup. Chill until very cold and serve.

Variation: Cook fruit with thin orange or lemon slices.

NUTRITION INFORMATION PER SERVING

Serving Size: approximately 1 cup

Calories: 226
Protein: ....1 g
Carbohydrate: ....60 g
Fat: ....less than 0.5 g
Cholesterol: ....0 mg
Sodium: ....47 mg
Fiber: ....3 g

Dietary Exchanges:
4 fruit

Lentil Soup

Serve with a tossed, mixed green salad, crusty French bread and fresh cantaloupe for dessert.

8 SERVINGS

1 large onion, chopped
4 stalks celery, sliced
4 cloves garlic, minced
2 16-oz. cans nonfat chicken broth
2 cups water
2 cups lentils, washed and picked over
1 large carrot, sliced
2 cups tomatoes, cut up
1 teaspoon dried thyme
2 tablespoons dried parsley
2 bay leaves
¼ teaspoon black pepper
  Tabasco sauce, several dashes
1 large potato, peeled and diced
  Nonfat cooking spray

NUTRITION INFORMATION PER SERVING

Serving size: 1½ cups

Calories: 154
Protein: ....11 g
Carbohydrate: ....28.5 g
Fat: ....less than 1 g
Cholesterol: ....0 mg
Sodium: ....482 mg
Fiber: ....0.5 g

Dietary Exchanges:
  1 starch, 2 vegetable and 1 very lean meat

Sauté onion, celery and garlic over medium heat in a 5-quart stock pot sprayed with nonfat cooking spray. Add broth, water, lentils and remaining ingredients except potatoes. Bring to a boil. Cover, reduce heat and simmer for approximately 1 hour. Add potatoes and continue cooking until potatoes are done.

Minestrone Soup

This Italian soup is typically made with many vegetables and grains. It's a very good way to use left-over vegetables. Freeze half for later use.

12 SERVINGS

10 cups water
¼ cup uncooked rice
¼ cup dry lentils
¼ cup dry green split peas
1 onion, chopped
2 cloves garlic, minced
4 stalks celery, sliced
1 cup tomato sauce
1 20-oz. pkg. (2½ cups) frozen mixed vegetables
2 teaspoons dried basil
1 teaspoon dried thyme
1 teaspoon dried oregano
⅛ teaspoon pepper
2 beef bouillon cubes or equivalent; fat-free, low-sodium, like MBT
½ cup whole-wheat pasta shells
4 cups coarsely shredded cabbage
2 cups fresh spinach, trimmed
   Herb and spice blend seasoning to taste (such as Mrs. Dash® or Salt-Free Spike®)
   Nonfat cooking spray

Using a large soup kettle, cook rice, lentils and split peas in 10 cups of water for 15 minutes. Sauté onions, garlic and celery in a skillet sprayed with nonfat cooking spray until tender.

Add onion mixture, tomato sauce, vegetables, seasonings and bouillon cubes to the soup kettle and cook another 15 minutes. Add pasta and cabbage and cook until tender. During the last 10 minutes of cooking, add the spinach. Adjust seasonings and thin with water if necessary.

NUTRITION INFORMATION PER SERVING

Serving Size: 1 cup

Calories: 80
Protein: ....4 g
Carbohydrate: ....17 g
Fat: ....less than 0.5 g
Cholesterol: ....0 mg
Sodium: ....136 mg
Fiber: ....0.5 g

Dietary Exchanges:
1 starch

Potato, Bean and Rice Soup

You can adapt any cream-or milk-based soup by substituting nonfat, cholesterol-free sour cream, flour and nonfat chicken broth. Double this recipe for another meal or freeze for later use.

6 SERVINGS

3 medium carrots, diced
½ cup diced celery
3 cloves garlic, minced
4 cups nonfat chicken broth
3 cups diced potatoes
1 cup cooked brown rice
2 teaspoons dried dill weed
2 tablespoons fresh parsley, snipped
1 16-oz. can (2 cups) navy beans, drained
½ cup nonfat, cholesterol-free sour cream
2 tablespoons whole-wheat flour
   Freshly ground black pepper to taste
   Nonfat cooking spray

Sauté carrots, celery and garlic in a soup kettle sprayed with nonfat cooking spray. Add broth, potatoes and rice and simmer covered for 15 minutes or until potatoes are done. Lightly mash the drained beans and add them to the potatoes.

In a small bowl, mix sour cream, flour and pepper. Stir into potato mixture and cook over medium heat until thickened. Cook 1 more minute stirring constantly.

NUTRITION INFORMATION PER SERVING

Serving Size: 1½ cups

Calories: 356
Protein: ....20.5 g
Carbohydrate: ....68.5 g
Fat:................................1.5 g
Cholesterol: ....0 mg
Sodium: ....275 mg
Fiber: ....1 g

Dietary Exchanges:
   3 starch, 3 vegetable and
   1 very lean meat

Split Pea Soup

This is a hearty, robust soup that is full of flavor. Leeks are an important ingredient in this soup. Serve with a whole-grain bread and a tossed green salad.

8 SERVINGS

2½ cups dry split peas (approximately 1 lb.)
6 cups water
5 cups nonfat chicken broth, divided
¾ cup chopped celery with some tender leaves
2 leeks, thinly sliced, washed well–white parts only
1 large onion, chopped
2 bay leaves
1½ cups peeled diced potatoes
1½ cups diced carrots
4 tablespoons imitation bacon bits
4 packets instant nonfat, low-sodium chicken broth (like MBT)
¼ teaspoon freshly ground black pepper
   Tabasco sauce to taste
   Herb and spice blend seasoning to taste
   Cracked pepper to taste.

In large soup kettle, combine the split peas and water. Bring to a boil, cook peas for 2 minutes. Remove from heat, cover and let stand 1 hour. Add 4 cups broth, celery, leeks, onion and bay leaves. Bring soup to a boil, reduce heat, cover pan and simmer soup for 1½ hours.

Add potatoes, carrots, imitation bacon bits and instant broth packets. Simmer for another 15 to 20 minutes (peas should disintegrate). If soup gets too thick, thin with remaining broth or water. Add pepper, Tabasco sauce and season to taste with herb and spice seasonings.

NUTRITION INFORMATION PER SERVING	
Serving Size: 1½ cups	
Calories:	141
Protein:	9.5 g
Carbohydrate:	24.5 g
Fat:	1 g
Cholesterol:	0 mg
Sodium:	263 mg
Fiber:	3.5 g

Dietary Exchanges:
1 starch, 1 vegetable and 1 very lean meat

Meatless Chili

Chili is very versatile. It can provide more meals than one. To begin with, cook cornmeal dumplings on top of the chili. It can also become a sauce for linguini, and finally, served as a topping for baked potatoes.

12 SERVINGS

1 large onion, chopped
1 large green pepper, seeded and chopped
3 16-oz. cans (6 cups) stewed tomatoes
1 16-oz. can (2 cups) pinto beans, drained and rinsed
1 16-oz. can (2 cups) kidney beans, drained and rinsed
1 16-oz. package (2 cups) frozen mixed vegetables
⅛ to ¼ teaspoon ground cloves
⅛ teaspoon allspice
2 tablespoons chili powder
1 tablespoon cumin
 Green chiles (optional)
 Tabasco sauce (optional)
 Nonfat cooking spray

Sauté onion and green pepper in a large soup kettle sprayed with nonfat cooking spray. Add the remaining ingredients and simmer until the flavors are blended and the vegetables are done. Heat and serve.

NUTRITION INFORMATION PER SERVING

Serving Size: 1 cup

Calories: 292
Protein: ....17 g
Carbohydrate: ....56.5 g
Fat: ....1.5 g
Cholesterol: ....0 mg
Sodium: ....321 mg
Fiber: ....1.5 g

Dietary Exchanges:
 3 starch and 3 vegetable

Polka Dot Chili

You can have this chili on the table in no time since most of these ingredients are probably staples in your kitchen. Serve in large soup bowl over a bed of rice along with a tossed salad.

8 SERVINGS

¾ cup chopped onion
½ cup mild green chiles
2 cloves garlic, minced
2 teaspoons chili powder
1 teaspoon cumin
1 teaspoon dried oregano
1 teaspoon sugar
⅛ teaspoon cloves or to taste
⅛ teaspoon cayenne pepper or to taste
3 large tomatoes, coarsely chopped
4 cups nonfat chicken broth
2 16-oz. cans (4 cups) cannellini beans, drained and rinsed
2 cups cooked rice (1 cup brown and 1 cup white rice)
   garnish: nonfat sour cream and cilantro, chopped

In large saucepan, sauté onions until tender, about 3 minutes. Add chiles, garlic, spices and tomatoes. Bring to a boil, reduce heat and simmer about 5 minutes. Add broth, bring to a boil; reduce heat and simmer covered for about 15 minutes to blend flavors.

Add beans and heat to serve. Serve over steaming rice and garnish each serving with 1 tablespoon sour cream and cilantro as desired.

NUTRITION INFORMATION PER SERVING

Serving Size: 1½ cups

Calories: 256
Protein: ....16 g
Carbohydrate: ....48 g
Fat: ....1.5 g
Cholesterol: ....0 mg
Sodium: ....198 mg
Fiber: ....1.5 g

Dietary Exchanges:
2 starch, 2 vegetable and
1 very lean meat

Bean and Pasta Stew

This bean and pasta dish is a good choice when time is short. All ingredients are cooked together in one kettle for easy preparation and clean up.

8 SERVINGS

1 cup chopped onion
½ cup chopped green pepper
3 cloves garlic, minced
1 16-oz. can (2 cups) stewed tomatoes
1 16-oz. can (2 cups) kidney beans, undrained
1 6-oz. pkg. small, whole-wheat pasta shells (about 3 cups cooked)
1 cup water
½ teaspoon dried oregano
1 teaspoon dried basil
1 16-oz. can (2 cups) garbanzo beans, undrained
Pepper to taste
Nonfat cooking spray

Sauté onions, green pepper and garlic in kettle sprayed with nonfat cooking spray. Add tomatoes, kidney beans, pasta shells, water and spices. Bring to a boil, cover and simmer until pasta is tender. Add garbanzo beans and pepper to taste. Heat thoroughly.

NUTRITION INFORMATION PER SERVING

Serving Size: approximately 1¼ cups

Calories: 195
Protein: ....9.5 g
Carbohydrate: ....38.5 g
Fat: ....1.5 g
Cholesterol: ....0 mg
Sodium: ....547 mg
Fiber: ....7.5 g

Dietary Exchanges:
  2 starch and 2 vegetable

Preparation Tip:

To reduce the sodium in this recipe, substitute salt-free tomatoes and add Mrs. Dash® or salt-free Spike to taste.

Potato and Vegetable Stew

Equally good hot or cold, this stew is a good choice for a summer picnic and it's even better the second day.

8 SERVINGS

1 large chopped onion
3 cloves garlic, minced
1 28-oz. can (3½ cups) Italian style stewed tomatoes
1 large green pepper, seeded and cut into chunks
6 small white potatoes, unpeeled and cut into
   1-inch pieces
1 teaspoon dried basil
1 teaspoon dried oregano
1 teaspoon mixed Italian herbs
½ teaspoon salt
2 cups frozen peas and carrots
   Nonfat cooking spray

Sauté onion and garlic in a large kettle which has been sprayed with a nonfat cooking spray. Add all remaining ingredients except peas and carrots. Bring to a boil, cover, reduce heat and continue cooking about 20 minutes or until potatoes are just tender. Add peas and carrots and continue cooking about 5 minutes or until stew is heated thoroughly.

NUTRITION INFORMATION PER SERVING

Serving Size: approximately 1¼ cups

Calories: 93
Protein: ....3 g
Carbohydrate: ....21.5 g
Fat: ....less than 0.5 g
Cholesterol: ....0 mg
Sodium: ....409 mg
Fiber: ....2 g

Dietary Exchanges:
1 starch and 1 vegetables

N o t e :

This is an excellent recipe to use new or red-skin potatoes in the spring. The flavor is extraordinary.

Vegetable Stew with Cornmeal Dumplings

In combination with the dumplings, this stew is a real winner. Feel free to substitute different vegetables—perhaps turnips or rutabagas for the potatoes.

8 SERVINGS

4 medium fresh tomatoes, peeled and cut up
2 cups tomato juice
2 nonfat beef broth packets, low-sodium variety like MBT
1 cup water
2 medium onions, chopped
2 cloves garlic, minced
¼ teaspoon pepper
½ cup nonfat broth or water

3 medium potatoes, peeled and quartered
2 carrots, sliced
1 cup fresh or frozen corn
1 16-oz. can (2 cups) garbanzo beans, drained and rinsed
1 cup fresh or frozen peas
   Tabasco to taste
½ cup sliced summer squash
2 tablespoons red wine
2 bay leaves
2 tablespoons Worcestershire sauce
¼ cup fresh parsley, snipped
3 tablespoons whole-wheat flour mixed in ½ cup broth
   Cornmeal Dumplings (page 194)

NUTRITION INFORMATION PER SERVING

Serving Size: approximately 1¼ cups (stew only)

Calories:	148
Protein:	5.5 g
Carbohydrate:	31.5 g
Fat:	1 g
Cholesterol:	0 mg
Sodium:	365 mg
Fiber:	2 g

Dietary Exchanges:
2 starch

In large soup kettle or dutch oven, combine first 8 ingredients and bring to a boil. Add potatoes and carrots and cook until just tender. Add remaining ingredients except flour and bring to a boil. (Can be prepared in advance up to this point). Just before serving remove bay leaves, add flour, heat to simmer and cook for 5 minutes to thicken.

Prepare **Cornmeal Dumplings** (see page 194) and drop in eight spoonfuls on top of the simmering stew. Cover and simmer until dumplings are done, approximately 20 minutes. Keep covered while cooking the dumplings. Serve stew over dumplings.

Chapter 8
Salads: Away with the Iceberg Lettuce!

When you think of salad, does an image of nearly white iceberg lettuce with pale pink tomatoes smothered in high-fat salad dressing come to mind? Think again! Salads can be a satisfying nutrient-dense, low-fat addition to a meal, or served as a main entrée.

For tossed salads, start with a base of greens other than iceberg lettuce. Not that iceberg lettuce doesn't have its place, but nutrient-packed spinach makes a fabulous salad as do the darker green lettuce varieties like romaine, escarole, and leaf. Add radicchio for color and a sharper taste. A mixture of baby greens is another fresh alternative. See the next page for a glossary of various greens.

Shredded carrots and tomato slices shouldn't exhaust your list of salad additions. Try chopped, bright red or yellow peppers, crisp bean sprouts, sliced squash or zucchini, fresh sprouts, chunks of broccoli and cauliflower, shredded purple cabbage, or chopped cucumber. Consider colorful, sliced baby vegetables. Sprinkle shredded nonfat cheese, a teaspoon of sunflower seeds, or toasted fat-free croutons on top.

Often fruit is overlooked in green salads, but fruit makes a great salad addition. Raspberries, strawberries, or sliced carambola (starfruit) team up well with fresh spinach. Sprinkle each serving with a half teaspoon of poppy seeds and drizzle with a flavored vinegar, such as raspberry. Chunks of apples go well with romaine or a mixture of escarole and red leaf lettuce, sprinkled with a little nonfat shredded cheese.

Leftover pasta or potato salad can be spooned into bowls lined generously with lettuce. You may want to add some bright red tomatoes, or red pepper strips for more crunch.

Make a southwestern salad by topping romaine lettuce with black beans, rice, fresh chopped tomatoes, and salsa. Finish with baked tortilla strips and dallops of nonfat, cholesterol-free sour cream.

Prepare salad ingredients in quantity and store them in a large container in the refrigerator. (Salad spinners work well for both draining and storing your salad greens). Greens, radishes, celery, carrots, cabbage, jicama, broccoli, cauliflower and cucumbers will keep well for 3 to 5 days. At serving time add tomatoes, onions, peppers, sprouts, etc., as you desire.

Salads don't have to be made with lettuce. Use a favorite vinegar on a medley of tomatoes, cucumbers, and onions. Or start with a base of flavored pasta (like spinach, lemon basil, or garlic) and add fresh fruit or a variety of chopped vegetables and black, cannellini or kidney beans. We think you'll enjoy our collection of varied salads.

Glossary of Greens

Arugula - Also called rocket or roquétte. A cruciferous vegetable with long, thin stems and small, flat green leaves somewhat resembling oak leaves. It has a peppery taste and is rich in Vitamin C and beta-carotene.

Belgian Endive - Also called French endive and known in Europe as "witloof chicory". Grows in small, oval heads of tightly closed creamy yellow or white leaves. The texture is velvety and crisp-edged with a bitter taste. While flavorful, it is low in nutrients. Serve in salads or creatively fill as an hors d'oeuvre.

Bibb Lettuce - A type of butterhead lettuce. Grows as a small head of loosely packed, succulent green leaves with a mild, sweet flavor.

Boston Lettuce - A type of butterhead lettuce. Grows round and loosely packed. Outer leaves are green, while inner leaves are light green and yellow with a buttery texture. Has a mild, sweet flavor.

Chicory - Also called curly endive. Grows as a loose head of lacy, green-edged outer leaves that curl at the tips, while the inner leaves are pale and yellow. Has a decidedly bitter taste, though the pale leaves are milder tasting.

Cress - Has very small, dark green leaves and a peppery taste.

Dandelion - Typically dark green leaves that grow wild. Pale young greens are best for salads. Greens should be used before the plant flowers as leaves will be milder tasting.

Escarole - Also called chicory escarole or Batavian endive. Grows as loosely packed, elongated leaves that are broader, less curly, a paler green, and milder in taste than curly endive. Slightly bitter in taste, the inner leaves are milder and best for salads.

Frisee - A member of the chicory family with leaves that range from pale green to creamy white. Mildly bitter in taste, it is the sweetest chicory.

Iceberg Lettuce - Also called crisphead lettuce. Grows as a large, firm, cabbage-like head with crisp, tightly packed leaves. The pale green to white leaves are very mild in flavor. It adds crunch to a salad but is rather low in nutrients.

Kale - Large leaves with curly edges and coarse texture that may be green, red, or purple and are a good source of Vitamin A. Small, young leaves are more tender and good for salads. More mature leaves should be cooked.

Looseleaf Lettuce - A variety of lettuces with large, loosely packed leaves that may be smooth or have ruffled edges, and are both tender and crisp in texture. Green in color, red leaf lettuce is also deep red at the edges. It is typically mildly flavored with young, soft leaves being the sweetest.

Mache - Also called lamb's lettuce, corn salad, or field lettuce. Grows as a loose head of small, velvety, delicate green leaves. It is best when young and has a mild, sweet, nutty taste. It is also high in beta-carotene.

Mesclun - Mixture of a variety of prepackaged young, tender greens. It may include arugula, mache, dandelion, Oakleaf lettuce, spinach, curly endive, radicchio, and various herbs.

Oakleaf Lettuce - A variety of loosely packed leaf lettuce resembling oak leaves. Green in color, it may also have a bronze or red color.

Radicchio - A member of the chicory family, it grows as a tender, cabbage-like head that may be round or elongated. The leaves are typically a purple-red with white ribs, though also grown in various shades of red and green. It has a slightly bitter and peppery taste. It is most often used in salad for color and flavor accent.

Red Cabbage - A cruciferous vegetable that grows in a tightly packed head of crisp, purple-red leaves. Imparting a somewhat strong flavor, it is most often used for color and flavor accent and is very high in Vitamin C.

Romaine - Also called cos lettuce. Grows as an elongated head of long, thick-ribbed, medium to dark green leaves, with more pale leaves in the center of the head. The lettuce used in Caesar salads, it has a crisp texture with a strong, tangy taste that makes a great salad base.

Sorrel - A member of the rhubarb family that grows both wild and cultivated, it has small, smooth and tender arrow-shaped leaves that somewhat resemble young spinach. The leaves may be light or dark green with a somewhat sharp, lemony flavor that are best for salads when young.

Spinach - Grows as long, smooth, heart-shaped leaves. There are a few varieties, ranging from flat and smooth to the more curly savoy varieties. Good spinach should have dark green leaves, smell somewhat sweet and have a slightly spicy taste. It is an excellent source of beta-carotene and folic acid.

Watercress - A cruciferous vegetable of the mustard family, it grows loosely with small, round, dark green and glossy leaves. It has a sharp, peppery, mustard flavor that is good on sandwiches or in salads.

Broiled Vegetable Salad

A colorful, tasty salad that you'll want to make often.

6 SERVINGS

2 large tomatoes, peeled and sliced
½ green pepper, cut into strips
½ red pepper, cut into strips
½ large sweet onion, sliced, rings separated
1 cup mushrooms, sliced
2 teaspoons capers
½ cup nonfat, cholesterol-free Italian dressing
1 cup nonfat Mozzarella cheese, shredded
   Sprigs of fresh basil, chopped

NUTRITION INFORMATION
PER SERVING

Serving Size: 1 portion

Calories: 62
Protein: ....6.5 g
Carbohydrate: ....8.5 g
Fat: ....less than 0.5 g
Cholesterol: ....2.5 mg
Sodium: ....431 mg
Fiber: ....1 g

Dietary Exchanges:
  1 vegetable and ½ very lean meat

In an 8 x 12-inch baking dish layer tomatoes, peppers, onion and mushrooms. Add capers. Pour dressing over the vegetables and top with shredded cheese. Broil to melt cheese. Just before serving add fresh basil. To serve this salad, carefully cut it into 6 portions and remove it from the baking dish with a wide spatula.

Carrot Salad

An adaptation of an old recipe made heart smart by using nonfat ingredients in the dressing.

NUTRITION INFORMATION
PER SERVING

Serving Size: approximately ⅔ cup

Calories: 184
Protein: ....2 g
Carbohydrate: ....47 g
Fat: ....less than 0.5 g
Cholesterol: ....0 mg
Sodium: ....83 mg
Fiber: ....4 g

Dietary Exchanges:
1 vegetable and 2½ fruit

8 SERVINGS

3 cups grated carrots
½ cup diced celery
1 cup pineapple tidbits, packed in own juice, drained
1 cup diced apple
¼ cup raisins or dried cherries
½ teaspoon celery seed
¼ cup nonfat, cholesterol-free mayonnaise
¼ cup nonfat plain yogurt
Freshly ground pepper

In a large bowl, combine all ingredients; mix well. Chill and serve.

Cole Slaw

16 SERVINGS

1 cup sugar
½ cup apple cider vinegar
½ cup water
1 tablespoon mustard seed
4 cups shredded cabbage
½ green pepper, chopped
1 roasted red pepper, seeded, peeled and cut up
3 stalks celery, diced
1 16-oz. can (2 cups) Three Bean Salad

Combine sugar, vinegar, water and mustard seed in a small sauce pan. Heat just until the sugar dissolves. Cool. Prepare vegetables accordingly. Add the cooled vinegar mixture to the prepared vegetables and fold into Three Bean Salad. Place in a tightly sealed refrigerator container and invert occasionally to mix. Best if made a day ahead.

Variation: This recipe can be made without the Three Bean Salad as a plain coleslaw.

NUTRITION INFORMATION PER SERVING

Serving Size: ½ *cup*

Calories: 80
Protein: ....1.5 g
Carbohydrate: ....20 g
Fat: ....less than 0.5 g
Cholesterol: ....0 mg
Sodium: ....119 mg
Fiber: ....2.5 g

Dietary Exchanges:
2 vegetable and ½ bread

Preparation Tip:

If you choose to substitute artificial sweetener for the sugar in this recipe you do not need to heat the liquid. Heat the mustard seeds in a dry pan over medium heat to release the flavor.

Confetti Rice Salad

Great as a main dish or as a side dish.

8 SERVINGS

Salad:

  3 cups cooked rice
  1 roasted red pepper cut into strips
  ⅓ cup diced red onion
  ¼ cup diced celery
  ¼ cup green pepper, cut into chunks
  1 cup frozen mixed vegetables, cooked
  ½ cup nonfat, cholesterol-free egg substitute, scrambled
  ½ teaspoon salt

Dressing:

  ½ cup nonfat, cholesterol-free mayonnaise
  2 tablespoons cider vinegar
  2 tablespoons sweet pickle relish
  1 teaspoon Dijon-style mustard
  2 teaspoons sugar
  ⅛ teaspoon black pepper

Combine first 8 ingredients in a large mixing bowl. Mix all dressing ingredients together in a small bowl and add to salad mixture. Toss lightly to coat rice and vegetables. Chill 2 hours.

NUTRITION INFORMATION PER SERVING

Serving Size: approximately 1 cup

  Calories: 151
  Protein: ....5 g
  Carbohydrate: ....30.5 g
  Fat: ....less than 1 g
  Cholesterol: ..less than 0.5 mg
  Sodium: ....312 mg
  Fiber: ....2 g

Dietary Exchanges:
  2 starch

Preparation Tip:

To roast peppers, broil whole for about 20 minutes or until the skins are black and blistered. Turn every 5 minutes. When blackened, place peppers in a paper bag to steam for about 15 minutes. When cooled, peel off skin, remove seeds and they're ready to use.

Cranberry Fluff

An excellent choice to include in your Thanksgiving dinner. A sugar substitute can replace the sugar in the recipe if so desired.

14 SERVINGS

2 cups ground cranberries, fresh or frozen
2 cups miniature marshmallows
½ cup sugar
2 cups apples, unpeeled and finely diced
1 cup halved green grapes
½ cup diced celery
2 small bananas, sliced

Combine cranberries, marshmallows and sugar together. Chill overnight. Add remaining ingredients. Chill and serve.

NUTRITION INFORMATION PER SERVING

Serving Size: approximately ⅔ cup

Calories: 82
Protein: ....0.5 g
Carbohydrate: ....21 g
Fat:....................................0 g
Cholesterol: ....0 mg
Sodium: ....7 mg
Fiber: ....1 g

Dietary Exchanges:
1½ fruit

Fresh Fruit Salad

Fruit flavored yogurt is the dressing for this salad. Read labels carefully as all yogurts are not alike. I usually buy a nonfat, cholesterol-free Dannon® 4.4-oz. six pack. The flavors will vary. Prepare just prior to serving.

6 SERVINGS

1 large banana, sliced
2 large red apples, unpeeled and cut in bite-size pieces
1 cup halved green grapes
2 kiwi fruit, peeled and cut in wedges
2 teaspoons celery seed
1 4.4-oz. carton nonfat, cholesterol-free yogurt

In medium bowl, combine banana, apples, grapes and kiwi. Stir the celery seed into the yogurt; add mixture to the fruit and toss gently to coat the fruit. Cover and chill before serving.

NUTRITION INFORMATION
PER SERVING

Serving Size: 1 cup

Calories: 94
Protein: ....1.5 g
Carbohydrate: ....23 g
Fat: ....0.5 g
Cholesterol: ....0 mg
Sodium: ....13 mg
Fiber: ....3 g

Dietary Exchanges:
  1½ fruit

Preparation Tip:

Many different fruits are good in this salad. Try combinations of orange sections, fresh pineapple, melon with mangos; or peaches, strawberries, papaya, with fresh blueberries or raspberries.

Italian Pasta Salad

This colorful, main dish salad is a perfect supper for a warm summer evening.

12 SERVINGS

3   cups uncooked rotini, or pasta of choice (6 cups cooked)
¼   cup nonfat Parmesan cheese
1   cup nonfat Italian dressing
3   cups broccoli, small flowerets and stem pieces, blanched
1   16-oz. can (2 cups) kidney beans, drained and rinsed
¾   cup red pepper, cut into chunks
½   cup sliced carrots
½   red onion, sliced and separated
1   teaspoon herb and spice blend seasoning (such as Mrs. Dash®)
    Cracked pepper

Cook pasta to desired doneness. Drain and rinse. In large bowl, mix all ingredients. Refrigerate several hours or overnight.

NUTRITION INFORMATION PER SERVING

Serving Size: 1 cup

Calories: 136
Protein: ....6 g
Carbohydrate: ....26.5 g
Fat: ....0.5 g
Cholesterol: ....1.5 mg
Sodium: ....309 mg
Fiber: ....3.5 g

Dietary Exchanges:
2 starch

Layered Party Slaw

A friend gave me this recipe years ago. Adjusting the dressing to use nonfat food products now available makes this heart-healthy and nutritious.

12 SERVINGS

Slaw:
- 4 cups finely chopped cabbage
- 1½ cups cauliflower or broccoli, cut into bite-size pieces
- 1½ cups frozen peas, thawed
- 1½ cups sliced fresh mushrooms
- ½ cup sliced green onions
- ½ teaspoon salt
- ½ teaspoon salt-free herb and spice blend seasoning
- 4 tablespoons imitation bacon bits
- *garnish:* tomato wedges and sprigs of parsley

Dressing:
- ⅔ cup nonfat, cholesterol-free mayonnaise
- ⅓ cup nonfat, cholesterol-free honey mustard dressing
- 1 teaspoon vinegar
- 1 teaspoon Dijon-style mustard
- 1½ teaspoons sugar

Slaw: In large glass bowl, layer cabbage, cauliflower, peas, mushrooms and onions. Sprinkle salt and other seasonings evenly between the layers.

Dressing: Combine all of the dressing ingredients together and spread dressing evenly over top of the vegetables. Cover and refrigerate overnight. Before serving, add imitation bacon bits, tomatoes and parsley.

NUTRITION INFORMATION PER SERVING

Serving Size: ¾ cup

Calories: 62
Protein: ....3 g
Carbohydrate: ....11.5 g
Fat: ....0.5 g
Cholesterol: ....0 mg
Sodium: ....272 mg
Fiber: ....1.5 g

Dietary Exchanges:
2 vegetable

Tip:

There are good, nonfat honey mustard dressings available in your supermarket. I buy mine from Chili's restaurant.

Lemony Vegetable Pasta

This salad is best when made early in the day so the flavors blend.

8 SERVINGS

Pasta:
- 3 cups cooked rotini pasta
- ½ cup frozen peas
- ½ cup coarsely grated carrots
- ¼ cup raisins
- 1 diced Granny Smith apple
- ¼ cup green onions
- ¼ cup diced celery
- ½ teaspoon celery seed
- 3 tablespoons fresh parsley, snipped

Dressing:
- ¾ cup plain, nonfat yogurt
- 1 tablespoon nonfat, cholesterol-free mayonnaise
- 3 tablespoons lemon juice
- 1 tablespoon Dijon-style mustard
- 1 tablespoon brown sugar
- ¼ teaspoon onion powder
- 2 teaspoons lemon zest
- ½ teaspoon herb and spice blend seasoning, to taste
  Lemon pepper to taste

NUTRITION INFORMATION PER SERVING

Serving Size: approximately ¾ cup

Calories:	132
Protein:	4.5 g
Carbohydrate:	28 g
Fat:	0.5 g
Cholesterol:	less than 0.5 mg
Sodium:	43 mg
Fiber:	1 g

Dietary Exchanges:
1 starch, 1 vegetable and ½ fruit

Pasta: Combine pasta, peas, carrots, raisins, apple, green onions and celery with celery seed and parsley.

Dressing: In large bowl, mix all dressing ingredients together and add to the pasta ingredients. Chill at least 2 hours or overnight.

Minestrone Salad

A salad to be enjoyed all year round, whenever a light lunch or supper is desired.

8 SERVINGS

Salad:

    2 cups uncooked elbow macaroni, plain or
       tri-colored (4 cups cooked)
    1 16-oz. can (2 cups) beans, kidney or pinto,
       drained and rinsed
    3 medium carrots, coarsely shredded or chopped
  1½ cups chopped celery
   ¼ cup fresh parsley, snipped

Dressing:

   ½ cup nonfat, sweet and sour salad dressing
    2 tablespoons red wine vinegar
   ¾ cup nonfat, cholesterol-free mayonnaise
       Herb and spice blend seasonings to taste
   ½ teaspoon lemon pepper
       garnish: 2 large tomatoes, sliced

Cook macaroni according to package directions. Cool. Place in a large bowl and toss with the beans, carrots, celery and parsley. Make a dressing of the salad dressing, vinegar, mayonnaise and seasonings. Pour over the macaroni mixture and toss to coat. Spoon salad into a large serving bowl; overlap tomato slices around the edge.

NUTRITION INFORMATION PER SERVING

Serving Size: approximately 1¼ cups

Calories: 205
Protein: ....7.5 g
Carbohydrate: ....41 g
Fat: ....1 g
Cholesterol: ....0 mg
Sodium: ....423 mg
Fiber: ....4.5 g

Dietary Exchanges:
  2 starch and 2 vegetable

Molded Gazpacho Salad

This recipe may be doubled and placed in a 6-cup decorative mold.

6 SERVINGS

2 cups stewed tomatoes, mashed
2 cloves garlic, minced
1 3-oz. pkg. sugar-free lemon-flavored gelatin
   Tabasco sauce, several dashes
2 teaspoons Worcestershire sauce
½ cup finely chopped green pepper
½ cup finely chopped, seeded, peeled cucumber
1 stalk celery, finely diced
2 green onions, thinly sliced, using some of green tops
¼ teaspoon lemon zest
¼ teaspoon black pepper
   garnish: nonfat, cholesterol-free mayonnaise or sour cream (optional)

Mash tomatoes and garlic or blend slightly in a blender. Measure 1 cup of tomato-garlic mixture into a saucepan. Heat to boiling.

Dissolve lemon gelatin in tomatoes heated to a boil. Add the remaining tomatoes and cool until mixture just begins to thicken. Add the remaining ingredients and pour into a decorative 3-cup mold or 6 individual salad molds. Cover and chill until set. Unmold on lettuce leaves and garnish with a teaspoon of nonfat, cholesterol-free mayonnaise or sour cream and a sprig of fresh parsley.

NUTRITION INFORMATION PER SERVING

Serving Size: ½ cup

Calories: 74
Protein: ....12.5 g
Carbohydrate: ....7 g
Fat: ....0 g
Cholesterol: ....0 mg
Sodium: ....249 mg
Fiber: ....1 g

Dietary Exchanges:
1 vegetable and 1 very lean meat

Pasta and Bean Salad

Chopped, fresh basil leaves are a nice addition to this salad.

NUTRITION INFORMATION
PER SERVING

Serving Size: ¾ cup

Calories: 109
Protein: ....8 g
Carbohydrate: ....18.5 g
Fat: ....0.5 g
Cholesterol: ....1.8 mg
Sodium: ....364 mg
Fiber: ....1 g

Dietary Exchanges:
1 starch and 1 vegetable

10 SERVINGS

½ cup nonfat yogurt
½ cup nonfat, cholesterol-free mayonnaise
1 tablespoon Dijon-style mustard
1 teaspoon dried dill weed
3 tablespoons fresh basil, chopped
1 cup uncooked rotini, cooked and drained
    (2 cups cooked)
1 16-oz. can (2 cups) pinto beans, drained and
    rinsed
2 cups fresh or frozen green beans, cooked and
    drained
1 large, roasted red pepper, seeded and cut up
1 cup nonfat Cheddar cheese, cubed or shredded
    Nonfat chicken broth to moisten, if desired
    Black pepper to taste

In small mixing bowl, combine yogurt, mayonnaise, mustard, dill weed and basil. Set aside.

Cook the rotini according to package directions. Drain and rinse. Cook the frozen beans to the tender crisp stage and drain. In large mixing bowl, combine rotini, pinto and green beans, roasted red pepper, cheese and black pepper with the dressing. Toss lightly to mix. Chill.

New Potato Salad with Vegetables

A refreshing change from the familiar salads made with mayonnaise. Served either hot or cold, it's best if made a day ahead.

8 SERVINGS

Salad:

- 1 lb. tiny new potatoes, unpeeled and quartered
- 2 cups brussels sprouts
- 1 cup sliced carrots
- 1 cup halved cherry tomatoes
- 1 cup coarsely chopped onion

Dressing:

- ⅓ cup red wine vinegar
- ⅓ cup nonfat Italian dressing
- 1 teaspoon dill weed
- ¼ cup chopped fresh parsley or 2 teaspoons dried parsley
- 1 teaspoon sugar
- ¼ teaspoon salt
- ⅛ teaspoon black pepper
- ½ cup fresh basil, chopped fine

NUTRITION INFORMATION PER SERVING
Serving Size: 1 cup
Calories: 104
Protein: ....2.5 g
Carbohydrate: ....24 g
Fat: ....0.5 g
Cholesterol: ....0 mg
Sodium: ....131 mg
Fiber: ....1 g
Dietary Exchanges: 1 starch and 1 vegetable

Boil potatoes, brussels sprouts and carrots in the same pan with a small amount of water—about 12 minutes. Drain. Add tomatoes and onions.

Make a dressing of the remaining ingredients and add to potatoes. Mix well. Add basil just prior to serving. Can be served either hot or cold.

Peanutty Fruit Salad

Use your favorite combination of fruit in season. The hint of peanut butter is a welcome surprise.

8 SERVINGS

NUTRITION INFORMATION PER SERVING

Serving Size: ⅔ cup

Calories: 67
Protein: ....1 g
Carbohydrate: ....15 g
Fat: ....1 g
Cholesterol: ....0 mg
Sodium: ....77 mg
Fiber: ....2 g

Dietary Exchanges:
1 fruit

Salad:
  2 medium red apples, cut into bite-size pieces
  1 banana, sliced
  1 navel orange, peeled and sectioned
  1 cup pineapple tidbits, drained, reserve juice
Dressing:
  ⅓ cup nonfat, cholesterol-free mayonnaise
  1 tablespoons pineapple juice
  2 teaspoon peanut butter (natural – oil on top)
  ⅛ teaspoon cinnamon
    Dash of nutmeg
    Lettuce leaves
    Paprika (optional)

Place all fruit in a medium-sized mixing bowl.

In small bowl, mix mayonnaise, pineapple juice, peanut butter, cinnamon and nutmeg until smooth. Pour over the prepared fruit and toss to coat. Place on lettuce leaves on individual salad plates. Sprinkle lightly with paprika if desired.

Spicy Black Bean Salad

Pectin, when mixed with water, creates a substance with a consistency much like oil. Add your favorite seasonings and you have a great dressing for salads, minus the fat.

6 SERVINGS

Dressing:
- ¼ cup nonfat chicken broth
- 1½ tablespoons powdered fruit pectin
- 3 tablespoons lime juice

Salad:
- 2 16-oz. cans (4 cups) black beans, drained and rinsed well
- ½ cup chopped red onion
- 1 jalapeño pepper, seeded and minced
- ¼ cup diced celery
- ⅓ cup snipped fresh cilantro
  Dash of red pepper
- 1 medium tomato, chopped

In small glass jar, combine broth, pectin and lime juice. Cover, shake well and set aside to thicken.

Place the remaining ingredients into a large mixing bowl. Add lime dressing and toss well. Chill 2 hours.

NUTRITION INFORMATION PER SERVING

Serving Size: approximately 1 cup

- Calories: 199
- Protein: ....12.5 g
- Carbohydrate: ....37.5 g
- Fat: ....less than 1 g
- Cholesterol: ....0 mg
- Sodium: ....37 mg
- Fiber: ....6 g

Dietary Exchanges:
  2 starch and 2 vegetable

Spinach Salad

A very attractive salad when arranged on individual salad plates. You will want to keep some of this dressing in your refrigerator for use on other salads. It's that good!

8 SERVINGS

½ lb. fresh spinach, cleaned with veins removed, torn into pieces

2 11-oz. cans Mandarin oranges, drained

1 sweet onion, thinly sliced and separated

1 16-oz. can (2 cups) garbanzo beans, drained and rinsed

5 tablespoons imitation bacon bits

Dressing:

⅓ cup rice vinegar

⅓ cup commercial nonfat sweet-and-sour dressing

⅓ cup orange juice concentrate

Pour dressing ingredients into a glass jar, shake and set aside.

Prepare spinach, mandarin oranges, onions and beans and place attractively in a large salad bowl. Just before serving, pour dressing over the salad; toss, sprinkle with imitation bacon bits and serve.

NUTRITION INFORMATION
PER SERVING

Serving Size: approximately 1 cup

Calories: 117
Protein: ....6 g
Carbohydrate: ....21 g
Fat:...................................2 g
Cholesterol: ....0 mg
Sodium: ....310 mg
Fiber: ....3.5 g

Dietary Exchanges:
2 vegetable and 1 fruit

N o t e :

Look for imitation bacon bits with less than 1 gm fat per 2 teaspoons and 0 mg cholesterol.

Summer Fruit Medley

You can enjoy this mealtime salad or finale for less than 170 calories! When fresh fruit isn't available, substitute canned pineapple chunks and mandarin oranges with apples.

4 SERVINGS

1 banana, sliced in ½-inch pieces
1 tablespoon lemon juice
1 cup sliced fresh strawberries
⅔ cup fresh raspberries
⅔ cup fresh blueberries
⅔ cup halved seedless grapes
4 tablespoons nonfat granola cereal

Dressing:
1 4.4-oz. container nonfat, cholesterol-free, fruit-flavored yogurt
1 tablespoon honey
   Pinch of ginger

NUTRITION INFORMATION PER SERVING
Serving Size: 1 cup
Calories: 168
Protein: ....2.5 g
Carbohydrate: ....42.5 g
Fat:...............................0.5 g
Cholesterol: ....0 mg
Sodium: ....20 mg
Fiber:...........................7.5 g
Dietary Exchanges:
½ starch and 2 fruit

Note:

See **Appendix D** for specific brands of nonfat granola cereal.

In medium mixing bowl, toss the banana with the lemon juice. Add the rest of the fruit and chill until serving time.

In small mixing bowl, combine all of the dressing ingredients and mix until smooth. Chill. At serving time, divide the fruit mixture between 4 parfait glasses or salad plates and top each with dollops of the dressing and a tablespoon granola per serving.

Variation: Layer fruit in parfait glasses and spoon small amounts of dressing between layers.

Summer Macaroni Salad

8 SERVINGS

Salad:
4 cups cooked elbow macaroni or pasta of choice
1 cup shredded carrots
1 cup frozen peas, cooked to thaw and plump
½ cup diced red onions
1 stalk celery, diced
½ cup coarsely chopped red pepper

Dressing:
⅔ cup nonfat, cholesterol-free mayonnaise
1 teaspoon celery seed
2 tablespoons sweet pickle relish
   Juice of half a lemon (1½ tablespoons)
½ teaspoon salt
   Pepper to taste

In large bowl, combine pasta with vegetables and toss lightly to mix. Combine mayonnaise, celery seed, relish, lemon juice, salt and pepper. Pour dressing over salad and mix lightly. Serve immediately or chill.

Chapter 9

Energizing Breakfasts

Eating breakfast every day is one of the best things that we can do for ourselves! To jump-start our day, our bodies need to "break the fast" that we've had while sleeping and to replenish its energy stores. Studies show that people who regularly eat breakfast have a better overall health profile and are better able to maintain a healthy body weight. An added bonus is we feel better!

Some people don't eat breakfast because they don't like typical breakfast foods such as eggs, toast or cereal. Others skip breakfast because they don't have time in the morning. We believe our breakfast recipes and ideas can address both issues.

Who says that breakfast has to be a bowl of cereal in the morning? A bowl of whole-grain cereal with skim milk and fruit is certainly a very healthy way to start the day, but there are many other options. Do you like pasta? How about that leftover cold spaghetti and marinara sauce in the refrigerator, or maybe fruit salad with fat-free crackers, even beans and rice reheated in the microwave. Don't feel confined by the rules of the majority!

No time because you're rushing off to work? Keep bagels on hand and grab one on your way out the door. A few seconds more, and it can be toasted and spread with fruit preserves. Keep small bottles of fruit juice or low-sodium vegetable juice on hand to take with you. Nonfat fruited yogurt is also an easy breakfast to have when you reach the office.

Here are other quick and easy breakfasts that can help fuel your day. Be creative!

Easy Breakfast Ideas

- Top a whole-wheat English muffin with a slice of tomato, sprinkled with shredded fat-free cheese and a little dill or oregano. Broil until cheese is melted.
- Fill a **Whole-Wheat Crêpe** (see page 193) with berries and top with nonfat plain or fruited yogurt. You might want to sprinkle it with a little brown sugar and/or cinnamon.

- Make a breakfast shake of nonfat plain yogurt, banana and other fresh fruit by whirring together in a blender. Add cinnamon or another favorite spice for more zing.
- Instead of skim milk, moisten a bowl of fat-free granola with apple juice and top with raisins or other dried fruit.
- Scramble nonfat, cholesterol-free egg substitute with any variety of chopped vegetables, and serve over whole-wheat toast topped with sprouts.
- Toast a whole-wheat bagel that's been sliced in half, spread with a thin layer of nonfat cream cheese, then sprinkle with raisins and top with banana slices for a bagel sandwich.
- Cooked cereal can make a healthy and satisfying breakfast. Pep it up by adding fruit or spices. Banana is a favorite, but don't forget about dried fruit like raisins, cherries, dates, figs, or pineapple. They can be added at serving time or cooked into the cereal. You can even try sprinkling oatmeal with nonfat granola.

Breakfast In A Glass

Equally good when made with apple juice or orange juice, this refreshing breakfast is a good way to use very ripe bananas.

1 SERVING

¾ cup cold pineapple juice
1 small ripe banana, cut in chunks
5 strawberries, sliced
¼ cup nonfat plain yogurt
1 tablespoon honey (optional)

Place all ingredients in a blender and process to the desired consistency.

NUTRITION INFORMATION PER SERVING

Serving Size: approximately 2 cups

Calories: 429
Protein: ....5.5 g
Carbohydrate: ....107 g
Fat: ....0.5 g
Cholesterol: ....1 mg
Sodium: ....51 mg
Fiber: ....4 g

Dietary Exchanges:
1 skim milk and 6 fruit

Preparation Tip:

Freeze very ripe bananas for future use in this recipe.

Banana Yogurt with Granola

1 SERVING

1 small banana
1 4.4-oz. container, nonfat, cholesterol-free
   banana yogurt
¼ cup blueberries
1 teaspoon brown sugar
   Dash cinnamon
¼ cup nonfat granola cereal

Combine all ingredients except granola cereal in a serving bowl. Top with granola cereal.

NUTRITION INFORMATION PER SERVING

Serving size: approximately 1½ cups

Calories: 281
Protein: ....10.5 g
Carbohydrate: ....63 g
Fat: ....less than 0.5 g
Cholesterol: ....0 mg
Sodium: ....110 mg
Fiber: ....5 g

Dietary Exchanges:
1 starch, 1 skim milk and 2 fruit

Grapefruit Surprise

A terrific breakfast or dessert that will tickle the fancy of your health-conscious friends.

2 medium pink grapefruit
4 teaspoons sugar, divided
3 egg whites, room temperature
¼ teaspoon cream of tartar
¼ cup sugar
  garnish: 2 maraschino cherries, cut in half

Cut the grapefruit in halves and loosen sections as though for serving, leaving fruit in the skins. Sprinkle 1 teaspoon sugar over each half.

Just before serving, make a meringue by beating the egg whites until foamy, adding cream of tartar and gradually adding ¼ cup of sugar. Continue beating until stiff peaks form.

Mound the meringue on top of each grapefruit half taking care to spread the meringue out to the edge of the grapefruit. Bake in a 350° oven for 10 minutes or until the meringue is baked and slightly brown on top. Garnish with half a maraschino cherry and serve immediately.

NUTRITION INFORMATION
PER SERVING

Serving Size: ½ grapefruit

Calories: 112
Protein: ....3.5 g
Carbohydrate: ....26 g
Fat: ....less than 0.5 g
Cholesterol: ....0 mg
Sodium: ....41 mg
Fiber: ....1.5 g

Dietary Exchanges:
1 starch and ½ fruit

Papaya with Lime Juice

Lime juice cuts the sweetness of the papaya and gives it added zest. Great for breakfast, a snack or dessert.

4 SERVINGS

4 cups papaya, peeled and cut up
  Juice of one lime

Prepare papaya. Pour lime juice over papaya and toss to coat. Spoon into individual serving dishes and serve immediately.

NUTRITION INFORMATION
PER SERVING

Serving Size: 1 cup

Calories: 57
Protein: ....1 g
Carbohydrate: ....14.5 g
Fat: ....less than 0.5 g
Cholesterol: ....0 mg
Sodium: ....4 mg
Fiber: ....1 g

Dietary Exchanges:
1 fruit

Oatmeal with Applesauce

Applesauce, raisins and spices in this recipe pep up an otherwise ordinary breakfast food.

1 SERVING

½ cup rolled oats, quick or regular
1 cup water
⅛ teaspoon salt
2 tablespoons raisins
⅓ cup applesauce
⅛ to ¼ teaspoon cinnamon
    Dash of nutmeg
1 tablespoon brown sugar (optional)

In small pan, combine the rolled oats, water, salt and raisins. Bring water to a boil, cook over medium heat for about 1 minute (regular oats, cook 5 minutes). When cereal is cooked remove from heat, add applesauce, cinnamon and nutmeg. Serve with sugar if desired.

NUTRITION INFORMATION
PER SERVING

Service Size: approximately 1½ cups

Calories: 293
Protein: ....6 g
Carbohydrate: ....64.5 g
Fat: ....3 g
Cholesterol: ....0 mg
Sodium: ....282 mg
Fiber: ....6 g

Dietary Exchanges:
  2 starch and 2 fruit

"Mosquito Coast" French Toast

This recipe is an adaptation of a breakfast served at a restaurant on the mosquito coast in Belize.

2 SERVINGS

    2   medium apples, peeled and sliced
    ½   cup water
    ¼   cup packed brown sugar
    ¼   cup maple syrup
    ⅛   teaspoon cinnamon
    ¼   cup nonfat, cholesterol-free egg substitute
    2   egg whites
    ¼   cup skim milk
    ⅛   teaspoon nutmeg
    4   slices low-fat, whole-wheat bread
    2   tablespoons nonfat, cholesterol-free sour cream
    ¼   cup raisins
        Nonfat cooking spray

Place apples, water, brown sugar, maple syrup and cinnamon in a medium saucepan and cook apples until tender but not mushy. Set aside and keep warm.

Combine the egg substitute, egg whites, skim milk and nutmeg and process in a blender until smooth. Coat both sides of each piece of bread in the egg mixture and cook on a griddle sprayed with a nonfat cooking spray, until both sides are a golden brown. Remove from griddle and spread the sour cream on two of the four slices of bread. Sprinkle with raisins, cover with the remaining slices of bread and top with the cooked apple mixture.

NUTRITION INFORMATION PER SERVING

Serving Size: 2 slices of bread and ½ of the apple topping

Calories: 548
Protein: ....15 g
Carbohydrate: ....115.5 g
Fat: ....3 g
Cholesterol: ....0.5 mg
Sodium: ....544 mg
Fiber: ....11.5 g

Dietary Exchanges:
2 starch, 1 skim milk and 5 fruit

Premier Pancakes

These pancakes are so good, and good for you, that you will want to fix them often. If you have any left, enjoy them plain or with a little applesauce as a midday snack.

MAKES 18, 3½-INCH PANCAKES

2 tablespoons cider vinegar plus skim milk to equal 1¼ cups
⅓ cup oatmeal
⅔ cup whole-wheat flour
⅓ cup all-purpose flour
2 teaspoons sugar
1 teaspoon baking powder
1 teaspoon baking soda
¼ teaspoon salt
⅓ cup nonfat, cholesterol-free egg substitute
1 egg white
½ teaspoon vanilla
Nonfat cooking spray

NUTRITION INFORMATION PER SERVING

Serving Size: 2 pancakes

Calories: 81
Protein: ....4 g
Carbohydrate: ....15 g
Fat: ....0.5 g
Cholesterol: ....0.5 mg
Sodium: ....222 mg
Fiber: ....1.5 g

Dietary Exchanges:
1 starch

In a 2-cup measuring cup combine the vinegar and skim milk. Let this mixture stand while measuring the remaining ingredients.

Process the oatmeal in a blender or food processor until coarsely ground.

Place all dry ingredients in a medium-size mixing bowl. In a separate small bowl beat the egg substitute, egg white and vanilla. Add the egg mixture and the vinegar milk to the dry ingredients and mix well. Cook without oil on a nonfat surface or griddle. Serve with your favorite fruits, syrups or **Raspberry Purée** (page 204).

Vegetable Omelette with Dill and Chives

2 SERVINGS

1 cup tomatoes, seeded, unpeeled and chopped
1 teaspoon fresh dill, chopped
1 teaspoon fresh chives, minced

   Nonfat cooking spray
1 small green pepper, chopped
1 medium onion, chopped
4 mushrooms, sliced
1 tablespoon fresh dill, chopped and divided
1 tablespoon fresh chives, minced and divided
½ cup nonfat, cholesterol-free egg substitute
4 egg whites

Combine first 3 ingredients and set aside. Coat a medium nonfat skillet with a nonfat cooking spray and gently sauté the green pepper, onion and mushrooms and half of the dill and chives. Set aside and keep warm.

Beat the egg substitute, and egg whites with the remaining dill and chives. Coat the skillet with nonfat cooking spray and place over medium heat until hot. Add the egg mixture; cook until done. To aid in cooking, it is sometimes helpful to use a spatula to lift the cooked egg while tipping the pan to allow the uncooked egg mixture to run onto the pan.

Add the cooked vegetables and fold in half. Loosen the omelette and gently slide it onto a serving dish, cut in half and spoon tomato mixture over the top.

NUTRITION INFORMATION PER SERVING

Serving Size: ½ omelette

Calories: 134
Protein: ....16 g
Carbohydrate: ....17 g
Fat:................................0.5 g
Carbohydrate: ....0 mg
Sodium: ....221 mg
Fiber: ....3 g

Dietary Exchanges:
1 very lean meat, 1 skim milk and 1 vegetable

Asparagus Quiche with Rice Crust

Cook up batches of white and brown rice and freeze them in 2 cup packages, 1 cup white and 1 cup brown. One package could be used in this recipe and shorten preparation time.

6 SERVINGS, 8 X 8" BAKING DISH

Crust:

    2 cups cooked rice
       (1 cup brown and 1 cup white rice)
    ¼ cup nonfat, cholesterol-free egg substitute
    2 teaspoons soy sauce
    ¼ teaspoon salt
       Black pepper
    2 teaspoons dried parsley
       Nonfat cooking spray

Filling:

    ½ lb. asparagus, trimmed and cut in 1-inch pieces
    1 cup shredded nonfat cheddar cheese
    ½ cup skim milk
    ½ cup evaporated skim milk
    ½ cup nonfat, cholesterol-free egg substitute
    2 egg whites
    ½ teaspoon dried basil
    ½ teaspoon dried tarragon
    ¼ teaspoon nutmeg
    ¼ teaspoon salt
    ¼ teaspoon black pepper
    2 tablespoons imitation bacon bits

Crust: Combine all crust ingredients and place in an 8 x 8-inch baking dish that has been sprayed with nonfat cooking spray. With moist fingers press the rice to the bottom of the pan. Prepare filling.

Filling: Steam asparagus 5 minutes. Place steamed asparagus onto the rice crust. Sprinkle cheese over the asparagus. Mix the remaining ingredients in a medium-size mixing bowl or blender and pour over the asparagus. Bake in a 350° oven for 30 minutes or until the center is set. Cool 5 minutes and serve.

NUTRITION INFORMATION PER SERVING

Serving Size: ⅙ of the quiche

    Calories: 188
    Protein: ....17 g
    Carbohydrate: ....24.5 g
    Fat: ....2 g
    Cholesterol: ....4 mg
    Sodium: ....528 mg
    Fiber: ....1 g

Dietary Exchanges:
    1 very lean meat, 1 skim milk
    and 1 starch

N o t e :

We have found that Carnation Lite® evaporated skim milk works extremely well in this recipe as it is cholesterol-free.

Vegetable Frittata

A one pan meal, similar to an omelette. Serve for breakfast, lunch or as an entrée - your choice. Summer squash, zucchini, mushrooms and tomatoes would be fine additions to this frittata.

4 SERVINGS

4 green onions, chopped, using some tops
3 cloves garlic, minced
Nonfat cooking spray
4 medium red-skin potatoes, unpeeled and cut in ½-inch cubes
1 cup broccoli flowerets
½ cup diced red pepper
Nonfat chicken broth for cooking, 1 tablespoon at a time
½ teaspoon dried basil
½ teaspoon dried thyme
½ teaspoon dried dill weed
1 cup nonfat, cholesterol-free egg substitute
4 egg whites, slightly beaten
¼ cup skim milk
½ cup shredded nonfat cheddar cheese
Pepper to taste
garnish: chunky salsa

Sauté onions and garlic in a 10-inch oven-proof skillet sprayed with a nonfat cooking spray. Add potatoes, broccoli, red pepper and herbs; adding chicken broth to cook vegetables as necessary. Cover but do not over-cook. In a small bowl, mix egg substitute, egg whites, and skim milk. Pour over the vegetables, sprinkle with cheese and bake in a 350° oven until egg is done in the center - approximately 10 minutes. Cut in quarters, top with 2 tablespoons salsa and serve.

NUTRITION INFORMATION PER SERVING

Serving Size: ¼ *frittata*

Calories: 150
Protein: ....17.5 g
Carbohydrate: ....19.5 g
Fat: ....less than 0.5 g
Cholesterol: ....2 mg
Sodium: ....363 mg
Fiber: ....less than 1 g

Dietary Exchanges:
1 very lean meat, 1 skim milk and 1 vegetable

N o t e :

Look for salsa with less than 100 mg of sodium per serving. Top each frittata with 2 tablespoons of your favorite chunky salsa.

Roasted Vegetable Strata

This strata is a grand choice for a weekend brunch. Roasting vegetables brings a special flavor to the strata and it frees the cook for other preparation.

9 PIECES, 9 X 9" BAKING DISH

5	slices whole-wheat bread, cubed and lightly toasted in oven
1½	cups red-skin potatoes, unpeeled and cut in ½-inch cubes.
1	cup carrots, ¼-inch slices
1	cup chopped onion
½	cup chopped red bell pepper
½	cup chopped green pepper
2	cloves garlic, minced
½	teaspoon dried basil
¼	teaspoon dried dill weed
	Nonfat cooking spray
1	7-oz. can mushroom pieces, drained or 1 cup fresh mushrooms, sliced
1	cup skim milk
1½	cups nonfat, cholesterol-free egg substitute
1	egg white
¼	teaspoon freshly ground black pepper
1	cup shredded fat-free cheddar cheese

Place toasted bread cubes in a 9 x 9-inch baking dish.

Place next 8 ingredients on a large flat baking sheet or in roaster sprayed with a nonfat cooking spray. Roast in a 425° oven for 20 to 25 minutes or until lightly browned. Stir vegetables after 10 minutes.

While vegetables are roasting combine milk, egg substitute, egg white, and black pepper. Set aside.

Remove vegetables from oven, add mushroom pieces to the vegetables and place on top of bread cubes. Pour milk mixture over the vegetables and bake at 375° for approximately 30 minutes or until the egg mixture is set. Add the cheese and continue baking for another 5 minutes. Serve immediately.

NUTRITION INFORMATION PER SERVING

Serving Size: 1 piece

Calories:	125
Protein:	11.5 g
Carbohydrate:	18.5 g
Fat:	1 g
Cholesterol:	2 mg
Sodium:	361 mg
Fiber:	3 g

Dietary Exchanges:
1 skim milk and 1 vegetable

N o t e s :

Select a whole-wheat bread with 1 g fat or less per slice. See **Appendix D** for specific brand names.

Chapter 10
Breads, Biscuits, Muffins & More

The breads and muffins in this chapter are great for breakfast, as a snack, or make great accompaniments for lunch or dinner. For breakfast or a snack, use fruit preserves, a thin layer of fat-free cream cheese, honey or applesauce as spreads. Moist and flavorful, breads don't need a spread at all!

If you're feeling bold and want a change in taste, you might want to try substituting a different fruit or vegetable than what is called for in the recipe. Speaking of substitutes, fruit purées or non-fat plain yogurt can often be used as a substitute for all or part of the oil called for in a recipe. These substitutions are discussed in further detail on page 50.

Boston Brown Bread

Baking this bread in four small loaves allows a few to be frozen for later use. Baking in cans makes round slices which are more interesting.

4 LOAVES; 32 SLICES

1½ cups raisins
1½ cups water
¾ cup sugar
2 tablespoons canola oil
¼ cup nonfat, cholesterol-free egg substitute
1 teaspoon vanilla
¾ cup whole-wheat flour
½ cup cornmeal
1½ cups all-purpose flour
2 teaspoons baking soda
1 teaspoon baking powder
½ teaspoon salt
    Nonfat cooking spray

In covered pan, boil the raisins in the water for 2 minutes. Set aside.

In large mixing bowl, cream sugar and oil; add egg substitute and vanilla and beat well.

In separate bowl, combine dry ingredients. Add flour and liquid alternately to the creamed mixture.

Spray four 16-oz. cans with nonfat cooking spray. Spoon batter into prepared cans, filling ½ full. Bake 30 minutes at 350°, reduce heat and bake for 30 minutes at 325°. Cut each loaf into 8 slices.

NUTRITION INFORMATION PER SERVING

Serving Size: 1 slice

Calories: 84
Protein: ....1.5 g
Carbohydrate: ....18 g
Fat: ....1 g
Cholesterol: ....0 mg
Sodium: ....100 mg
Fiber: ....1 g

Dietary Exchanges:
1 starch

Dr. Pepper® Apricot Bread

This bread recipe is an adaptation of a recipe given me by a friend who collects Dr. Pepper® memorabilia. The Dr. Pepper® is a nice, fruity addition to the apricots.

TWO 8 X 4" LOAF PANS; 32 SLICES

- 1 cup sugar
- ¼ cup nonfat plain yogurt
- ¼ cup nonfat, cholesterol-free egg substitute
- 1 tablespoon vanilla
- 1 6-oz. pkg. apricots, finely diced
- 2 cups all-purpose flour
- ¾ cup whole-wheat pastry flour
- 2 teaspoons baking soda
- 1 teaspoon baking powder
- ¼ teaspoon salt
- 1 12-oz. can Dr. Pepper®, boiling
  Nonfat cooking spray

NUTRITION INFORMATION PER SERVING

Serving Size: 1 slice

Calories: 81
Protein: ....1.5 g
Carbohydrate: ....19 g
Fat: ....0 g
Cholesterol: ....0 mg
Sodium: ....85 mg
Fiber: ....1 g

Dietary Exchanges:
1 starch

In small mixing bowl, combine the sugar, yogurt, egg substitute and vanilla. Set aside. Measure and blend all dry ingredients into a large mixing bowl. Dredge apricots in flour mixture. Add the yogurt mixture and Dr. Pepper to the dry ingredients and mix only to completely moisten.

Pour into two 8 x 4-inch loaf pans sprayed with nonfat cooking spray. Bake at 350° for approximately 35 minutes or until a toothpick inserted in the middle comes out clean.

Lemon Poppy Seed Bread

This moist, lemony bread is a perfect choice for your morning coffee break.

8 ½" x 4 ½" LOAF; 20 SLICES

1¾ cups all-purpose flour
2½ teaspoons baking powder
¼ teaspoon salt
3 tablespoons liquid Butter Buds®
¾ cup sugar
2 tablespoons lemon juice
1 tablespoon lemon zest
¼ cup nonfat, cholesterol-free egg substitute
½ cup evaporated skim milk
1 tablespoon poppy seeds
2 egg whites
    Nonfat cooking spray

Glaze
1 tablespoon lemon juice
1 tablespoon sugar

In medium bowl, combine flour, baking powder and salt. Set aside. In mixing bowl, combine liquid Butter Buds®, sugar, lemon juice and lemon zest. Add egg substitute and beat well. Gradually stir in flour mixture alternately with evaporated milk until just blended. Begin and end with flour. Add poppy seeds. In a separate bowl, beat egg whites until stiff and fold them into the batter. Pour into an 8½ x 4½-inch loaf pan that has been sprayed with nonfat cooking spray and coated with flour. Bake at 350° for 40 to 45 minutes or until a toothpick inserted in the center comes out clean. Cool 5 minutes. Remove from pan and brush with the glaze.

Glaze: Combine 1 tablespoon lemon juice and 1 tablespoon sugar in a small pan. Bring to a boil and cook for about 2 minutes until syrupy. Spread evenly over the top of the warm bread.

NUTRITION INFORMATION PER SERVING

Serving Size: 1 slice

Calories: 82
Protein: ....2.5 g
Carbohydrate: ....17.5 g
Fat: ....less than 0.5 g
Cholesterol: ....0 mg
Sodium: ....87 mg
Fiber: ....0.5 g

Dietary Exchanges:
1 starch

Preparation Tip:

Zest is the colored part of the lemon without the bitter white membrane. Zesters can be purchased in a kitchen shop.

Carrot Muffins

Whole-wheat pastry flour is flour made from the whole grain of wheat and milled many times more than regular flour. It creates light, moist cakes, muffins and breads.

16 MUFFINS

1¼ cups whole-wheat pastry flour
1¼ cups all-purpose flour
1 teaspoon cinnamon
¼ teaspoon ginger
½ teaspoon salt
1½ teaspoons baking powder
1 teaspoon baking soda
½ cup dried cherries or cranberries
1 cup nonfat plain yogurt
½ cup packed brown sugar
¼ cup nonfat, cholesterol-free egg substitute
2 egg whites
½ cup applesauce
1½ cups grated carrots
Nonfat cooking spray

NUTRITION INFORMATION PER SERVING
Serving size: 1 muffin
Calories: 123
Protein: ....4 g
Carbohydrate: ....26.5 g
Fat: ....less than 0.5 g
Cholesterol: ....less than 0.5 mg
Sodium: ....179 mg
Fiber: ....2 g
Dietary Exchanges:
1 starch, 1 vegetable and ½ fruit

In large mixing bowl, combine all dry ingredients. Add dried cherries and coat them with flour. In another bowl, combine the remaining ingredients. Add the liquid ingredients to the flour mixture and mix by hand only until the flour is moistened.

Spoon into muffin tins that have been sprayed with a nonfat cooking spray. Bake at 400° for 15 minutes or until a toothpick inserted in the center comes out clean.

Date Bran Muffins

16 MUFFINS

2 cups All Bran® cereal
1¼ cups skim milk
½ cup sugar
¼ cup nonfat, cholesterol-free egg substitute
½ cup nonfat plain yogurt
1 cup all-purpose flour
2 teaspoons baking powder
½ teaspoon baking soda
½ teaspoon cinnamon
1 cup chopped dates
  Nonfat cooking spray

In large mixing bowl, combine the cereal, milk, sugar, egg substitute and yogurt. Set aside for 5 minutes to soften the cereal.

In small bowl, combine flour, baking powder, baking soda, cinnamon and dates. Add the flour mixture to the milk-cereal mixture and stir just until all the flour is moistened. Spray tins with nonfat cooking spray and fill muffin tins ¾ full. Bake at 400° for 15 to 18 minutes or until center tests done when a toothpick is inserted in the center.

Oatmeal Applesauce Muffins

12 MUFFINS

1½ tablespoons vinegar plus skim milk
   to equal 1 cup
 1 cup quick rolled oats
 ½ cup all-purpose flour
 ¾ cup whole-wheat flour
 1 teaspoon cinnamon
 ⅛ teaspoon ginger
 ½ cup raisins
1½ teaspoons baking powder
 ½ teaspoon baking soda
 ¼ teaspoon salt
 ½ cup applesauce
 ⅓ cup packed brown sugar
 2 egg whites
   Nonfat cooking spray

NUTRITION INFORMATION PER SERVING

Serving Size: 1 muffin

Calories: 131
Protein: ....4.5 g
Carbohydrate: ....27 g
Fat: ....1 g
Cholesterol: ..less than 0.5 mg
Sodium: ....141 mg
Fiber: ....3 g

Dietary Exchanges:
  1 starch and 1 fruit

Add vinegar to the skim milk and set aside. In large bowl, combine rolled oats, flours, cinnamon, ginger, raisins, baking powder, baking soda, and salt.

In small bowl, combine vinegar-milk mixture with applesauce, brown sugar and egg whites. Add liquid ingredients to dry ingredients and stir just until all ingredients are moistened. Divide batter equally among 12 muffin cups that have been sprayed with nonfat cooking spray. Bake at 400° for 20 to 25 minutes or until a toothpick inserted in the center comes out clean. Cool 10 minutes and remove from tins.

Pumpkin Spice Muffins

12 MUFFINS

NUTRITION INFORMATION
PER SERVING

Serving Size: 1 muffin

Calories: 144
Protein: ....4 g
Carbohydrate: ....33 g
Fat:................................0.5 g
Cholesterol: ....0 mg
Sodium: ....122 mg
Fiber: ....2.5 g

Dietary Exchanges:
1 starch and 1 fruit

¾ cup canned pumpkin
½ cup honey
½ cup nonfat, cholesterol-free egg substitute
½ cup unsweetened applesauce
2 tablespoons skim milk
1 teaspoon vanilla
1¾ cups whole-wheat pastry flour
⅓ cup packed brown sugar
2 teaspoons baking powder
¼ teaspoon salt
1 teaspoon cinnamon
½ teaspoon nutmeg
Nonfat cooking spray

In large bowl, mix together the pumpkin, honey, egg substitute, applesauce, milk and vanilla. In another bowl, combine the flour, brown sugar, baking powder, salt, cinnamon and nutmeg. Combine the dry with the wet ingredients and mix well.

Spoon batter equally into 12 muffin cups that have been sprayed with nonfat cooking spray. Bake at 350° for 20 to 25 minutes or until a toothpick inserted in the center comes out clean. Cool and remove from the tin.

Whole Wheat Blueberry Muffins

Nonfat yogurt replaces the oil in these moist, wholesome muffins.

16 MUFFINS

    1 cup whole-wheat pastry flour
    1 cup all-purpose flour
    1 tablespoon baking powder
    1 teaspoon baking soda
    ½ cup packed brown sugar
    3 egg whites lightly beaten
    ¾ cup nonfat plain yogurt
    1 cup skim milk
    1 teaspoon vanilla
    ¾ cup fresh or frozen blueberries
       Nonfat cooking spray

In large mixing bowl, combine all dry ingredients. In a separate bowl, combine egg whites, yogurt, skim milk and vanilla; add mixture to the flour, stirring only to moisten flour. Fold in the blueberries. Spoon batter into muffin cups that have been sprayed with nonfat cooking spray, filling each cup ⅔ full. Bake at 425° for 20 to 25 minutes or until a toothpick inserted in center comes out clean.

NUTRITION INFORMATION PER SERVING

Serving Size: 1 muffin

    Calories: 96
    Protein: ....3.5 g
    Carbohydrate: ....20.5 g
    Fat: ....less than 0.5 g
    Cholesterol: ..less than 0.5 mg
    Sodium: ....138 mg
    Fiber: ....1.5 g

Dietary Exchanges:
    1 starch and ½ fruit

Preparation Tip:

If fresh or frozen blueberries aren't available use a 16-oz. can of blueberries, drained and rinsed very well.

Cheese Biscuits

These biscuits are best if eaten as they come out of the oven.

14 BISCUITS

2⅓ cups low-fat Pioneer Biscuit Mix®
 1 cup nonfat shredded pizza cheese
 ½ cup skim milk
 ¾ cup nonfat plain yogurt
     Nonfat cooking spray

Measure biscuit mix into a large bowl and add pizza cheese. Stir to coat the cheese. Add milk and yogurt and stir just until all the dry ingredients are moistened. Drop by spoonfuls onto a baking sheet that has been sprayed with nonfat cooking spray. Bake at 400° for approximately 10 minutes or until a toothpick inserted in the center of a biscuit comes out clean. Serve immediately.

Shortcake Biscuits

These biscuits make wonderful strawberry or peach shortcake.

10 BISCUITS

2⅓ cups low-fat Pioneer Biscuit Mix®
 ½ cup skim milk
 ¾ cup nonfat plain yogurt
 ¼ cup sugar
     Nonfat cooking spray

In large bowl, combine all ingredients together, making certain all the biscuit mix is moistened. Drop by spoonfuls onto a 9-inch round baking dish that has been sprayed with nonfat cooking spray. Bake at 400° for 15 minutes or until a toothpick inserted into the center comes out clean.

NUTRITION INFORMATION
PER SERVING

Serving Size: 1 biscuit

Calories: 123
Protein: ....5.5 g
Carbohydrate: ....28.5 g
Fat: ....less than 0.5 g
Cholesterol: ....1.5 mg
Sodium: ....411 mg
Fiber: ....0.5 g

Dietary Exchanges:
1 starch and ½ skim milk

Note:

Please see **Appendix D** for purchasing information on Pioneer Biscuit Mix®, available in most supermarkets.

NUTRITION INFORMATION
PER SERVING

Serving Size: 1 biscuit

Calories: 172
Protein: ....4 g
Carbohydrate: ....44 g
Fat: ....0.5 g
Cholesterol: ....0.5 mg
Sodium: 495
Fiber: ....0.5 g

Dietary Exchanges:
2 starch and 1 fruit

Whole Wheat Crêpes

Crêpes freeze well. Keep some in your freezer to fill for a speedy dinner.

12 CRÊPES

¼ cup nonfat, cholesterol-free egg substitute
2 egg whites
1 cup skim milk
⅔ cup whole-wheat flour
    Nonfat cooking spray

NUTRITION INFORMATION PER SERVING
Serving Size: 1 crêpe
Calories: 37
Protein: ....3 g
Carbohydrate: ....6 g
Fat:..............................0.5 g
Cholesterol: ....0 mg
Sodium: ....29 mg
Fiber: ....1 g
Dietary Exchanges:
½ starch

In a blender or medium bowl, mix ingredients together on medium speed. Batter should be smooth. Cover and allow the batter to rest for an hour or so before cooking the crêpes.

To make crêpes, heat a 6-inch nonstick skillet that has been sprayed with nonfat cooking spray. Pour 2 tablespoons of batter into the pan and tip the pan allowing the batter to cover the bottom of the pan. Cook for about one minute, allowing it to brown before turning. Then turn and cook the other side. Remove from pan, cool and stack between pieces of wax paper.

Cornmeal Dumplings

Serve with hot vegetable stew for a delicious meal.

8 DUMPLINGS

1   cup flour
¾   cup yellow cornmeal
3   teaspoons baking powder
¼   teaspoon salt
1   tablespoon extra light margarine
⅓   cup plus 2 tablespoons skim milk
3   egg whites

In medium-size mixing bowl, combine dry ingredients together; set aside. Melt margarine, add to the milk and egg whites and beat slightly with a fork. Add milk mixture to the dry ingredients and stir well. Drop dough by spoonfuls onto the top of the hot stew (**Vegetable Stew**, page 147). Cover and simmer until done, approximately 20 minutes.

NUTRITION INFORMATION PER SERVING

Serving Size: 1 dumpling

Calories: 117
Protein: ....4.5 g
Carbohydrate: ....22 g
Fat:................................1.5 g
Cholesterol: ..less than 0.5 mg
Sodium: ....229 mg
Fiber: ....2 g

Dietary Exchanges:
1½ starch

N o t e :

An extra light margarine contains 6 g fat per tablespoon. See **Appendix D** for specific brand names.

Hungarian Kugel

This recipe, given to me by a friend, can be served as an accompaniment to a vegetable entrée or as a dessert.

8 X 8" BAKING DISH; 9 PORTIONS

4 oz. fine eggless noodles (about 2 cups cooked)
½ cup nonfat cottage cheese
½ cup nonfat, cholesterol-free sour cream
¾ cup skim milk
½ cup nonfat, cholesterol-free egg substitute
2 egg whites
½ cup sugar
1 teaspoon vanilla
   Dash or two of nutmeg
½ cup raisins
2 tablespoons sugar
1½ teaspoons cinnamon

NUTRITION INFORMATION PER SERVING

Serving Size: 1 portion

Calories: 165
Protein: ....7.5 g
Carbohydrate: ....33 g
Fat: ....less than 1 g
Cholesterol: ....1.5 mg
Sodium: ....111 mg
Fiber: ....1 g

Dietary Exchanges:
2 starch

Cook noodles until very done, about 20 minutes. Drain and set aside.

In medium bowl and using an electric mixer, combine cottage cheese, sour cream, skim milk, egg substitute, egg whites, sugar, vanilla and nutmeg. Add the noodles and raisins and mix well. Place in an 8 x 8-inch baking dish and sprinkle with a mixture of cinnamon and sugar. Bake at 350° for approximately 45 minutes or until set.

Stollen

This is my mother's recipe. I substituted candied fruit for the nutmeats and yogurt for the margarine. Otherwise the recipe is the same. It's a nice gift for friends at holiday time.

TWO 8 X 3¾" LOAF PANS; 32 SLICES

2¼ cups all-purpose flour
¾ cup sugar
3 teaspoons baking powder
½ teaspoon salt
½ teaspoon baking soda
1 cup candied fruit and peel, chopped in small pieces
¼ cup nonfat, cholesterol-free egg substitute or 2 egg whites
¾ cup orange juice
1 tablespoon grated orange rind
¼ cup nonfat plain yogurt

In large mixing bowl, mix together dry ingredients. Add dried fruit to the flour mixture and coat well. In another bowl, combine egg substitute, orange juice, grated orange rind and yogurt. Add the wet ingredients to the dry ingredients and mix well. Pour into two 8 x 3¾-inch loaf pans and bake for 35 minutes at 350°.

NUTRITION INFORMATION PER SERVING

Serving Size: 1 slice

Calories: 126
Protein: ....2.5 g
Carbohydrate: ....29 g
Fat: ....less than 0.5 g
Cholesterol: ....0 mg
Sodium: ....163 mg
Fiber: ....0.5 g

Dietary Exchanges:
1 starch and 1 fruit

"Mosquito Coast" French Toast, page 176, Breakfast In A Glass, Page 173 and
Whole Wheat Blueberry Muffins, page 191

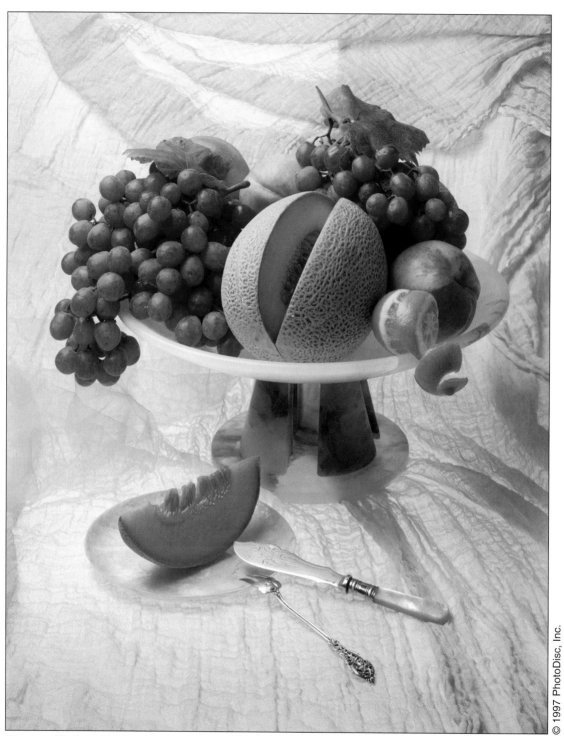

Desserts To Live For!

Chapter 11
Desserts To Live For

Desserts can and do fit into an ultra low-fat eating pattern. You don't have to give up rich flavor and enjoyment just because you're cutting back on fat. There are so many ways to adjust desserts to make them more healthful, and the continual appearance of new fat-free products on supermarket shelves make it easy to enjoy old favorites without the guilt.

Not only will this chapter give you some great recipes, it's also chocked full of hints and suggestions to make luscious, low-fat desserts.

Crusts

Many new food products make pies and quiche more adaptable. Since crusts tend to be the high-fat culprits, we have many ideas and suggestions to keep pies low in fat and cholesterol. The **Pumpkin Pie** recipe (see page 221) in this chapter makes its own crust, or you can adapt your favorite pumpkin pie recipe and bake it without a crust as a custard in a pie pan, custard cups or a casserole dish.

Health Valley® fat-free cookies can be ground into crumbs for use with cheesecakes or pies that previously required graham cracker crusts. For a crust covering the bottom and sides of an 8 or 9-inch pie plate or springform pan, you will need a full package of cookies (1¾ cups crumbs). As these cookies are moist and sweet, you will not need to add any juice or sweetener. Simply moisten your fingers and press the crumbs firmly into the pan.

If the filling bakes inside the crust, partially bake the crust for a crispier result. Place the empty shell in a 375° oven for 4 or 5 minutes and let it cool for about 10 minutes before adding the filling. If the filling is not baked inside the crust, bake the empty crust at 375° for 5 to 8 minutes or just until the edges begin to darken. Cool and add the filling.

Rice or grated potatoes make a fine crust for quiche. you will find a recipe for a rice crust with the **Asparagus Quiche** recipe (see page 179). Grape Nuts® (cereal makes a tasty crust in the **Apple Tart** recipe (see page 217).

Dessert Tips

- Try the following recipe if you would like to add a nonfat whipped topping to your dessert:

  In a mixing bowl, combine about 1 cup nonfat dry milk powder with 1 cup ice water. Beat until peaks form. Add 3 tablespoons sugar and 1 teaspoon vanilla. Beat until stiff. Use immediately.

- Fresh fruit makes a refreshing dessert. Increase flavor and interest by stirring in fresh lime juice and topping with a mixture of nonfat plain yogurt and honey sprinkled with cinnamon and/or nutmeg.

- Plain angel food cake becomes an elegant dessert when served with raspberry purée and sliced kiwi fruit. Make raspberry purée by processing a 10-ounce package of raspberries in a blender with 1 tablespoon of powdered sugar or honey until smooth.

- Fruit purées allow for healthier baking. They can be substituted in equal amounts for the oil in cake recipes. Pick a purée that is compatible with your recipe. For example, prune purée replaced the oil in the **Chocolate Raspberry Cake** (see page 208). You might use applesauce or a pear purée in an applesauce cake.

- When cutting back or eliminating fat, add an extra teaspoon of baking powder to ensure that your product rises as it should.

Pineapple Baked Alaskas

4 SERVINGS

- 4 pineapple rings
- 3 egg whites, room temperature
- ¼ teaspoon cream of tartar
- ¼ cup sugar
- 2 cups nonfat, cholesterol-free frozen vanilla yogurt
  garnish: chocolate sauce and a sprig of mint

Drain pineapple rings, dry well and set aside. Scoop 4 portions of nonfat frozen yogurt (which will be placed on the pineapple) and put them on a tray in the coldest section of your freezer until just before serving.

At serving time, beat egg whites until foamy. Add cream of tartar and continue beating as you gradually add sugar. Beat until stiff peaks are formed.

To assemble the Alaskas, place the pineapple rings on a wooden cutting board, place a scoop of frozen yogurt on each ring. Frost each scoop with beaten egg whites taking care to cover all of the yogurt. Bake in a 400° oven about 5 to 10 minutes until meringue is lightly browned. Drizzle with chocolate sauce if you choose and garnish with fresh mint, serve immediately.

NUTRITION INFORMATION PER SERVING

Serving Size: 1 baked Alaska

Calories: 161
Protein: ....6.5 g
Carbohydrate: ....33.5 g
Fat: ....0 g
Cholesterol: ....0 mg
Sodium: ....107 mg
Fiber: ....less than 1 g

Dietary Exchanges:
1 skim milk and 1 fruit

Preparation Tip:

You will need to work quickly when you assemble these because the frozen yogurt melts a bit faster than regular ice cream. Set your freezer at its coldest setting and take frozen yogurt scoops out one at a time to frost them.

Lemon Soufflé

My Dad asked for this tart, lemony dessert every year on his birthday. Mom baked it in an unbaked pie shell. By using the fat-free spread, and an egg substitute and eliminating the pie crust the fat has been reduced to a trace. It's a very delicious soufflé.

6 SERVINGS

3 tablespoons Fleischmann's® fat-free, squeezable spread
⅔ cup sugar
½ cup plus 1 tablespoon nonfat, cholesterol-free egg substitute
Juice and zest of 2 small lemons (6 tablespoons of juice)
4 tablespoons flour
1½ cups skim milk
3 egg whites, stiffly beaten
garnish: fresh raspberries

In large bowl, cream the sugar with the fat-free spread. Add egg substitute, lemon juice, lemon zest and flour. Beat well. Add milk, mixing well.

In separate bowl, beat egg whites into stiff peaks and carefully fold into the lemon mixture. Pour mixture into 6 individual 1 ½-cup ramekins and place in a 9 x 13-inch pan with about 1-inch hot water. Bake at 325° about 45 minutes or until golden brown. Top each serving with 2–3 tablespoons of fresh raspberries and serve immediately.

NUTRITION INFORMATION PER SERVING

Serving Size: 1 ramekin

Calories: 157
Protein: ....7 g
Carbohydrate: ....33 g
Fat: ....less than 0.5 g
Cholesterol: ....1 mg
Sodium: ....160 mg
Fiber: ....1 g

Dietary Exchanges:
1 skim milk and 1 fruit

Variation:

For an entirely different looking dessert, let the soufflé cool, then invert the ramekins onto individual dessert plates and circle each serving with **Raspberry Purée** (see page 204)

Melon Granita

A granita is very much like a sorbet but easier to make. It can be made with a variety of fruit, however, the fruit you choose must be ripe and at the peak of perfection. Prepare and freeze granita in freezer bags to be enjoyed in the off season.

4 PORTIONS

1 medium cantaloupe (approximately 1½ lbs when seeded and peeled)
¼ cup superfine sugar
 Juice of 1 lemon or to taste
 garnish: fresh berries or mint sprigs

Peel and seed the cantaloupe and cut into medium-size pieces. Place all ingredients in blender and process until smooth.

Place mixture into two ice-cube trays. Freeze until ready to use. To serve, place 6 or 7 melon cubes (one serving) in the bottom of a food processor and process until it becomes a coarse mixture. Repeat for additional servings.

Garnish with fresh blueberries or sprigs of mint.

NUTRITION INFORMATION PER SERVING

Serving Size: 1 portion

Calories:	106
Protein:	1.5 g
Carbohydrate:	26.5 g
Fat:	0.5 g
Cholesterol:	0 mg
Sodium:	16 mg
Fiber:	1.5 g

Dietary Exchanges:
 1½ fruit

V a r i a t i o n :

Peaches, papaya and mangos make excellent variations. You may need to adjust the sugar according to the sweetness of the fruit you choose. Take care not to over sweeten as it detracts from the natural flavor of the fruit.

Meringues with Raspberry Purée

Meringues are an elegant dessert and the combinations of fruit and nonfat, frozen yogurts are limited only by your imagination.

6 MERINGUES

Meringues:
3 egg whites, room temperature
½ teaspoon vanilla
¼ teaspoon cream of tartar
⅛ teaspoon salt
½ cup sugar

Raspberry Purée:
1 10-oz. pkg. frozen raspberries
1 tablespoon honey
garnish: raspberry or strawberry fan

Heat oven to 225°. Line cookie sheet with brown paper.

Meringues: In large bowl, beat egg whites at high speed with an electric mixer until frothy. Add vanilla, cream of tartar and salt. Continue beating until soft peaks form. Gradually add sugar 1 tablespoon at a time, beating until stiff peaks form and sugar dissolves. Do not underbeat.

Using a heaping tablespoonful for each meringue, spoon onto prepared pan. Form 6 individual meringues. Make a deep well in center of each, spreading meringues to 3-inch circles. Bake at 225° for 1 hour or until crisp and very lightly browned. Turn oven off; leave meringues in oven for at least 1 hour with door closed. Remove from oven and carefully remove paper from meringues. Cool completely.

Raspberry Purée: In blender, process raspberries until seeds disappear. Add honey and continue blending.

Fill with fresh fruit and drizzle with Raspberry Purée or with a nonfat frozen yogurt. Garnish.

NUTRITION INFORMATION PER SERVING

Serving Size: 1 meringue with 2 tablespoons purée

Calories: 104
Protein: ....2.5 g
Carbohydrate: ....24 g
Fat: ....0 g
Cholesterol: ....0 mg
Sodium: ....72 mg
Fiber: ....20 g

Dietary Exchanges:
1½ fruit

N o t e :

If filling with a nonfat, cholesterol-free frozen yogurt add an additional 90 calories, 4 g protein, and 18 g carbohydrate for each ½ cup.

Dessert Crêpes

Make these to freeze and fill with sweetened nonfat yogurt cheese and fresh fruit. You'll be just minutes away from a delicious dessert.

30 CRÊPES

¼ cup nonfat, cholesterol-free egg substitute
2 egg whites
2 tablespoons sugar
1 cup all-purpose flour
1 cup whole-wheat pastry flour
2¼ cups skim milk
　　Nonfat cooking spray

NUTRITION INFORMATION PER SERVING

Serving Size: 1 crêpe

Calories: 41
Protein: ....2 g
Carbohydrate: ....8 g
Fat: ....0 g
Cholesterol: ..less than 0.5 mg
Sodium: ....17 mg
Fiber: ....0.5 g

Dietary Exchanges:
½ starch

In blender, combine all ingredients and blend until smooth. Let batter rest for 1 hour. Blend once more before cooking.

Heat a 6-inch nonstick skillet over medium heat. Pour 2 tablespoons of batter into the pan and immediately tilt the pan, swirling the batter to cover the bottom of the pan in a thin layer. Cook approximately 1 minute or until brown. Carefully turn with a spatula and continue cooking the other side. Remove from pan, cool and stack between pieces of wax paper. Wrap unused crêpes for freezing.

Preparation Tip:

Spray the skillet lightly with nonfat cooking spray as you cook the first few crêpes. As the pan becomes seasoned you won't need to spray anymore.

Strawberry Crêpes

Crêpes are fun, economical, delicious, easy to make and they freeze well.

6 CRÊPES

2 cups sliced fresh strawberries
¼ cup sugar
½ cup nonfat cottage cheese
½ cup nonfat, low-cholesterol sour cream
¼ cup powdered sugar
½ teaspoon vanilla
6 **Dessert Crêpes** (see page 205)

Wash and hull strawberries, leaving 3 with hulls for garnish. Slice strawberries, add granulated sugar and set aside.

Using an electric mixer or food processor, whip cottage cheese until smooth. Stir in sour cream and powdered sugar and vanilla and continue beating until mixture is smooth.

With each **Dessert Crêpe** brown side down, fill with about 2 tablespoons of cheese mixture and a proportional share of the strawberries, reserving about ½ cup of cheese for tops. Roll each crêpe and top with a dollop of cheese and ½ strawberry, fanned.

Carrot Cake with Rum Sauce

Nonfat plain yogurt replaces the oil in in this traditional carrot cake recipe. This cake makes every meal a special occasion, as every bite is moist and flavorful.

9 X 13" BAKING PAN; 15 PIECES

1½ cups sugar
1 cup crushed pineapple packed in juice, drained
¼ cup nonfat, cholesterol-free egg substitute
1¼ cups nonfat plain yogurt
2 teaspoons vanilla
3 cups grated carrots, loosely spooned into cup
2 cups all-purpose flour
2 teaspoons baking soda
1½ teaspoons baking powder
2 teaspoons cinnamon
⅛ teaspoon cloves
⅛ teaspoon nutmeg
½ teaspoon salt
½ cup raisins
    Nonfat cooking spray
    Rum Sauce (see page 224)

NUTRITION INFORMATION PER SERVING
Serving Size: 1 piece
Calories: 180
Protein: ....4 g
Carbohydrate: ....41.5 g
Fat: ....0.5 g
Cholesterol: .....less than 0.5 g
Sodium: .... 244 mg
Fiber: ....1.5 g
Dietary Exchanges:
1 starch, 1 vegetable and 1 fruit

In medium bowl, combine sugar, pineapple, egg substitute, yogurt, vanilla and carrots. Stir to blend thoroughly.

In large bowl, combine flour, soda, baking powder, cinnamon, cloves, nutmeg, salt and raisins. Add liquid ingredients to the dry ingredients. Mix well by hand.

Pour into a 9 x 13-inch baking pan sprayed lightly with nonfat cooking spray. Bake at 350° for 40 minutes or until a toothpick inserted in center comes out clean. Serve with **Rum Sauce**, (see page 224) if desired. Makes 15 servings.

Chocolate Raspberry Cake

Who said chocolate cake couldn't be enjoyed on a fat-free eating plan?

NUTRITION INFORMATION PER SERVING

Serving Size: 1 piece

Calories: 252
Protein: ....3 g
Carbohydrates: ....60.5 g
Fat: ....less than 0.5 g
Cholesterol: ..less than 0.5 mg
Sodium: ....164 mg
Fiber: ....1 g

Dietary Exchanges:
2 starch and 2 fruit

N o t e :

Prunes with tapioca are not acceptable for this recipe. When making batters without fat, it's important to avoid over mixing so do not use an electric mixer, mix by hand. This cake is best if made and eaten within two days.

8 X 8" BAKING PAN; 9 PIECES

1 cup plus 2 tablespoons sifted cake flour
½ cup cocoa powder
1 cup sugar
1 teaspoon baking soda
½ teaspoon baking powder
⅛ teaspoon salt
½ cup skim milk
2 2½-oz. jars prune purée baby food
2 egg whites, lightly beaten with a fork
1 teaspoon vanilla
½ cup boiling water
1 heaping teaspoon instant decaffeinated coffee granules
½ cup seedless raspberry preserves

Frosting:
1 cup powdered sugar, sifted
2 tablespoons cocoa
1½ to 2 tablespoons skim milk
¼ teaspoon vanilla

In large mixing bowl, sift all dry ingredients together. Set aside.

In small bowl, combine milk, prunes, egg whites and vanilla. Add the liquid ingredients to the dry ingredients and stir only until mixed. Add instant coffee granules to the boiling water and stir into the batter until blended.

Pour into an 8 x 8-inch baking pan and bake for 30 minutes at 350°. When cake is cool, invert on a plate and slice into two layers. Spread the raspberry preserves between the layers. Prepare frosting and frost the top and sides of the cake. Serve.

Hawaiian Wedding Cake

Fruit cocktail can be substituted for the crushed pineapple in this recipe.

9 X 13" BAKING PAN; 15 PIECES

2 cups all-purpose flour
2 teaspoons baking soda
1½ cups sugar
1 teaspoon salt
1 20-oz. can crushed pineapple
¼ cup egg substitute
2 egg whites
2 teaspoons vanilla
¼ cup powdered sugar
  Nonfat cooking spray

Measure and mix all ingredients except powdered sugar and nonfat cooking spray together in one large bowl. Pour batter into a 9 x 13-inch baking pan that has been lightly sprayed with nonfat cooking spray. Bake for 35 minutes at 350°. Dust with powdered sugar before serving.

NUTRITION INFORMATION PER SERVING
Serving Size: 1 piece
Calories: 167
Protein: ....2.5 g
Carbohydrate: ....39.5 g
Fat: ....less than 0.5 g
Cholesterol: ....0 mg
Sodium: ....260 mg
Fiber: ....1 g
Dietary Exchanges:
2 starch

Raspberry Parfait

Any combination of cake, fruit, puddings, fat-free yogurts and preserves make this an elegant dessert.

1 SERVING

½ cup angel food cake, cut in ½-inch cubes
⅓ cup nonfat, plain yogurt
1 teaspoon honey
⅛ teaspoon vanilla
½ cup fresh raspberries
1 tablespoon seedless raspberry jam
1 teaspoon broken slivered almonds, approximately 7 pieces
1 teaspoon rum
1 tablespoon fat-free whipped topping

Cut angel food cake into ½-inch cubes. Combine yogurt, honey and vanilla.

Layer the following ingredients into a parfait glass or other 1-cup capacity.

Half of the angel food cake, half of the yogurt-honey mixture, ½ tablespoon jam, 1 teaspoon almonds and half of the raspberries. Repeat the layers again adding the rum (instead of the almonds) to the last layer of cake. Top with fat-free whipped topping. The parfait will be prettier if you place the jam and the raspberries close to the side of the glass.

NUTRITION INFORMATION PER SERVING

Serving Size: 1 parfait glass

Calories: 257
Protein: ....7.5 g
Carbohydrate: ....50.5 g
Fat: ....2 g
Cholesterol: ....1.5 mg
Sodium: ....134 mg
Fiber: ....3 g

Dietary Exchanges:
2 starch, ½ skim milk and 1 fruit

N o t e :

Like many processed fat-free products, whipped toppings should be used in moderation. While it is essentially fat-free in small quantities, it can add significant amounts of fat and sugar to the diet when eaten in large quantities.

Company Cheesecake

Cheesecake without the guilt! Serve plain or glazed with fresh fruit or a light canned pie filling.

8" SPRINGFORM PAN; 12 PIECES

4 cups nonfat plain yogurt
9 Health Valley®, fat-free cookies (orange pineapple)
3 egg whites
1 cup fat-free cottage cheese
2 tablespoons flour
¾ cup sugar
1½ tablespoons orange juice concentrate
1 teaspoon vanilla
    garnish: fruit (optional)

NUTRITION INFORMATION PER SERVING

Serving Size: 1 piece

Calories: 134
Protein: ....8 g
Carbohydrate: ....25 g
Fat: ....less than 0.5 g
Cholesterol: ....3 mg
Sodium: ....165 mg
Fiber: ....1 g

Dietary Exchanges:
  1 skim milk and 1 starch

The day before serving, make yogurt cheese by placing yogurt in a large strainer that has been lined with a piece of heavy paper towel or coffee filter. Place strainer over a bowl, cover and refrigerate over night. The next morning discard the liquid in lower bowl.

In blender, crumble the cookies, 3 or 4 at a time. Place crumbs in an 8" springform pan. Wetting your fingers slightly, press the crumbs evenly over the bottom of the pan. Bake the crust 5 minutes at 350°. Remove from oven and set aside to cool.

In blender or food processor, process egg whites and cottage cheese until smooth. Add yogurt cheese, flour, sugar, orange juice and vanilla. Process until well blended, scraping down the sides of the container. Pour the filling over the prepared crust and bake at 325° for approximately 1 hour or until the filling is done in the middle. Do not overbake. Chill.

Cherry, Apple, Oatmeal Cookies

Lighter Bake® has been substituted for the fat in these cookies. The apples and dried cherries make them moist and chewy.

MAKES ABOUT 1½ DOZEN COOKIES

¼ cup dried cherries
½ cup water
⅓ cup Lighter Bake®
1 teaspoon vanilla
¼ nonfat, cholesterol-free egg substitute
⅓ cup packed brown sugar
¼ cup granulated sugar
¾ cup flour
1½ cups quick oats
½ teaspoon baking powder
½ teaspoon baking soda
½ teaspoon cinnamon
⅛ teaspoon nutmeg
¼ teaspoon salt
½ cup grated apple, unpeeled
   Nonfat cooking spray

In small bowl, soak the cherries in the water, Set aside.

In large bowl, mix Lighter Bake®, vanilla, egg substitute and sugars. In another large bowl, combine the flour, quick oats, baking powder, baking soda, cinnamon, nutmeg, and salt. Drain the cherries, pressing out excess moisture. Add the cherries and grated apples to the flour mixture and toss to coat them with the flour. Chill.

Drop by tablespoons onto a baking sheet that has been sprayed with nonfat cooking spray. Bake at 350° for 15 to 18 minutes or until done.

NUTRITION INFORMATION PER SERVING

Serving Size: 1 cookie

Calories: 116
Protein: ....3 g
Carbohydrate: ....24 g
Fat: ....1 g
Cholesterol: ....0 mg
Sodium: ....70 mg
Fiber: ....2 g

Dietary Exchanges:
½ fruit and 1 starch

Preparation Tip:

When using a nonfat cooking spray in baking cakes, muffins or cookies, use very sparingly as too much of the spray tends to make the product tough on the bottom.

Note:

The 1 g of fat in each cookie is primarily polyunsaturated and monounsaturated fat from the oats.

Molasses Crinkles

Blackstrap molasses heightens the flavor in these popular cookies and substituting Lighter Bake® for the margarine in the original recipe eliminates the fat.

ABOUT 1¹/₂ DOZEN COOKIES

¼ cup Lighter Bake®
¼ cup Blackstrap molasses
¼ cup nonfat, cholesterol-free egg substitute
²/₃ cup sugar
2 teaspoons baking soda
2 cups flour
1 teaspoon cinnamon
½ teaspoon cloves
½ teaspoon ginger
¼ teaspoon salt
    Nonfat cooking spray

In medium-size mixing bowl, combine first three ingredients, mixing well. Add dry ingredients to the liquid mixture and stir until all ingredients are moistened. Chill.

Shape into walnut-size balls, roll in granulated sugar and place on a cookie sheet sprayed with nonfat cooking spray. Flatten slightly with the bottom of a glass.

Bake at 375° for 10 minutes or until done.

NUTRITION INFORMATION PER SERVING

Serving Size: 1 cookie

Calories: 99
Protein: ....1.5 g
Carbohydrate: ....23 g
Fat: ....less than 0.5 g
Cholesterol: ....0 mg
Sodium: ....128 mg
Fiber: ....0.5 g

Dietary Exchanges:
  1 fruit and ½ starch

N o t e :

Lighter Bake® is made from a blend of dried plums and apples. It is a 100 percent fat- and cholesterol-free fat replacement for baking. Please see page 241 for manufacturer information.

Chocolate Bars a l'Orange

8 X 8" BAKING PAN; 16 BARS

Bars:
½ cup unsweetened applesauce
¾ cup sugar
4 egg whites
1 teaspoon vanilla
⅔ cup all-purpose flour
½ cup cocoa powder
½ teaspoon baking powder
¼ teaspoon salt
Nonfat cooking spray

Orange Frosting:
½ cup powdered sugar, sifted
2 teaspoons fresh orange juice
1 teaspoon orange zest (divided)

Chocolate Glaze:
3 tablespoons cocoa powder
1½ teaspoons cornstarch
½ teaspoon sugar
½ teaspoon canola oil
1 tablespoon skim milk
⅓ cup corn syrup
½ teaspoon vanilla

NUTRITION INFORMATION
PER SERVING

Serving Size: 1 bar

Calories: 103
Protein: ....2 g
Carbohydrate: ....24.5 g
Fat: ....0.5 grams
Cholesterol: ....0 mg
Sodium: ....65 mg
Fiber: ....less than 1 g

Dietary Exchanges:
1 starch and ½ fruit

Bars: Measure the applesauce and sugar into a medium-size mixing bowl. Using an electric mixer, beat until mixture becomes light and fluffy. Add egg whites one at a time, beating after each addition. Add vanilla and mix well.

In separate bowl, combine flour, cocoa powder, baking powder and salt. Add the applesauce mixture to the dry ingredients and beat until the batter is smooth. Pour batter in an 8 x 8-inch baking dish that has been sprayed with a nonfat cooking spray. Bake in a 350° oven for 20 minutes or until a toothpick inserted in the center comes out clean. When cool, frost with the orange frosting and drizzle 1 tablespoon of the chocolate glaze over the frosting.

Frosting: Mix all ingredients together, saving ¼ teaspoon of the orange zest for later use. Frost the cooled brownies.

Glaze: Place all ingredients except vanilla, in a small saucepan and cook over medium heat, stirring constantly until mixture comes to a gentle boil and is thickened. Add vanilla. Cool slightly and drizzle 1 tablespoon of the glaze over the frosted bars. Sprinkle the remaining ¼ teaspoon of orange zest over the bars. Cut into 16 bars.

Pineapple Date Bars

9 X 13" BAKING PAN; 24 BARS

1 20-oz. can crushed pineapple with juice
2 cups chopped dates
3 cups quick oats
½ cup whole-wheat pastry flour
½ cup all-purpose flour
1 cup orange juice
½ cup packed brown sugar
1 banana, mashed
½ teaspoon cinnamon
⅛ teaspoon cloves
1 teaspoon salt

Cook the pineapple and dates until thickened. Remove from heat and set aside.

In separate bowl, combine the remaining ingredients and mix with a fork as though cutting pastry dough. Add more orange juice 1 tablespoon at a time if the mixture is too dry. Press one-half of the crumb mixture into a 9 x 13-inch baking pan. Spread the cooked fruit over the crumbs. Top with the remaining crumbs and bake for 30 minutes at 350°. Cut with a pizza cutter.

Apple Tart

Grape Nuts® cereal makes a flavorful, crunchy crust for this dessert. You may want to serve with a small, $1/4$-cup scoop of nonfat, cholesterol–free frozen vanilla yogurt.

10" TART PAN; 8 PORTIONS

1⅓ cups Grape Nuts®
¾ cup apple juice concentrate, divided
3 large tart apples, sliced
½ teaspoon cinnamon
⅛ teaspoon nutmeg
1 tablespoon plus 1 teaspoon cornstarch
⅛ cup water
¼ cup apple jelly

NUTRITION INFORMATION PER SERVING
Serving Size: 1 portion

Calories:	176
Protein:	2.5 g
Carbohydrate:	43 g
Fat:	0.5 g
Cholesterol:	0 mg
Sodium:	141 mg
Fiber:	2.5 g

Dietary Exchanges:
½ starch and 1½ fruit

Mix cereal with ¼ cup of the apple juice concentrate. Let sit for a few minutes for the cereal to absorb the juice. With wet fingers press the cereal over the bottom of a 10-inch tart pan with removable bottom.

Arrange apples in concentric circles on the crust and sprinkle with cinnamon and nutmeg. Cover with foil and bake at 350° for 30 minutes until apples are tender but not mushy. Check after about 20 minutes. Let cool.

Mix cornstarch with water and add to remaining ½ cup of apple juice concentrate. Add apple jelly and cook to thicken. Spoon over the apples as a glaze.

Key Lime Chiffon Pie

A grand dessert to serve your guests or take to a potluck. An artificial sweetener can be used in place of the sugar.

NUTRITION INFORMATION PER SERVING

Serving Size: 1 piece

Calories: 150
Protein: ....6.5 g
Carbohydrate: ....32 g
Fat: ....0 g
Cholesterol: ....1.5 mg
Sodium: ....173 mg
Fiber: .... 1.5 g

Dietary Exchanges:
2 starch

N o t e s :

Key lime is a specific kind of lime with a light yellow juice. It is not the green lime normally sold in supermarkets. It gets its name because it is grown in the Florida Keys. Buy bottles of Key lime juice in your supermarket.

Choose a flavor of Health Valley® cookies that is compatible with the filling, perhaps orange or Hawaiian fruit.

7¹/₂ X12" BAKING PAN; 12 PIECES

1 6½-oz. pkg. Health Valley® cookies
1 envelope unflavored gelatin
¼ cup water
1 12-oz. can evaporated skim milk
8 oz. Philadelphia Free® cream cheese
1 cup plus 1 tablespoon sugar
5 tablespoons Key lime juice
1 tablespoon lime zest

Crust: Using a blender, chop 4 or 5 cookies at a time into uniform crumbs. The package will yield approximately 1½ cups of crumbs. Moisten fingers and press crumbs over the bottom of a 7½ x 12-inch baking pan, reserving some of the crumbs to sprinkle on top. Bake for about 5 minutes at 375°. Cool.

Filling: Soften gelatin in water and warm it slightly in microwave to dissolve. Place evaporated milk in a large mixing bowl. Slowly add gelatin to the evaporated milk, mix well and refrigerate until thickened but not set, about 45 minutes to an hour. Whip at high speed until volume doubles and soft peaks form-about 10 minutes. Place the mixture in the refrigerator or freezer for awhile if it loses it's chill and then continue whipping.

In separate bowl, beat cream cheese, gradually adding sugar and continue beating until sugar is dissolved. Add Key lime juice and lime zest. Fold cream cheese mixture carefully into the whipped milk mixture taking care to completely combine the two. Pour into the prepared crust. Sprinkle reserved crumbs over the top and chill.

Double Chocolate Mint Pie

7¹/₂ X 12" BAKING DISH; 12 PIECES

- 1 6½-oz. pkg. Health Valley® Double Chocolate cookies
- 1 envelope unflavored gelatin
- ¼ cup water
- 1 12-oz. can evaporated skim milk
- 8 oz. Philadelphia® Free cream cheese
- 1 cup plus 1 tablespoon sugar
- 2½ tablespoons creme de cacao
- 2½ tablespoons green creme de menthe

NUTRITION INFORMATION PER SERVING	
Serving Size: 1 piece	
Calories:	205
Protein:	6.5 g
Carbohydrate:	38.5 g
Fat:	0 g
Cholesterol:	1.5 mg
Sodium:	142 mg
Fiber:	2 g
Dietary Exchanges:	
2 starch and ½ fruit	

Crust: Using a blender, chop 4 or 5 cookies at a time into uniform crumbs. The package will yield approximately 1½ cups of crumbs. Moisten fingers and press crumbs over the bottom of a 7½ x 12-inch pan, reserving some of the crumbs to sprinkle on top. Bake at 375° for about 5 minutes. Cool.

Filling: Soften gelatin in water and warm it slightly in microwave to dissolve. Place evaporated milk in large mixing bowl. Slowly add gelatin to the evaporated milk, mix well and refrigerate until thickened but not set, about 45 minutes to an hour. Whip at high speed until volume doubles and soft peaks form—about 10 minutes. Place the mixture in the refrigerator or freezer for awhile if it loses it's chill and then continue whipping.

In separate bowl, beat cream cheese, gradually adding sugar and continue beating until sugar is dissolved. Add creme de cacao and creme de menthe. Fold cream cheese mixture carefully into the whipped milk mixture taking care to completely combine the two. Pour into the prepared crust. Sprinkle reserved crumbs over the top and freeze until about 15 minutes before serving.

Peach Cobbler

Change the fruit as you wish. Fresh blueberries substitute nicely for peaches. When you don't have fresh fruit use a canned pie filling.

8 X 8" BAKING DISH; 5 PORTIONS

Filling:
- 3 cups peeled, sliced peaches
- ¾ cup water
- ⅓ cup sugar
- ¼ teaspoon cinnamon
    Dash of nutmeg
- 2 teaspoons cornstarch

Batter:
- 1 tablespoon light margarine, melted
- ½ cup sugar
- ¼ cup nonfat, cholesterol-free egg substitute
- ½ cup flour
- ¼ teaspoon salt
- ½ teaspoon baking powder
- 1 teaspoon vanilla

Filling: In medium sauce pan, combine all filling ingredients and cook until the mixture becomes clear. Place in an 8 x 8-inch baking dish. Prepare the batter.

Batter: In small mixing bowl, cream the melted margarine with the sugar. Add the remaining ingredients and mix well. Spoon the batter over the fruit and bake at 400° for 20 minutes or until top is browned.

NUTRITION INFORMATION
PER SERVING

Serving Size: 1 portion

Calories:	238
Protein:	3.5 g
Carbohydrate:	54 g
Fat:	1.5 g
Cholesterol:	0 mg
Sodium:	174 mg
Fiber:	2 g

Dietary Exchanges:
1 starch and 2½ fruit

Pumpkin Pie

The whole-wheat pastry flour in this recipe settles to make a crust. Substituting liquefied, imitation butter sprinkles and butter flavoring for the melted margarine eliminates the fat without sacrificing flavor.

9" PIE; 8 PIECES

1   12-oz. can evaporated skim milk
2   cups canned pumpkin
½   cup nonfat, cholesterol-free egg substitute
¾   cup sugar
2   teaspoons vanilla
⅓   cup whole-wheat pastry flour
¾   teaspoon baking powder
½   teaspoon salt
2   tablespoons liquid imitation butter sprinkles
¼   teaspoon butter flavoring
1   teaspoon cinnamon
½   teaspoon ginger
½   teaspoon cloves

In large bowl, mix all ingredients together. Blend well. Pour into a 9-inch pie pan and bake for 50 to 55 minutes at 350°.

NUTRITION INFORMATION
PER SERVING

Serving Size: 1 piece

Calories: 156
Protein: ....6 g
Carbohydrate: ....33.5 g
Fat: ....less than 0.5 g
Cholesterol: ....0 mg
Sodium: ....253 mg
Fiber: ....2 g

Dietary Exchanges:
  2 starch

N o t e s :

I prefer Carnation Lite® evaporated skim milk because it is cholesterol-free.

Liquefy Molly McButter® or Butter Buds® according to package directions.

Flan and Philly

4 SERVINGS

4 oz. fat-free cream cheese, room temperature
1 3-oz. box Flan mix
2 cups skim milk
  garnish: freshly sliced peaches

Place cream cheese in medium-size mixing bowl. Set aside.

Pour contents of caramel package (included with the boxed flan mix) into 4 custard cups. Blend flan mix with 2 cups skim milk in saucepan. Cook over medium heat until mixture comes to a boil, stirring constantly. Slowly add the flan mixture to the cream cheese and blend well. Slowly pour over the caramel. Chill 1 hour or until firm. Invert on individual dessert plates and garnish with ¼ cup sliced peaches, per serving.

NUTRITION INFORMATION
PER SERVING

Serving Size: 1 custard cup

Calories: 167
Protein: ....9 g
Carbohydrate: ....32 g
Fat: ....less than 0.5 g
Cholesterol: ....4.5 mg
Sodium: ....205 mg
Fiber: ....less than 1 g

Dietary Exchanges:
1 skim milk and 1 fruit

Rice Pudding

This delicious pudding can be made in minutes when using pre-prepared packages of frozen cooked rice from the freezer.

1½-QT. BAKING DISH; 6 PORTIONS

- 2 cups cooked rice (1 cup white rice, 1 cup brown rice)
- 2 egg whites
- ¼ cup nonfat, cholesterol-free egg substitute
- 1 cup skim milk
- ⅔ cup nonfat, cholesterol-free coffee creamer
- ⅓ cup sugar
- 1 teaspoon vanilla
- ¼ cup golden raisins
- ¼ teaspoon cinnamon
- ⅛ teaspoon nutmeg

NUTRITION INFORMATION PER SERVING

Serving Size: 1 portion

Calories: 182
Protein: ....5.5 g
Carbohydrate: ....34.5 g
Fat: ....less than 1 g
Cholesterol: .....less than 1 mg
Sodium: ....69 mg
Fiber: ....1 g

Dietary Exchanges:
2 starch

N o t e :

One of our favorite brands of coffee creamer is CoffeeMate®.

Place rice in a 1½-qt. baking dish. In another bowl, beat the egg whites and egg substitute slightly with a fork. Add the milk, coffee creamer, sugar, vanilla and raisins; stir to blend. Pour milk and egg mixture over the rice and stir. Sprinkle cinnamon and nutmeg over the top.

Set the baking dish in a larger, deep pan and add boiling water to a depth of ¾-inch. Bake uncovered for approximately 45 minutes at 350°. Halfway through the baking time stir the pudding. It's done when the milk is absorbed and the custard is set. Do not over bake.

Rum Sauce

1 CUP; 8 SERVINGS

NUTRITION INFORMATION
PER SERVING

Serving Size: 2 tablespoons

Calories: 53
Protein: ....2 g
Carbohydrate: ....10 g
Fat: ....less than 0.5 g
Cholesterol: ....1 mg
Sodium: ....67 mg
Fiber: ....0 g

Dietary Exchanges:
½ skim milk

¼ cup sugar
1 tablespoon plus 1 teaspoon cornstarch
⅛ teaspoon salt
½ cup evaporated skim milk
½ cup skim milk
2 tablespoons nonfat, cholesterol-free egg substitute
1 tablespoon rum
¼ teaspoon vanilla
¼ teaspoon butter flavoring

In saucepan, combine sugar, cornstarch and salt. Gradually add evaporated skim milk and skim milk, cook over medium heat until mixture thickens. Beat a small amount of the sauce into the egg substitute and then add all the egg mixture to the sauce and keep cooking until mixture boils. Remove from heat and stir in rum, vanilla and butter flavoring.

Makes enough sauce for about 8 pieces of cake. Excellent with **Carrot Cake** (see page 207).

References

Conway, Linda Glick, ed. *The New Professional Chef,* 5th ed. The Culinary Institute of America. Van Nostrand Reinhold, New York, NY, 1991.

Coyle, Patrick L. *The World Encyclopedia of Food.* Facts on File, Inc. New York, NY, 1982.

Ensminger, A.H., et al. *Foods and Nutrition Encyclopedia, Volumes I & II.* Pegus Press, Clovis, CA, 1983.

Messina, Mark, PhD, and Virginia Messina, MPH,RD. *The Dietitian's Guide to Vegetarian Diets: Issues and Applications.* Aspen Publishers, Inc., Gaithersburg, MD, 1996.

Ornish, Dean, MD. *Dr. Dean Ornish's Program for Reversing Heart Disease: The Only System Proven to Reverse Heart Disease Without Drugs or Surgery.* Ballantine Books, New York, NY, 1990.

Ornish, D., MD. *Stress, Diet & Your Heart: A Lifetime Program for Healing Your Heart Without Drugs or Surgery.* Penguin Books USA, Inc., New York, NY, 1982.

Pennington, Jean A.T., PhD,RD, ed. *Bowes and Church's Food Values of Portions Commonly Used, 16th ed.* J.B. Lippincott Company, Philadelphia, PA, 1994.

Rombauer, Irma S. and Marion Rombauer Becker. *Joy of Cooking.* The Bobbs-Merrill Company, Inc., Indianapolis, IN, 1964.

Rosso, Julee. *Great Good Food.* Crown Publishers, Inc., New York, NY, 1993.

Sheldon, M., MD. *The Wellness Encyclopedia of Food and Nutrition: How to Buy, Store, and Prepare Every Variety of Fresh Food.* University of California at Berkeley. Dickey, Thomas, et al, eds. REBUS, New York, NY, 1992.

Vegetarian Diets. *J American Diet Assoc.* 1993; 93:1317-1319.

Suggestions for Further Reading

Fat and Cholesterol Counter. The American Heart Association. Time Books/Random House, 1991.

FDA/USDA Food Labeling Education Information Center, National Agricultural Library, 10301 Baltimore Blvd., Room 304, Beltsville, MD 20705-2351, (301) 504-5719.

"Label Facts for Healthful Eating", The Mazer Corporation, Creative Services Division, 2501 Neff Rd., Dayton, OH 45414.

Ornish, Dean. *Stress, Diet and Your Heart.* New York: Penguin Books, 1982.

Ornish, Dean. *Dr. Dean Ornish's Program for Reversing Heart Disease.* New York: Ballantine Books, 1990.

Ornish, Dean. *Eat More, Weigh Less.* New York: HarperCollins Publishers, Inc., 1993.

Pennington, Jean A.T. *Bowes & Church's Food Values of Portions Commonly Used.* 16th ed. Philadelphia: J.B. Lippincott Company, 1994.

Pope-Cordle, Jamie and Martin Katahn. *The T-Factor Fat Gram Counter.* New York: W.W. Norton & Company, 1991.

U.S. 1997 Soy Foods Directory. Stevens, R. and J.A. Stevens, eds. Indiana Soybean Development Council, 1997. (800) 301-3153.

Appendix A
Metropolitan Height and Weight Tables

As discussed in **Chapter 2: Nutrition & Lifestyle**, use the MetLife Height & Weight Tables as a guide for determining your optimal fat intake. These are not provided as a recommendation for your optimal weight, but as a tool for determining fat intake only.

Find your height in inches on the chart and follow to the column of your frame size to determine reasonable body weight (reasonable as based on lowest mortality). A quick method for determining your frame size: Wrap the thumb and middle finger of your dominant hand around the wrist of your other arm. If your finger and thumb do not touch, you have a large frame; if they touch, you have a medium frame; if they overlap you have a small frame. Use this weight range with the formulas in **Chapter 2** to determine your optimal daily fat intake.

Metropolitan Height and Weight Tables

MEN				WOMEN			
Height Feet Inches	Small Frame	Medium Frame	Large Frame	Height Feet Inches	Small Frame	Medium Frame	Large Frame
5 2	128–134	131–141	138–150	4 10	102–111	109–121	118–131
5 3	130–136	133–143	140–153	4 11	103–113	111–123	120–134
5 4	132–138	135–145	142–156	5 0	104–115	113–126	122–137
5 5	134–140	137–148	144–160	5 1	106–118	115–129	125–140
5 6	136–142	139–151	146–164	5 2	108–121	118–132	128–143
5 7	138–145	142–154	149–168	5 3	111–124	121–135	131–147
5 8	140–148	145–157	152–172	5 4	114–127	124–138	134–151
5 9	142–151	148–160	155–176	5 5	117–130	127–141	137–155
5 10	144–154	151–163	158–180	5 6	120–133	130–144	140–159
5 11	146–157	154–166	161–184	5 7	123–136	133–147	143–163
6 0	149–160	157–170	164–188	5 8	126–139	136–150	146–167
6 1	152–164	160–174	168–192	5 9	129–142	139–153	149–170
6 2	155–168	164–178	172–197	5 10	132–145	142–156	152–173
6 3	158–172	167–182	176–202	5 11	135–148	145–159	155–176
6 4	162–176	171–187	181–207	6 0	138–151	148–162	158–179

(Weights at age 25–59 based on lowest mortality. For men, weight in pounds according to frame, in indoor clothing weighing 5 lbs., shoes with 1" heels. For women, weight in pounds according to frame, in indoor clothing weighing 3 lbs., shoes with 1" heels).

Source of basic data: 1979 Build Study, Society of Actuaries and Association of Life Insurance Medical Directors of America, 1980.

Reprinted courtesy of Statistical Bulletin, Metropolitan Life Insurance Company.

Appendix B

Tying it all Together: Sample Menus

Creating well-balanced low-fat meals that include a variety of foods is so simple! Following are some ideas using the recipes found in *Vegetarian Cooking for Healthy Living*.

Remember, if you are trying to follow Dr. Ornish's Reversal Diet which strictly limits your cholesterol and fat intake for the day, you may need to be a little more careful with your meal planning. For example, Dr. Ornish's Reversal Diet limits cholesterol intake to 5 milligrams a day. (That's about the amount in a cup of skim milk.) If you prepare a recipe that is going to give you 6 milligrams of cholesterol, you would want to try to eat only cholesterol-free foods for the rest of the day.

If you're simply trying to eat healthier, and allow your fat and cholesterol intake to be a little more liberal, you can feel comfortable eating any combination of the foods in this book along with other low-fat selections.

Calorie content of the meals is not provided as we do not advocate counting calories. However, protein content averages 60 grams per menu.

These sample menus are not meant as a diet to be followed strictly. You may choose to use only a portion of the sample menu, perhaps a recipe or a meal to be added to your favorite foods. These are simply *suggestions* meant to give you an idea of great tasting combinations for *Vegetarian Cooking for Healthy Living* recipes, and to get you started in the right direction of planning and preparing healthy meals!

Menu Planner

It is assumed that any reference to items not found as recipes in *Vegetarian Cooking for Healthy Living*, such as salad dressings, cookies, breads, spreads and yogurts are to be nonfat, cholesterol-free when available. Recipes found in *Vegetarian Cooking for Healthy Living* are noted with an *.

Menu 1

BREAKFAST	Whole Wheat Blueberry Muffins* Scrambled Eggbeaters with salsa Orange juice
LUNCH	Vegetable Pita Sandwich* Blackeyed Peas and Corn* Red grapes
DINNER	"Ground Beef" Casserole* Green and Yellow Mixit* Tossed Salad with Honey Mustard Dressing Summer Fruit Medley*
EVENING SNACK	Rice Pudding* and cookie

Menu 2

BREAKFAST	Vegetable Frittata* Whole wheat toast with preserves Fruit juice
LUNCH	Lentil Patties with Tomato Chutney* Coleslaw* Sliced honeydew Melon Granita*
DINNER	Broccoli and Mostaccioli* Green Beans with raspberry vinaigrette Carrot Salad* Crusty French bread with yogurt cheese and chives
EVENING SNACK	Chocolate Bars a l'Orange*

Menu 3

BREAKFAST	Roasted Vegetable Strata*
	Sliced melon
	Herbal tea
LUNCH	Lemony Vegetable Pasta*
	Sliced tomatoes
	Assorted breads and yogurt cheese spread
	Sliced kiwi with blackberries
DINNER	Crêpes with Hearty Bean Filling*
	Carrots and Grapes*
	Steamed broccoli
	Key Lime Chiffon Pie*
EVENING SNACK	Breakfast in a Glass*

Menu 4

BREAKFAST	Vegetable Omelette with Dill and Chives*
	Multigrain bread with apple butter
	Fruit juice
LUNCH	Polka Dot Chili*
	Tossed salad with orange basil dressing
	Corn muffin (Resources)
	Fresh fruit compote
DINNER	Vegetable Masala*
	Basmati Rice*
	Strawberry Crêpes*
EVENING SNACK	Premier Pancake* with applesauce

Menu 5

BREAKFAST	Broiled pink grapefruit
	Premier Pancakes* with syrup or fruit
	4 ounces skim milk
LUNCH	Vegetable Frittata*
	Bibb lettuce and mandarin orange salad
	Date Bran Muffin*
DINNER	Fulla Beans Casserole*
	Cooked barley with chopped onion and carrot
	Steamed young asparagus
	Sliced tomatoes with chopped fresh basil
EVENING SNACK	Raspberry Parfait*

Menu 6

BREAKFAST	Raisin bread toast with cinnamon yogurt cheese Melon wedge with blueberries Orange juice
LUNCH	Asparagus Quiche* Whole grain bread Fruit Soup*
DINNER	Cornbread Hot Tamale Pie* Steamed baby zucchini Layered Party Slaw*
EVENING SNACK	Pineapple Date Bar*

Menu 7

BREAKFAST	Breakfast in a Glass* Oatmeal Applesauce Muffin*
LUNCH	Minestrone Soup* Baco's, Lettuce and Tomato Sandwich* Fresh Berries
DINNER	Lentil Casserole* Orange Rice* Spinach Salad* Molasses Crinkle Cookie* with frozen yogurt
EVENING SNACK	Whole Wheat Crêpe* filled with fruited yogurt

Menu 8

BREAKFAST	Mosquito Coast French Toast* Sliced melon Caribbean blend juice
LUNCH	Lentil Soup* Crisp vegetables (baby carrots, red pepper strips, celery) Fresh plum
DINNER	Szechuan Asparagus with Vermicelli* Garden salad with sweet and sour dressing Sliced tomatoes Carrot Cake with Rum Sauce*
EVENING SNACK	Refried Beans* with baked whole wheat pita wedges

Menu 9

BREAKFAST	Oatmeal with Applesauce* Whole-wheat bagel with herbed cream cheese 4 oz. skim milk
LUNCH	Sloppy Joe* New Potato Salad with Vegetables* Fresh melon
DINNER	Linguini with Pineapple Salsa* Sautéed snow peas and mushrooms Baby greens with raspberry vinaigrette Apple Tart*
EVENING SNACK	Dr. Pepper® Apricot Bread*

Menu 10

BREAKFAST	Banana Yogurt with Granola* Whole-wheat toast with preserves Fruit juice
LUNCH	Veggie burger (Resources) on whole-wheat bun with lettuce, tomato, onion Oven Fried Potatoes* Spicy Black Bean Salad* Watermelon
DINNER	Cabbage Rolls* Steamed cauliflower with fresh dill Curly endive and watercress salad with Orange Vinaigrette (see Spinach Salad recipe*)
EVENING SNACK	Carrot Muffin*

Menu 11

BREAKFAST	Pumpkin Spice Muffin* with yogurt cheese spread Dried apricots Fruit juice
LUNCH	Potato, Bean and Rice Soup* Cucumber sandwich with Hummus* Mixed berries
DINNER	Vegetable Stew with Cornmeal Dumplings* Peanutty Fruit Salad on Greens* Chocolate Raspberry Cake*
EVENING SNACK	Popcorn and sliced apple

Menu 12

BREAKFAST	Lemon Poppy Seed Bread*
	Strawberry yogurt
	Herbal tea
	Fruit juice
LUNCH	Pasta and Bean Salad*
	Whole-grain bread with herbed cream cheese
	Sliced kiwi
DINNER	Calzones with Marinara Sauce*
	Fresh Asparagus with Lemon Sauce*
	Mixed greens with Italian dressing
	Papaya with Lime Juice*
EVENING SNACK	Cherry, Apple, Oatmeal Cookie*
	4 oz. skim milk

Menu 13

BREAKFAST	Whole Wheat Crêpe* filled with yogurt cheese, and sliced strawberries and bananas
	Fruit juice
LUNCH	Minestrone Salad*
	Pumpernickel bread with vegetable spread
	Fresh pear
DINNER	Penne with Artichokes and Leeks*
	Spinach Salad*
	Whole grain bread
	Lemon Souffle*
EVENING SNACK	Tortilla chips and salsa

Menu 14

BREAKFAST	Broiled bagel with tomato, cheese and basil
	Fresh fruit
	Orange juice
LUNCH	Veggie Submarine Sandwich*
	Cabbage Soup*
	Red grapes
DINNER	Tortilla Black Bean Casserole*
	Sweet corn on the cob
	Sliced tomatoes in tarragon vinegar
	Double Chocolate Mint Pie*
EVENING SNACK	Lemon Poppy Seed Bread*

Appendix C
Reading Food Labels

Before you can stock your low-fat vegetarian kitchen, you need to understand how to decipher food labels, which can be a daunting task. Reading labels is an important skill because it makes you aware of your nutritional intake. Thanks to the Nutrition Labeling and Education Act of 1993, it's much easier to determine product ingredients. Prior to the 1993 legislation, food labels frequently displayed inaccurate nutritional information. The Nutrition Facts label found on all products lists ingredients in a useful and straightforward manner. The diagram on the next page illustrates how the Nutrition Facts label displays information.

Even though the Nutrition Facts label contains much useful information, we caution you against broadly studying its contents. You may find it easier to focus on one nutritional concern at a time. For example, focus initially on fat content, since it's such in integral part of a low-fat vegetarian dietary lifestyle.

To determine how a food fits into your dietary plan, use the following approach. After reading the section in **Chapter 2** about calculating your daily fat intake, study the Nutrition Facts label on a product you wish to use. First, scan the information in the Total Fat category. This lists the number of grams of fat in a single serving. Next, study the information on saturated fats, polyunsaturated fats and monounsaturated fats. Remember that you want to avoid saturated fats. If you feel that a food is unacceptable, check the serving size. This is important because the amount that the manufacturer lists as a serving may not be what you would normally eat. For instance, if the serving size is 1 cup, but you would normally eat 2 cups of a particular food, you will need to double the Amount Per Serving information.

In addition to the fat information provided in Nutrition Facts, familiarize yourself with specific label claims about fat and cholesterol. In order for a manufacture to include these claims on a food label, the food must meet government guidelines listed on page 236.

Food label at a Glance

The new food label can be found on food packages in your supermarket. Reading the label tells more about the food and what you are getting. What you see on the food label–the nutrition and ingredient information–is required by the government.

Nutrition Facts Title
The new title "Nutrition Facts" signals the new label.

Serving Size
Similar food products now have similar serving sizes. This makes it easier to compare foods. Serving sizes are based on amounts people actually eat.

New Label Information
Some label information may be new to you. The new nutrient list covers those most important to your health. You may have seen this information on some old labels, but it is now required.

Vitamins and Minerals
Only two vitamins, A and C, and two minerals, calcium and iron, are required on the food label. A food company can voluntarily list other vitamins and minerals in the food.

Label Numbers
Numbers on the nutrition label may be rounded for labeling.

Nutrition Facts
Serving Size 1 cup (228g)
Servings Per Container 2

Amount Per Serving

Calories 90   Calories from Fat 30

	% Daily Value*
Total Fat 3g	**5%**
Saturated Fat 0g	**0%**
Cholesterol 0mg	**0%**
Sodium 300mg	**13%**
Total Carbohydrate 13g	**4%**
Dietary Fiber 3g	**12%**
Sugars 3g	
Protein 3g	

Vitamin A 80%	•	Vitamin C 60%
Calcium 4%	•	Iron 4%

* Percent Daily Values are based on a 2,000 calorie diet. Your daily values may be higher or lower depending on your calorie needs:

	Calories:	2,000	2,500
Total Fat	Less than	65g	80g
Sat Fat	Less than	20g	25g
Cholesterol	Less than	300mg	300mg
Sodium	Less than	2,400mg	2,400mg
Total Carbohydrate		300g	375g
Dietary Fiber		25g	30g

Calories per gram:
Fat 9 • Carbohydrate 4 • Protein 4

© 1993 National Food Processors Association

% Daily Values
% Daily Values shows how a food fits into a 2,000 calorie reference diet.

You can use % Daily Value to compare foods and see how the amount of a nutrient in a serving of food fits in a 2,000 calorie reference diet.

Daily Values Footnote
Daily Values are the new label reference numbers. These numbers are set by the government and are based on current nutrition recommendations.

Some labels list the daily values for a daily diet of 2,000 and 2,500 calories. Your own nutrient needs may be less than or more than the Daily Values on the label.

Calories Per Gram
Some labels tell the approximate number of calories in a gram of fat, carbohydrate, and protein.

Nutrition Claims

Following are nutrition claims found on the front of food labels, along with definitions, that relate to the fat and cholesterol content of foods. They are often put on labels to get your attention and entice you to purchase a product, so it's helpful to know what they mean.

Fat Free - less than 0.5 grams of fat per serving

Low Fat - 3 grams or less fat per serving

Reduced Fat/Less Fat - at least 25% less fat than the original product

Saturated Fat Free - less than 0.5 grams saturated fat per serving

Low Saturated Fat - 1 gram or less saturated fat, and no more than 15% of calories from saturated fat

Reduced or Less Saturated Fat - at least 25% less saturated fat than the original product

Cholesterol Free - less than 2 milligrams cholesterol, and 2 grams or less saturated fat per serving

Low Cholesterol - 20 milligrams or less cholesterol, and 2 grams or less saturated fat per serving

Reduced or Less Cholesterol - at least 25% less cholesterol, and 2 grams or less saturated fat than the original product

Additional Label Reading Hints

Foods that contain a fat-free or nonfat label shouldn't be viewed as an opportunity to eat additional portions. Such foods may contain small amounts of fat, so over-indulging could lead to exceeding your daily fat allowance. The ingredients label explains whether the product has added fat or whether the food contains any high-fat ingredients. The label lists the ingredients in order from the most to the least amounts. For example, if soybean oil is listed as the last ingredient, the product contains less oil than other ingredients. A product that lists oil as one of the first ingredients should be considered with caution.

In addition, fat-free does not mean calorie-free. Some consumers mistakenly believe that if a food carries a fat-free label, they can eat as much as they want without gaining weight. While there is some truth to this in regard to naturally fat-free or low-fat foods like fruits, vegetables and whole-grains, many of the highly processed fat-free foods contain high levels of sugar and may therefore be high in calories. Don't be surprised to find that a fat-free version of a processed food has more calories in a serving than the original, higher-fat version. In other words, the fat-free label shouldn't be used to justify over-indulging.

Be sure to check the ingredients list for oils that are 'hydrogenated' or 'partially hydrogenated'. This means the oil has undergone a process that makes it more solid and results in trans fatty acids. These fatty acids act like saturated fat and increase blood cholesterol levels. Unfortunately, the amount of trans fatty acids are not listed on the Nutrition Facts label. You will want to treat them like saturated fat, though, and limit consumption of foods containing them.

Take note, also, of the fiber content in foods. By following the guidelines set forth in this book, you will naturally eat a high-fiber diet, but you should still carefully consider the products that you purchase and choose high-fiber items when possible. The Nutrition Facts label lists dietary fiber under Total Carbohydrate information. The recommended daily fiber intake is between 20 and 35 grams of fiber a day.

Foods that bear the label claim 'good source of fiber', 'contains fiber', or 'provides fiber' contain between three and five grams of fiber per serving. Foods that are 'high fiber', 'rich in fiber', or an 'excellent source of fiber' contain at least five or more grams per serving. In addition, because of fiber's association with lowering cholesterol levels and decreasing cancer risk, a label must declare the level of total fat per serving if the food is high in fat (more than three grams per serving). This prevents the manufacturer from enticing consumers with the claim of high fiber and the reality of high fat.

Finally, become familiar with the Daily Values and Percent Daily Values on the Nutrition Facts label. Daily Values are simply label reference numbers based on current nutrition recommendations. On most labels, the amounts listed are for 2000 and 2500 calorie diets. The amounts listed represent dietary guidelines, to be used for reference, not dietary laws.

The Percent Daily Values indicate how a particular food fits into a 2000-calorie reference diet. The Percent Daily Values also assist you in determining whether your daily intake of a nutrient fits within current recommendations. For example, based on the 2000-calorie diet, if your total Percent Daily Value for your sodium intake on a given day adds up to 100%, then your diet fits within the sodium recommendations.

As you create your dietary plan, keep in mind that the Daily Value for fat and cholesterol will be higher than the recommendations in this book. The recommendations for Daily Value averages are based on the AHA recommendation that 30% of one's calories come from fat and that cholesterol intake should be limited to no more than 300 milligrams per day. Consequently, you may find it most helpful to use only the Amount Per Serving information for fat and cholesterol. This gives you all the information that you need for determining your daily intake.

Although this section doesn't constitute a complete discussion on food labels, it does provide enough information for you to begin educating yourself about label reading. If you feel that you need more information, consult the "Suggestions for Further Reading" list on page 226.

Appendix D
Commercial Food Buying Guide

Resources and Mail Order Directory

This list does not intend to cover all of the acceptable products available to consumers but it gives the reader a place to start.

Bacon Pieces - imitation, 1.5 grams fat or less per serving

Bac'n Pieces ....McCormick Co., Inc.
Consumer Affairs
Hunt Valley, MD 21031-1100
1-800-632-5847

Bac-O's....................................General Mills, Inc.
Minneapolis, MN 55440
1-800-328-6787

Mario Bacon Bits ....Westin, Inc.
Omaha, NE 68106

Baked Beans - Vegetarian, fat-free, cholesterol free

B & M ....B & M Consumer Affairs
P. O. Box 66719
St. Louis, MI 63166-6719

Bush's ....Bush Bros. and Co.
P. O. Box 52330, Department C
Knoxville, TN 37950-2330

Heinz.......................................H. J. Heinz Co.
Pittsburgh, PA 15212

Beans, box meals

Bean Cuisine............................Reily Foods Co.
640 Magazine Street
New Orleans, LA 70130
1-800-692-7895

Beans, canned

Eden Organic fat-free, low-salt .....Eden Foods, Inc
Clinton, MI 49236

Randall Mixed Beans..................Randall Food Products, Inc.
Tekonsha, MI 49092

Beans, refried - fat-free

Bearitos ....Little Organic Foods
Carson, CA 90746

Old El Paso ....Old El Paso Foods Co.
Consumer Affairs
P. O. Box 66719
St. Louis, MO 63166-6719
1-800-325-7130

Bean Salad - canned - fat-free

Hanover Three Bean Salad ....Hanover Foods Corp.
Hanover, PA 17331

Read Garden Salad....................Princeville Canning Co.
Princeville, IL 61559

Three Bean Salad ....The Pillsbury Co.
2866 Pillsbury Center
Minneapolis, MN 55402-1464
1-800-998-9996

Breads and Dinner Rolls

Bridgford Frozen Bread Dough .....Bridgford Foods Corp.
P. O. Box 3773
Anaheim, CA 92803
1-800-854-3255

California Goldminer....................Pioneer French Baking Co.
Sourdough Flute   Venice, CA 90291
(no sugar added, 99% fat-free)

Healthy Life, Light, Whole-wheat, .Lewis Bakeries
Light Italian, Light White   P. O. Box 6471
(99% fat-free/cholesterol-free bread)   Evansville, IL 47719-0471

Italian Bread Sticks.....................Moose Bros. Food Systems
P. O. Box 780
Sioux Falls, SD 57101
1-800-336-3288

Quick Loaf - fat-free...................Daily Bread Co., Inc.
P. O. Box 1091
Portsmouth, NH 03802-1091
1-800-635-5668

Great Harvest Bread Co..............Franchises - check local area

Rhodes Bake-N-Serv...................Rhodes Bake-N-Serv
Roll Dough fat-free   Box 25487
Salt Lake City, UT 84125
1-800-876-7333

Burgers - Meatless - 2.5 grams fat or less per patty

Boca Burgers ....Boca Burger Co.
fat-free   Ft. Lauderdale, FL 33305

Better 'n Burgers ....Worthington Foods, Inc.
(Morningstar Farms)   Worthington, OH 43085
1-800-243-1810

Garden Burgers ....Wholesome and Hearty Foods, Inc.
Veggie Medley, fat-free   Portland, OR 97214
1-800-636-0109

Harvest Burgers (Green Giant)......The Pillsbury Co.
• Italian Style   2866 Pillsbury Center
• Southwest Style   Minneapolis, MN 55402-1464
• Original Flavor   1-800-998-9996

Spicy Black Bean Burger ....Worthington Foods
(Morning Star Farms) 1g fat per patty   Worthington, OH 43085

Butter and Oil Replacement

Lighter Bake..............................Sun-Diamond Growers of CA
Pleasanton, CA 94588
1-800-417-2253

Butter Sprinkles - imitation

Butter Buds...............................Cumberland Packing Corp.
Department B B
2 Cumberland Street
Brooklyn, NY 11205

Molly McButter ....Alberto-Culver USA, Inc.
Melrose Park, IL 60160

Cake Mixes - fat and cholesterol-free

Sweet Rewards..........................General Mills, Inc.
Minneapolis, MN 55440
1-800-328-6787

Cheese, alternatives, fat, lactose and cholesterol-free

Soya Kaas.................................American Natural Snacks
Jalapeño, Monterrey Jack   St. Augustine, FL 32085-1067

Cheese, shredded and sliced - nonfat, less than 5 mg cholesterol per serving

Alpine Lace ....Alpine Lace Brands, Inc.
Maplewood, NJ 07040

Bordens - slices.........................Borden, Inc.
Columbus, OH 43215

Fame Slices ....Fame Marketing
cholesterol free   Dayton, OH 45429

Healthy Choice ....Con Agra
Consumer Affairs Department
P. O. Box 3768
Omaha, NE 68103-0768
1-800-323-9980

Kraft Slices Sharp cheddar only....Kraft, Inc.
cholesterol free   Glenview, IL 60025
1-800-634-1984

Polly-O......................................Pollio Dairy Products
Mineola, NY 11501

Smart Beat ....Smart Beat Foods
cholesterol free   Div. GFA Brands, Inc.
Cresskill, NJ 07626-0397

Weight Watchers........................Heinz Nutrition Products, Inc.
P. O. Box 57
Pittsburgh, PA 15230

Cheese, Cream - nonfat, less than 5 mg cholesterol per serving

Healthy Choice ....Con Agra Consumer Affairs
Department B C
P. O. Box 3768
Omaha, NE 68103-0768
1-800-323-9980

Philadelphia Free ....Kraft, Inc.
Glenview, IL 60025
1-800-634-1984

Cheese, Parmesan - fat-free

Kraft Grated Cheese Topping........Kraft, Inc.
   cholesterol-free   Glenview, IL 60025
1-800-323-0768

Weight Watchers.........................Weight Watchers Food Co.
P. O. Box 57
Pittsburgh, PA 15230

Cheese, Ricotta - nonfat, less than 5 mg cholesterol per serving

M Maggios ....M Maggios
Philadelphia, PA 19148

Polly-O ....Pollio Dairy Products
Mineola, NY 11501

Chips - 1.5 grams or less fat per serving

Baked Tostitos ....Frito-Lay, Inc.
   1 gram fat per serving   Dallas, TX 75235-5224
1-800-352-4477

Childers ....Childers Food Products, L. P.
1307 W. Morehead Street
Charlotte, NC 28208
1-800-322-4632

Guiltless Tortilla Chips.................Guiltless Gourmet, Inc.
3709 Promontory Pt. Dr. #131
Austin, TX 78744-1139
1-800-723-9541

Louise's ....A T G T B T, Inc.
Louisville, KY 40299

Baked Lays Low-Fat ....Frito Lay, Inc.
Dallas, TX 75235-5224

Jay's Low-Fat.............................Jay's Foods, L. L. C.
Chicago, IL 60628

Cocoa Mix - fat-free, cholesterol free

Carnation ....Nestle Beverage Co.
345 Spear St.
San Francisco, CA 94105

Swiss Miss ....Hunt Wesson, Inc.
P. O. Box 4800
Fullerton, CA 92634

Coffee Creamers - fat-free, cholesterol-free

CoffeeMate ....Nestle Beverage Co.
San Francisco, CA 94105
1-800-NESTLE-4

International Delight....................M Star, Inc.
5956 Sherry Lane
Dallas, TX 75225

1-800-441-3321

Rich's ....Rich Products Corporation
Buffalo, NY 14240 USA
1-800-356-7094

Cold Cuts - fat-free, cholesterol-free

Deli Slices.................................Yves Fine Foods, Inc.
Vancouver, B. C., Canada V6A 2A8

Veggie Bacon ....Yves Fine Foods, Inc.
Vancouver, B. C., Canada V6A 2A8

Cookies and Bars - fat-free

Archway....................................Archway Cookies, Inc.
Battle Creek, MI 49016

Elfin Delight...............................Keebler Co.
Customer Relations
1 Hollow Tree Lane
Elmhurst, IL 60626

Famous Amos ....Famous Amos Cookie Corporation
Atlanta, GA 30346

Frookie ....R. W. Frookies, Inc.
P. O. Box 1649
Sag Harbor, NY 11963-0060

Greenfield ....Greenfield Healthy Food Co. Inc.
P. O. Box 1200
Southport, CT 06490

Health Valley ....Health Valley Foods, Inc.
16100 Foothill Blvd.
Irwindale, CA 91706-7811
1-800-423-4846

Jammers...................................Auburn Farms, Inc.
P. O. Box 348180
Sacramento, CA 95834

Newtons and Snack Well ....Nabisco Foods
East Hanover, NJ 07936
1-800-NABISCO

Cottage Cheese - fat-free

Breakstones .... Kraft General Foods
5 mg cholesterol per ½ cup   Glenview, IL 60025
1-800-323-0768

Friendship ....Friendship Dairies, Inc.
cholesterol-free   Friendship, NY 14739

Couscous

Marrakesh Express......................Marrakesh Express
Melting Pot Foods
1145 Westgate
Oat Park, IL 60301

Crackers - fat-free

Health Valley ....Health Valley Foods, Inc.

16100 Foothill Blvd.
Irwindale, CA 91706-7811
1-800-423-4846

Krispy Saltines...........................Sunshine Biscuit, Inc.
677 Larch Ave.
Elmhurst, IL 60126

Mr. Phipps, Premium Saltines ......Nabisco Foods
Snack Wells   East Hanover, NJ 07936
1-800-NABISCO

Zesta Saltines ....Keebler Co.
1 Hollow Tree Lane
Elmhurst, IL 60126

Dips - fat-free

Guiltless Gourmet ....Guiltless Gourmet, Inc.
3709 Promontory Point, Dr.
Austin, TX 78744-1139
1-800-723-9541

Enrico's ....Ventre Packing Co. Inc.
6050 Court Street Road
Syracuse, NY 13206

Hain ....Hain Pure Food Co., Inc.
24 Jericho Turnpike
Jericho, NY 11753

Saguaro Cool Coyote...................Saguaro Food Products
860 E. 46th St.
Tucson, AZ 85713
1-602-884-8049

Zapata.....................................Zapata Foods
Dallas, TX 75236

Egg Substitute - fat-free, cholesterol-free

Better'n Eggs.............................Worthington Foods, Inc.
Worthington, OH 43085
1-800-243-1810

Egg Beaters..............................Nabisco Foods, Inc.
East Hanover, NJ 07936
1-800-622-4726

Scramblers................................Worthington Foods, Inc.
Worthington, OH 43085
1-800-243-1810

Second Nature ....M Star, Inc.
5956 Sherry Lane
Dallas, TX 75225
1-800-441-3321

Evaporated Skim Milk - fat-free

Carnation Lite............................Nestle Food Co.
  cholesterol free   Glendale, CA 91203
1-800-854-8935

Pet Light ....Pet Incorporated

5 mg cholesterol	St. Louis, MI 63102
	1-800-325-7130

Granola - fat-free

Health Valley ....Health Valley Foods, Inc.
16100 Foothill Blvd.
Irwindale, CA 91706-7811
1-800-423-4846

Gravy - fat-free

Heinz Fat Free ....H. J. Heinz company
Pittsburgh, PA 15212

Hot Dogs - fat-free, cholesterol-free

Smart Dogs................................Lightlife Foods, Inc.
P. O. Box 870
Greenfield, MA 01302
1-800-274-6001

Veggie Wieners...........................Yves Fine Foods, Inc.
Vancouver B. C. Canada V6A 2A8

Ice Cream / Frozen Yogurt - nonfat, cholesterol-free

Edy's ....Edy's Grand Ice Cream
5929 College Ave.
Oakland, CA 94618
1-800-301-0542

Food Lion..................................Food Lion, Inc.
Salisbury, NC 28145-1330

Haagen-Dazs.............................The Haagen-Dazs Co., Inc.
Teaneck, NJ 07666
1-800-726-6455

Kemps......................................Marigold Foods, Inc. Plant 27-621
Minneapolis, MN 55414
1-800-726-6455

McArthur T G Lee........................McArthur Dairy, Inc.
Ft. Lauderdale, FL 33313
1-800-301-0542

Sealtest ....Good Humor Breyers Ice Cream
P. O. Box 19007
Green Bay, WI 54307-9007

TCBY ....TCBY Systems, Inc. Plant #480925F
Little Rock, AR 72201

Margarines / Vegetable spreads - nonfat, cholesterol free

Fleischman's fat-free...................Nabisco Foods
  squeezable bottle   East Hanover, NJ 07936
1-800-NABISCO

I Can't Believe It's Not Butter.......Van Den Bergh Foods Co.
  fat-free   Lisle, IL 60532
1-800-735-3554

Promise Ultra ....Van Den Bergh Foods Co.
  fat-free   Lisle, IL 60532

Smart Beat ....Heart Beat Foods
          1-800-735-3554
DIV. GFA Brands
P. O. Box 397
Cresskill, NJ 07626-0397

Mayonnaise 1 gm fat or less per tablespoon

Hellman's Low Fat ....Best Foods Division
CPC International, Inc.
Englewood Cliffs, NJ 07632-9975

Kraft Free...................................Kraft, Inc.
Glenview, IL 60025
1-800-323-0768

Kraft Miracle Whip Free ....Kraft, Inc.
Glenview, IL 60025
1-800-323-0768

Noodles - cholesterol free

Muellers....................................Best Foods Division
CPC International, Inc.
Englewood Cliffs, NJ 07632-9976

No Yolks....................................Foulds, Inc.
Libertyville, IL 90640

Pastries/Baked Goods/Mixes - 0.5 gm fat or less per serving, cholesterol-free

Entenman's...............................Entenman's, Inc.
Bay Shore, NY 11706

Krusteze - muffin mix ....Continental Mills, Inc.
 fat-free   Consumer Relations Department
P. O. Box 88176
Seattle, WA 98138
1-800-457-7744

Pioneer - biscuit mix ....Pioneer Flour Mills
San Antonio, TX 78291
1-800-235-8186

Calhoun Bend Mill ....Calhoun Bend Mill, Inc.
 (If use egg substitute and skim 3615 Fourth Street
 milk, no added fat in directions) Jonesville, LA 71343

Pizza Sauce - fat-free

Boboli.......................................Boboli Co.
White Birch Rd. Industrial Park
Hazelton, PA 18201

Old Fashioned Foods..................Old Fashioned Foods, Inc.
Mayville, WI 53050
1-800-346-0154

Potatoes, fat-free

Simply Potatoes........................North Star Co.
3171 Fifth St. S. E.
Minneapolis, MN 55414
1-800-556-7827

Pretzels - fat-free

Eagle ....Eagle Snacks, Inc.
P. O. Box 27238
St. Louis, MO 63118
1-800-426-4851

Old Dutch ....Old Dutch Foods
P. O. Box 64627
St. Paul, MN 55113

Jay's..Jay's Foods, Inc. L.L.C.
Chicago, IL 60628

Rold Gold..................................Frito-Lay, Inc.
Dallas, TX 75235-5224
1-800-352-4477

Pudding - fat-free, cholesterol-free

Hunts Fat-Free Snack Pack..........Hunt-Wesson, Inc.
P. O. Box 4800
Fullerton, CA 92634

Jello Free ....Kraft General Foods, Inc.
Box FRE-VC
White Plains, NY 10625
1-800-431-1001

Swiss Miss ....Hunt-Wesson, Inc.
P. O. Box 4800
Fullerton, CA 92634

Rice Cakes - fat-free

Hain ....Hain Pure Food Co., Inc.
Consumer Affairs
P. O. Box 66967
St. Louis, MO 63166-6967

Quaker.......................................Quaker Oats Co.
P. O. Box 049003
Chicago, IL 60604-9003

Roman Meal ....Roman Meal Co.
601 Main St., Suite 500
Vancouver, WA 98660

Rice, Grains and Bean Products

Fantastic Foods ....Fantastic Foods, Inc.
Petaluma, CA 60301

Indian Harvest - rice bread ....Indian Harvest
P. O. Box 428
Bemidji, MN 56619-0428
1-800-346-7032

Salad Dressing - fat-free

Good Seasons ....General Foods Corp.
Box GSSD-FFI
White Plains, NY 10625
1-800-431-1003

Herb Magic ....William B. Reily and Co., Inc.
New Orleans, LA 70130
1-800-535-1961

Hidden Valley ....The HVR Co.
Department A
Oakland, CA 94612
1-800-537-2823

Kraft...Kraft, Inc.
Glenview, IL 60025
1-800-323-0768

Marie's ....Campbell Soup Co.
Camden, NJ 08103-1701
1-800-257-8443

Marzetti's..................................T. Marzetti Co.
Columbus, OH 43229

Naturally Fresh ....Naturally Fresh
1000 Naturally Fresh Blvd.
Atlanta, GA 30349

Old Dutch ....Old Dutch Co.
Division of Root Co.
P. O. Box 2540
Daytona Beach, FL 32115

Pfeiffer......................................Pfeiffer Foods
Wilson, NY 14172

Pritikin ....Pritikin Systems, Inc.
P. O. Box 049003
Chicago, IL 60604-9003

S & W Vintage Lites ....S & W Fine Foods, Inc.
San Ramon, CA 94583-1338
1-800-742-3853

Walden Farms ....W F I Corp.
Linden, NJ 07036

Wish Bone ....Thos. J. Lipton, Inc.
Englewood, Cliffs, NJ 07632

Soups and Broth

Campbell's Healthy Request ....Campbell Soup Co.
Camden, NJ 08103-1701
1-800-257-8443

Health Valley ....Health Valley Foods, Inc.
16100 Foothill Blvd.
Irwindale, CA 91706-7811
1-800-423-4846

MBT Instant Broth Packets ....Borden, Incorporated
Columbus, OH 43215-3799

Swanson's Vegetable Broth.........Campbell Soup Co.
Camden, NJ 08103-1701
1-800-257-8443

Weight Watchers........................H. J. Heinz
Instant broth packets   Pittsburgh, PA 15212

Sour Cream - fat-free

Breakstones ....Kraft General Foods
Less than 5 mg cholesterol   Glenview, IL 60025
per 2 tablespoons   1-800-323-0768

Land O Lakes ....Land O Lakes, Inc.
Less than 5 mg cholesterol   Arden Hills, MN 55126
per 2 tablespoons   1-800-328-4155

Naturally Yours...........................M Star, Inc.
Cholesterol-free   5956 Sherry Lane
                                    Dallas, TX 75225
                                    1-800-441-3321

Soybean Products

Just Like Ground.........................Yves Fine Foods, Inc.
                                    Vancover, B.C. Canada V6A 2A8

ADM Midland Harvest.................The Mail Order Catalog
Herb 'n Spice, Chili, Taco Mix,   P. O. Box 180
Sloppy Joes   Summertown, TN 38483
                                    1-800-695-2241

TVP ....The Mail Order Catalog
                                    P. O. Box 180
                                    Summertown, TN 38483
                                    1-800-695-2241

Soyfood Directory

Editors: ....Stevens & Associates, Inc.
                                    4816 N. Pennsylvania St.
                                    Indianapolis, IN 46205
                                    1-800-301-3153

Spaghetti/Pasta Sauce - 1 g fat or less per ½ cup serving

Campbell's Healthy Request ....Campbell Soup Co.
                                    Camden, NJ 08103-1701
                                    1-800-257-8443

Classico ....International Specialties Co.
                                    180 E. Broad St.
                                    Columbus, OH 43215

Del Monte.................................Del Monte Foods
                                    San Francisco, CA 94105
                                    1-800-543-3090

Enrico's ....Ventre Packing Co., Inc.
                                    6050 Court Street Road
                                    Syracuse, NY 13206

Healthy Choice ....Con Agra
                                    P. O. Box 3768
                                    Omaha, NE 66103-0768
                                    1-800-323-9980

Hunts Lite ....Hunt Wesson, Inc.
                                    P. O. Box 4800
                                    Fullerton, CA 92634

Health Valley ....Health Valley Foods, Inc.

16100 Foothill Blvd.
Irwindale, CA 91706-7811
1-800-423-4846

Muir Glen Organic, fat-free...........Muir Glen Organic
P. O. Box 1498
Sacramento, CA 95812

Pritikin ....Pritikin Systems, Inc.
P. O. Box 9003
Chicago, IL 60604-9003

Ragu Lite ....Van Den Bergh Foods Co.
Lisle, IL 60532
1-800-328-7248

Yogurt - nonfat

Dannon, plain.............................Dannon Co., Inc.
  5 mg cholesterol   P. O. Box 44235
  per 1 cup serving   Jacksonville, FL 32231-4235
1-800-321-2174

Dannon, fruit, six pack, ...Dannon Co., Inc.
  nonfat, cholesterol-free   see above address

TCBY - Fat-Free Fantasy ....Mid America Dairyman, Inc.
  cholesterol-free   Springfield, MO 65802

Whipped Topping - fat-free, cholesterol-free

Cool Whip Free ....Kraft Foods, Inc.
Box CWF-8
White Plains, NY 10625
1-800-431-1001

Kraft..Kraft Foods, Inc.
Box KF
White Plains, NY 10625
1-800-538-1998

Reddi Whip ....Beatrice Cheese, Inc.
Waukesha, WI 53186

Appendix E
Enjoying Food Away From Home

Are you concerned that healthy eating habits might prevent you from eating out? Don't worry. Dining at a restaurant or social event doesn't have to jeopardize your health or ruin your plans for healthy eating. However, it does require some creativity. Here are some suggestions for healthy dining in various situations.

Dining Out

Dining out poses its own set of problems for those seeking healthier fare. Cooks often use butter and oil liberally and most restaurants serve large portions. Admittedly, many people enjoy a heaping plate of food, however, they often don't realize that one large entree could realistically serve two or three people. Keeping this in mind, diners should always exercise portion control. Eat only what you want, and if there are leftovers, take them home to be savored for lunch the next day. Or, if you're dining with a companion, try ordering separate salads and sharing one entrée.

We encourage you to view restaurants as a resource in your attempts to eat healthy meals. As a paying customer, you reserve the right to express your dietary considerations and to question servers about food preparation. This type of request has become common-place as more people pursue healthful dining. In fact, the National Restaurant Association recently featured meatless main dishes in its 150,000 member restaurants. In addition, a Gallup Poll indicated that 1 out of every 5 restaurant customers looks for a restaurant that serves vegetarian cuisine and 1 out of every 3 diners orders vegetarian dishes when they are available. Therefore, you should feel comfortable asserting your wishes in a restaurant. Consider the server your best line of dietary defense.

As you study the menu, try to choose items that are steamed, baked, broiled, grilled or stir-fried. For example, ask for stir-fried vegetables that have been prepared on a dry grill or steamed in a small amount of broth or wine. Order your entrée without meat and avoid selections described as buttered, creamed, fried and sautéed.

Also avoid rich gravies or sauces such as Alfredo and Hollandaise.

When all else fails, we recommend ordering a traditional tomato or vegetable sandwich. Every restaurant can prepare a tomato sandwich and it's interesting to see how the results differ among eating establishments. To reduce the fat content of your sandwich, ask for unbuttered bread and eliminate mayonnaise. Prepared with lettuce, sprouts or onion, tomato sandwiches are a good choice when you're in a hurry. Dill pickles, mustard and vinegar work equally well on sandwiches and a side of broth-based soup rounds out a meal nicely.

When studying a menu, remember to look at the side dishes offered by the restaurant. If you see an acceptable item that accompanies an entrée, ask whether the restaurant will serve it separately. Or, consider choosing a combination of vegetables, rice, baked potato, fruit and salad, which add variety to a meal and are satisfying.

When enjoying the multitude of items offered on the salad bar, choose lots of fresh vegetables to maximize the nutritional value of your meal. Vegetables such as carrots, broccoli, cauliflower and tomatoes contain many nutrients, as do peppers, peas and mushrooms. Chickpeas (garbanzo beans), onions and fruit complement the taste of other vegetables while adding nutrients to a meal. Fresh spinach or dark green lettuce should also be used on salads as they contain more nutrients than pale iceberg lettuce. Avoid high-fat creamy pasta, potato salad, cheese, olives, croutons, eggs and meat, as well as any vegetables that have been marinated in oil.

Many restaurants now serve nonfat salad dressings. However, if they don't, ask that the regular dressing be served on the side. Then, dip the tip of your fork into the dressing before eating your salad. You'll be surprised at how little dressing you use and the amount of flavor you find! In addition, flavored vinegars make a good dressing substitute. Squeezing fresh lemon juice over salad and adding fresh cracked pepper also improves the taste of a salad.

When ordering an egg dish from the menu, ask that it be prepared with a nonfat, cholesterol-free egg substitute. Also, read the menu carefully to ensure that the restaurant uses an egg substitute that is cholesterol-free and not merely low in cholesterol. Don't be afraid to inquire further if the menu doesn't offer adequate information about food preparation.

If you decide to order a vegetable omelette, request vegetables that have been cooked on a dry grill, or on one that has been sprayed with nonfat cooking spray (and forego the cheese). Hash brown potatoes are also acceptable when cooked on a dry grill. Although they won't be crisp, they will be flavorful.

Some restaurants include heart healthy or low calorie specials on their menus. These aren't always a good choice. The preparation and ingredient descriptions as well as the nutritional analysis should be carefully read before ordering. You can request that an entrée or side dish be altered slightly to meet your dietary stipulations. For example, you request a dish prepared without chicken, cheese, nuts or other unacceptable ingredients.

When ordering bread products with your meal, ask for unbuttered dinner rolls and bread sticks. Many restaurants serve honey or fruit preserves with bread, or they may sprinkle breadsticks with garlic powder. Some foods that appear healthy may contain more fat than you realize. For example, muffins contain as much fat as a couple of doughnuts. For a grand finale, order frozen fruit sorbet for dessert. Or, try fresh fruit with a splash of Grand Marnier.

Ethnic Restaurants

Chinese

Most Chinese restaurants serve a 'Happy Buddha' which is an assortment of vegetables served over rice. It can be ordered in a variety of sauces and you can boost the protein content by ordering it with tofu (soybean curd) or sietan (also known as wheat meat). Mooshu vegetables without eggs, a savory combination of vegetables wrapped in paper-thin Chinese pancakes spread with plum sauce, offer increased flavor and decreased fat. When ordering appetizers, avoid egg rolls and fried wanton chips in favor of clear vegetable-broth soup. Request steamed rice with you entrée rather than fried rice.

Italian

Italian restaurants usually offer a meatless marinara or tomato sauce over pasta. Pasta primavera, steamed vegetables over pasta, often served with a splash of white wine or broth for moistness, presents another low-fat vegetarian option. Pizza baked without cheese and topped with fruit or vegetables tastes delicious. Also, consider Minestrone soup because it is meatless and prepared in a light tomato broth.

Mexican

Ordering food in a Mexican restaurant presents some difficulties. If possible, choose a restaurant that prepares its foods authentically, without adding lard or frying ingredients. Some acceptable choices include corn tortillas, perhaps filled with black beans and salsa, and plain white rice mixed with beans (also prepared without fat) and chopped onions. Corn tortillas make a better choice than white flour tortillas because the white flour variety are usually prepared with lard. Order a few baked corn tortillas to break into chips and dip into salsa. Avoid refried beans as they are usually prepared with highly saturated lard and high-fat guacamole.

Indian/Middle Eastern

When choosing Indian or Middle Eastern cuisine, focus on the use of vegetables and grains such as rice, couscous and bulgur. Request dishes prepared without meat or chicken. Middle Eastern foods contain many spices and are consequently very flavorful, so eliminating meat from an entrée does not lessen its flavor. Lentils, frequently used in Indian food, offer a high-fiber source of protein.

Fast Food

Fast food restaurants pose their own set of problems for diners seeking low-fat vegetarian foods. Fortunately, the choices are getting better. Try to choose a fast-food establishment that offers a salad bar. Then, add beans or chickpeas to your meal for more protein. Baked potatoes topped with vegetables taste great, and if the restaurant doesn't offer bread, ask for a plain or toasted bun. Some establishments even offer high-fiber whole-wheat bread or buns. If submarine sandwiches are available, order a veggie sub topped with tomato, lettuce, peppers, pickles and onions. Top it with mustard, a splash of vinegar and pepper. For your beverage, avoid soda and order fruit juice instead.

As a Guest

Dining as a guest while trying to maintain a certain nutrition lifestyle can be challenging. However, it is possible to navigate potentially awkward social situations. We suggest that when responding to an invitation, you explain your dietary preferences to the hosts. Ask them not to prepare anything special for you. Once your hosts understand the situation, they should not be offended if you don't eat the entrée. There will usually be a variety of side dishes for you to sample. And, if it seems appropriate, you can offer to bring a specially prepared dish.

You can also take steps to limit your fat intake before attending a dinner party. For example, eat a bit before you leave home. That way you won't be ravenous and will find it easier to eat smaller portions. In addition, if you anticipate eating more fat at dinner, cut back on your fat intake during the rest of the day.

When staying in someone's home, whether overnight or for a week, bring some of your own groceries. Although your host would probably never admit it, the thoughtfulness will be appreciated. They won't worry about how to feed you, and you won't worry about finding acceptable foods to eat.

Potluck dinners are not a problem if you plan ahead. Take a main dish for yourself, like **Baked Vegetable Packets** (see page 102), as well as a dish to pass. There will usually be other dishes that you can eat. You should never avoid the chance to socialize with your family and friends just because you're avoiding certain foods.

Travel

Just as you plan every other aspect of your trip, dining while travelling takes some extra planning. On long car trips, for example, consider packing a small cooler filled with fresh fruit and juices, fat-free yogurt, chopped raw vegetables, or maybe even some salad (don't forget utensils). Pack a bag of fat-free pretzels, chips, crackers and air-popped popcorn. Then, eat at an outdoor rest stop rather than inside a bland, confining fast-food restaurant.

At your lodging destination, ask the desk clerk to suggest a restaurant that might accommodate your dietary needs. Perhaps the clerk can suggest a health food restaurant or an acceptable restaurant chain familiar to you. Check the Yellow Pages for additional options.

Most airlines accommodate vegetarian passengers who request vegetarian meals in advance. We suggest asking for vegetarian meals when you book your ticket (be sure to also ask for a nondairy meal). Then, approximately a week before your trip, call the airline to verify that your request is in their computer.

Planning to book a cruise? Ask your travel agent whether the cruise line offers a vegetarian menu. While vegetarian entrées sometimes contain too much fat and are full of eggs, there will usually be one or two items that meet your dietary needs. Meatless marinara or tomato sauces can usually be found. Cruise lines also offer their passengers a wide array of fresh fruits and vegetables. Breakfasts on a cruise offer more options because cruise lines usually serve a variety of hot and cold cereals along with skim milk. If the cruise line doesn't offer what you need, ask them to purchase it at the next port. Good service is important on a cruise and they will accommodate you if they can.

Pack some fruit and fat-free crackers and snack bars when you make long trips. Unless you are diabetic or suffer from hypoglycemia (low blood sugar), your health won't be adversely affected if you miss a meal. While your aim should be to relax and enjoy the trip, it's always good to plan for delays. We hope that the suggestions offered in this Appendix help relieve some of the concern you feel about dining away from home and maintaining the standards of your nutrition lifestyle.

Subject Index

Alcohol, 19

American Heart Association diet guidelines, 9, 12

Amino acids, 24-25

Anti-oxidants, 14, 27-28

Atherosclerosis, 13
anti-oxidants and, 27-28

Beans and legumes, 11, 21, 26, 28-29, 53-58
as protein source, 26, 28
cooking times, yields, chart, 58
glossary of, 55-57

Breakfast
ideas, 171-172
importance of, 171

Caffeine, 19, 20

Calcium
osteoporosis and, 31
sources, 29, 31
supplements, 31-32

Calories
determining intake, 23-24

Cancer
anti-oxidants and, 27-28
development, 14
fiber and, 27
soy products and, 28
risk, 14

Carbohydrate
as fuel, 14-15
calories, 13

Cholesterol
effects of fat on, 22-23
fiber and, 26-27
food labels and, 234-238
guidelines for intake, 19
in dairy products, 29
reduction, 8, 12
soy products and, 28-29

Cooking
baking, 41-42
methods, 40-42
substitutions, chart, 50-51

Dairy products
as protein source, 25, 29
in diet, 11, 19, 20, 25, 29

Desserts, ideas, 199-200

Dining out, 251-255
ethnic restaurants, 253-255
travel, 255-256

Eating habits
change, 17-18

Egg whites
as protein source, 29
in baking, 41
in diet, 11, 19

Equipment, kitchen 39-40

Fat
body storage, 14
calories, 13
determining intake, 23-24
food labels and, 234-238
food preparation and, 49-50
guidelines for intake, 19, 22-24
monounsaturated, 23, 49
oxidative damage, 14
polyunsaturated, 22-23
saturated, 13, 22
substitutions for, 41, 183, 200

Fatty acids
essential, 22
trans, 23, 237

Fiber
benefits of, 26-27
cautions, 27
definition, 27
in cooking, 42
on food labels, 235, 237-238
recommended intake, 27

Fluids
and fiber, 27

Food Guide Pyramid, Vegetarian, 20, 21

Food labels, 234-238
nutrition claims, 234, 236
sample, Nutrition Facts, 235

Food log, 18, 23

Food presentation, 45

Fruit
in salads, 149
nutrients in, 27-28
recommended amount, 27

shopping for, 35-36

Glucose
fiber and, 27

Grains
cooking times, yields, chart, 80
fiber in, 27
glossary of, 76-79
in cooking, 75
pasta, see Pasta
purchasing, 36
rice, see Rice

Hydrogenation, 22-23, 237

Hypertension, 12
salt and, 29-30

Iron, 31

Legumes, see Beans and legumes

Margarine, 49-50

Menus, sample, 228-233
protein in, 228

Metabolism
and muscle mass, 14

Metropolitan Height and Weight Tables, 227
use of, 24, 227

Oils, in cooking, 49-50

Organic products, 36

Ornish, MD, Dean
diet guidelines, 9, 19, 228
Dr. Dean Ornish's Program for Reversing
Heart Disease, 7, 12, 24

Pantry, stocking basics, 37-39

Pasta, 75, 83
cooking times, yields, chart, 83
in salad, 149

Protein
calories, 13
combining, 25-26, 29
definitions, 25
excess, 25
needs, 24-25

Rice, 44, 75, 81-82
cooking times, yields, chart, 82
glossary of, 81-82

Salad, 39-40, 44, 149
greens, glossary of, 150-152

Salt
and hypertension, 29-30
sodium in, 29-30
reduction in food, 51-52

Seasonings, 42-43, 46-47
extracts, 42
herbs and spices, 42
imitation butter flavor, 42
for vegetables, 46-47
vinegars, 47-48

Sodium
and hypertension, 29-30
recommendations, 29
reduction, 51-52

Soy products
as protein source, 28-29
in diet, 25, 28-29

Sugar, in diet, 30

Supplements, vitamin and mineral, 27, 31-32

Time savers, 43-44

Vegetables
in cooking, 46, 101, 125
recommended amount, 27
shopping for, 35-36

Vegetarian Cooking for Healthy Living
diet principles, 15, 19

Vegetarian diet
definition, 11
Position Paper, American Dietetic Association,
12
ultra low-fat, benefits of, 12-14

Vinegars, 47-48

Vitamin B12, 31

Weight
determining reasonable, 24, 227
fiber and, 26-27
loss, 8, 12-14, 24
management, 13

Yogurt cheese, 48-49

Food and Recipe Index

BEANS AND LEGUMES - MAIN DISHES
see also Legumes
Bean and Pasta Stew, 145
Bean Lasagna, 59, 26
Beans and Vegetables with Rice, 60
Black Beans and Rice, 61
Broccoli and Tofu Bake, 62
Crêpes with Hearty Bean Filling, 63
Fulla Beans Casserole, 64, 230
Lentil Casserole, 65, 231
Lentil Patties with Tomato Chutney, 66, 229, 26
Picante Black Bean Casserole, 67, 26
Quick and Easy Baked Beans, 68
Refried Beans, 69
Super Bowl Beans, 70
Three Bean Casserole, 71
Tofu Stuffed Shells, 72
Tortilla Black Bean Casserole, 73, 233, 26
Tostadas, 74, 26
Biscuits
Cheese, 192
Shortcake, 192
Bread Crumbs, 46
BREADS, 183, see also Muffins
Boston Brown, 184
Dr. Pepper Apricot, 185, 232
Lemon Poppy Seed, 186, 233
Stollen, 196
Breakfast Ideas, 171-172
BREAKFASTS
Asparagus Quiche with Rice Crust, 179, 199, 231
Banana Yogurt with Granola, 173, 232, 26
Breakfast In A Glass, 173, 230, 231
Grapefruit Surprise, 174
Papaya with Lime Juice, 174, 233
Oatmeal with Applesauce, 175, 232
"Mosquito Coast" French Toast, 176, 231, 26
Premier Pancakes, 177, 230
Roasted Vegetable Strata, 181, 230, 26
Vegetable Frittata, 180, 229, 230
Vegetable Omelette with Dill and Chives, 178, 230
Cakes
Carrot Cake with Rum Sauce, 207, 231
Chocolate Raspberry, 208, 232
Hawaiian Wedding, 209
COOKIES AND BARS
Cherry, Apple, Oatmeal, 212, 233
Chocolate Bar a l'Orange, 214, 229
Molasses Crinkles, 213, 231
Pineapple Date Bars, 216, 231
CRÊPES, 44
Crêpes with Hearty Bean Filling, 63, 230, 26
Dessert, 205

Strawberry, 206, 230, 26
Whole Wheat, 193, 231, 233
Crusts, 199
DESSERTS
Apple Tart, 217, 232
Company Cheesecake, 211
Dessert Crêpes, 205
Flan and Philly, 222
Lemon Souffle, 202, 233
Melon Granita, 203, 229
Meringues with Raspberry Purée, 204
Peach Cobbler, 220
Pineapple Baked Alaska, 201
Raspberry Parfait, 210, 230, 26
Rice Pudding, 223
Strawberry Crêpes, 206
Dessert Tips, 199-200
Dumplings, Cornmeal, 194
Flavor Boosters, 42-43
Food Presentation, 45
Grains, 75-80
Cooking Times, yields, chart ,80
Glossary of, 76-79
Greens, Glossary of, 150-152
Herb and Spice Mix
"Ground Beef" Casserole, 90, 26
Hungarian Kugel, 195
Legumes, 53-58
Cooking Times, yields, chart, 58
Glossary of, 55-57
MUFFINS, see also Breads
Carrot, 187, 232
Date Bran, 188, 230
Oatmeal Applesauce, 189, 231
Pumpkin Spice, 190, 232
Whole Wheat Blueberry, 191, 229
Oils, Margarines and Imitations, 41, 49-50
Pasta, 75, 83
Cooking Times and yields, 83
PASTA - MAIN DISHES
Bean and Pasta Stew, 145
Broccoli and Mostaccioli, 86, 229, 26
Cabbage and Noodles, 87
Creamy Fettuccine, 89, 26
Jackpot Casserole, 91
Linguini with Pineapple Salsa, 92, 232
Penne with Artichokes and Leeks, 94, 233, 26
Szechuan Asparagus with Vermicelli, 96, 231, 26
Tomato Lasagna Rollups, 97, 26
Vegetable Lasagna, 98, 26
Pies
Double Chocolate Mint, 219, 233

33

...uiche with Rice Crust, 179
...85, 230
... and Vegetables with Rice, 60, 26
...ck Beans and Rice, 61
Confetti Rice Salad, 156
Corn, Bean and Rice Goulash, 105, 26
"Ground Beef" Casserole, 90, 229
Orange, 93, 231
Pilaf, 93
Potato, Bean and Rice Soup, 141
Rice Pudding, 223, 229
Spanish Rice and Beans, 95
Vegetable Kabobs Over Rice, 110
Rice, cooking times and yields, 82
Rice, Glossary of, 81-82
Roasted Red Peppers, 43, 46
SALAD, 149-150, see also Greens, Glossary of
Broiled Vegetable Salad, 153
Carrot Salad, 154, 229
Cole Slaw, 155, 229
Confetti Rice Salad, 156
Cranberry Fluff, 157
Fresh Fruit, 158
Italian Pasta, 159, 26
Layered Party Slaw, 160, 231
Lemony Vegetable Pasta, 161, 230
Minestrone Salad, 162, 233, 26
Molded Gazpacho Salad, 163
Pasta and Bean Salad, 164, 233, 26
New Potato Salad with Vegetables, 165, 232
Peanutty Fruit Salad, 166, 232
Spicy Black Bean Salad, 167, 232
Spinach Salad, 168, 231, 233
Summer Fruit Medley, 169, 229
Summer Macaroni Salad, 26, 170
Salad Dressing, 48, 156, 160-162, 165-170
SANDWICHES, 125
Baco's, Lettuce and Tomato, 127, 231
Cucumber, 128, 232
Egg, 129
Sloppy Joes, 132, 232
Vegetable Pita, 133, 229, 26
Veggie Submarine, 134, 233, 26
Sauces
Lemon, 113
Raspberry Purée, 204
Rum, 224, 231
Sweet and Spicy Tomato, 123
Tomato Chutney, 122
Vegetable Spaghetti, 124

SOUPS, CHILIES AND CHOWDERS, 125-126
Cabbage, 135, 233
Corn and Potato Chowder, 136
Country Bean, 137
Fruit, 138, 231
Lentil, 139, 231
Meatless Chili, 143
Minestrone, 140, 231, 26
Polka Dot Chili, 144, 230, 26
Potato, Bean and Rice, 141, 232, 26
Split Pea, 142
Spreads, 43
Hummus, 130
Refried Beans, 69, 231
Tomato Chutney, 122
Stews
Bean and Pasta, 145
Potato and Vegetable, 146
Vegetable Stew with Cornmeal Dumplings, 147, 26
Substitutions, 41-42, 50-51
Tofu
Tofu Stuffed Shells, 72, 26
Broccoli and Tofu Bake, 62
Tomato Chutney, 122
Texturized Vegetable Protein (TVP), 38
Cornbread Hot Tamale Pie, 88, 231, 26
Mashed Potato Pie, 109
Sloppy Joes, 132, 232, 26
VEGETABLE - MAIN DISHES
Baked Vegetable Packets, 102, 255
Broccoli Ricotta Crêpes, 103, 26
Cabbage Rolls, 106, 232, 26
Calzones, 104, 233, 26
Corn, Bean and Rice Goulash, 105
Gratin of Vegetables, 108
Mashed Potato Pie, 109
Potato and Vegetable Stew, 146
Vegetable Kabobs Over Rice, 110
Vegetable Masala, 112, 230
Vegetable Stew with Cornmeal Dumplings, 147
Vegetable Stir-fry, 111, 26
Vegetable Seasoning Chart, 47
VEGETABLES, 46, 101, 125
Asparagus with Lemon Sauce, 113, 233
Black-eyed Peas and Corn, 114, 229, 26
Buttercup Squash with Peas and Onions, 115
Carrots and Grapes, 116, 230
Green and Yellow Mixit, 117, 229
Green Beans in Creamy Tomato Sauce, 117
Oven Fried Potatoes, 118, 232
Stuffed Zucchini, 119
Sweet and Sour Cabbage with Apples, 120
Sweet Potato Pone, 121
Vinegars, 47-48
Raspberry Vinegar, 48
Yogurt Cheese, 48-49